"FOR
TEXAS,
I WILL"

The History of Memorial Stadium

by
Richard Pennington

Library of Congress Catalog Card Number: 92–72615

Publisher's Cataloging in Publication Data

Pennington, Richard, 1952-
 "For Texas, I Will": The History of Memorial Stadium / Richard Pennington

 Includes
  Index
  Bibliography

ISBN 1-881825-01-9

FIRST EDITION

Published by

Historical Publications
15705 *Hilcroft Cove* • *Austin, Texas* 78717-5331

Printed and bound in the United States of America

This book is dedicated to C. B. Smith, 1903-1992. A Texas track star during the stadium's early years, he did more than anyone else to document Longhorn sports history.

Foreword

Richard Pennington is to be complimented for a great amount of research work that has brought back memories to all of us. His book cuts an interesting story that almost makes Memorial Stadium seem alive.

I had a lot of fun reliving moments and learning things that I didn't know happened there. I had the sense of the games . . . and the great moments such as our UCLA game in 1970. I remember the crowd that day, and I'm not sure we could have won that game anywhere else. That day, the stadium was alive.

The Freddie Steinmark scoreboard reminds me of a little guy with a big heart who never quit, and it really kind of sums up the stadium. Memorial Stadium is a bunch of individuals passing the baton, and no one passed a larger baton than Freddie. With each era of the stadium, you think of the people who have gone before.

I know I had those thoughts when it came my time to occupy a little space on that field. I remembered those who had been there in front of me, and the groundwork they had laid for us.

You can't invent a feeling, but if your blood runs orange, this book will cause that tingly sensation of goose bumps on your arms and legs. It's a wonderful feeling!

Darrell Royal

Preface

Its abbreviation is "STD," building number 9710 on the official University of Texas inventory. Few people would deny that Memorial Stadium, one of UT's oldest structures, has been the scene of much athletic drama during nearly 70 years.

You can find plenty of newspaper and magazine articles about the stadium's history and the football games and track meets it has hosted. But nothing in depth has been done, and a fair amount of misinformation has arisen over time, so I endeavor to tell the whole story.

I want to keep alive—or perhaps revive—the memory of some people who played major roles in the building of Memorial Stadium and in its early years. Aside from a handful of UT historians, who today remembers H. J. Lutcher Stark, L. Theo Bellmont, William McGill, Max Fichtenbaum or Jake Bleymaier? Who has heard of Louis Jordan and the other Texans who fought and died in World War I? They provided the inspiration to construct the stadium, which was an urgent practical necessity in 1924.

The university was 41 years old before Memorial Stadium was built on a hillside east of Waller Creek. This far predates the formation of the University of Texas System, with campuses in farflung cities like El Paso, Arlington, Tyler and Brownsville. So without meaning to disparage those schools, by "UT" I refer only to the flagship institution located in Austin, the state capital.

A few words about myself will suffice. I am a native of Dallas, a 1975 UT graduate with a deep, but not obsessive, interest in Longhorn athletics. I trace the genesis of this book to a remark made by my brother, Randy, in the summer of 1976. During one of his rare visits to Austin, we dropped by the stadium to look around, and he said "You know, most people aren't aware of just what a historic building Memorial Stadium is and all the great things that have happened here." I mumbled an assent, yet his words rolled around my head for nearly 14 years until I began the project.

I want to acknowledge the following people, who have kindly provided various amounts of financial assistance during the research, writing and editing of the book: Lex Acker, Ann Caswell Allison, Rooster Andrews, Dr.

Jay Arnette, David C. Bland, Jr., Jack Blanton, Dr. John Breen (in honor of Heinie Pfannkuche), Charles Brewer, John Butler, Harley Clark, Moton Crockett, Darrell S. David, Frank Denius, Noble Doss, Tim Doss, Dr. Marion Ford, Margaret Bellmont Gray, Joe Greenhill, Frank Guthrie, Drew Kennard, Bobby Lackey, Jerry LeVias, Clyde Littlefield, Jr., William Luedecke, Pat Luther, Doug Lynch, Karl Kamrath, Jr. (in honor of Karl Kamrath, Sr.), Velma Keller, Dr. Charles Mallett, B. J. "Red" McCombs, Bob Miller, Dr. Mitch Moore, Dr. Warren F. Neely, Knox Nunnally, Dr. Don Patrick, Nelson Puett, Jr., Dr. Nasser al-Rashid, Jim Raup, Travis Raven, Benno C. Schmidt, Wally Scott, J. Shelby Sharpe, A. M. Simmons, C. B. and Johanna Smith, Weldon Smith, John G. Taylor, Jerry Thompson, Brian Ullom, Robert C. Vaughn, William Caswell Ward and Dick Wilkowski.

While I have written with complete editorial independence, I remained open to feedback from all quarters. At the start, UT men's athletic director DeLoss Dodds recognized the value of a history of the stadium and has been supportive of this project. So have other current and former members of the entire athletic department, including Bill Sansing, Bob Rochs, Al Lundstedt, Darrell Royal, Dr. J. Neils Thompson, David McWilliams, Ken Dabbs, Bill Little, Doug Messer, Robert Brewer and John Mackovic.

I appreciate the interest shown by Roy Vaughan, executive director of the Ex-Students' Association. The court of final appeal on UT history is Dr. Margaret Berry. She has freely imparted her knowledge, as has architect Lex Acker of the UT System Office of Facilities Planning and Construction.

In addition to me, four people comprise the book's publication "team": Weldon Smith, Ted Bellmont, John Knaggs and Ron Nielsen; Smith, along with Eloise Blades, Hal Hillman, Homer and Pat Luther, James R. Moffett, Robert Parker, Louis Pearce, Jr., and John and Jerry Thompson, have generously helped underwrite the book's publication costs. I thank them, along with the object of my affection, Kathy Monte, who has witnessed the project's development for the last two years. Robert Reed and Jo Zarboulas have performed several technical tasks along the way and offered stinging critiques.

I must also give a belated pat on the back to the anonymous person(s) who put together two large scrapbooks detailing the funding and construction of the stadium in the 1920s. These scrapbooks, located in UT's Collections Deposit Library, proved invaluable to my research.

It has been a challenge, and a satisfying one, to learn about Memorial Stadium's evolution into an arena capable of holding more than 80,000 people. In the process, I have gained a deeper appreciation for the rich history of my alma mater. I hope that this book, published on the eve of the 100th season of Longhorn football, might do the same for others.

Richard Pennington
Austin, Texas

Photo Credits

(**Front dust jacket**) © Reagan Bradshaw, 1990; (**front endsheet**) UT Center for American History; **1.** UT Center for American History; **2.** UT Center for American History; **3.** UT Center for American History; **4.** UT Ex-Students' Association; **5.** UT Sports Information; **6.** Austin History Center; **7.** UT Sports Information; **8.** UT Sports Information; **9.** UT Sports Information; **10.** UT Center for American History; **11.** UT Sports Information; **12.** UT Center for American History/*Austin American-Statesman;* **13.** UT Sports Information; **14.** UT Sports Information; **15.** UT Center for American History; **16.** UT Sports Information; **17.** UT Sports Information/*Dallas Morning News;* **18.** UT Sports Information; **19.** UT Sports Information; **20.** UT Center for American History; **21.** UT Sports Information/*Austin American-Statesman;* **22.** Lockwood, Andrews & Newnam; **23.** UT Center for American History; **24.** UT Sports Information; **25.** UT Sports Information; **26.** UT Center for American History; **27.** UT Sports Information; **28.** UT Sports Information; **29.** UT Sports Information; **30.** UT Center for American History; **31.** UT Sports Information; **32.** UT Sports Information; **33.** UT Sports Information; **34.** UT Sports Information; **35.** UT Sports Information; **36.** UT Sports Information; (**back endsheet**) UT Sports Information; (**author photo**) Kathleen Monte; (**back dust jacket**) UT Center for American History.

(Book/Dust Jacket Design by Ron Nielsen. Typesetting-Text by David Nielsen, Historical Publications. Typesetting-Dust Jacket by Valerie Milligan, SciTran. Books printed and bound by BookCrafters, U.S.A.; Fredricksburg, Virginia.)

Table of Contents

Before Memorial Stadium

A necdotal evidence exists that a group of University of Texas students engaged in a game of "football" with Bickler's German and English Academy in December 1883, just weeks after UT first opened its doors. More like rugby than football as we now know it, this informal contest was staged on a rough plot of ground east of Congress Avenue between the Capitol and the university. As darkness settled, the Bickler's students, who had scored two goals, declared themselves winners.

A few other such pickup games were played on or near the Forty Acres in succeeding years, but not until 1893 did anything like a football team representative of the school emerge. On December 16 of that year, Texas played what is recognized as its first "home" football game, against a club from San Antonio at Dam Baseball Park, close by the Colorado River. The 21-man team, led by captains Paul McLane and James Morrison, drew 600 fans to the first Austin game on a cold, wet day.

Later, they moved two miles north of campus to Hyde Park, roping off a grass field near the home of famed sculptor Elisabet Ney. Spectators stood or sat on the sidelines, some of them in horse-drawn carriages. Other "Varsity" home football games took place at the Hyde Park fairgrounds. There, Texas and its opponents played in the middle of an erstwhile horse-driving track.

One of the team's most stalwart fans, chemistry professor Edgar Everhart, grew tired of going all the way out to Hyde Park to watch the games. In 1895, he urged that a permanent football field be set up east of the UT campus, on a sparsely settled area covered with cedar trees and mesquite bushes. Everhart's plan of leveling a hill and constructing bleachers near the future site of Memorial Stadium was a visionary one. While some work was actually done, he soon left the university, and without his leadership, the project died.

HOME AT LAST

Only in 1896 did Texas get a campus-area home for football. The location of Varsity Athletic Field at the southeast corner of Speedway and 24th Street (now the location of Taylor Hall) was not really part of the campus, but sat adjacent to it. The UT gridiron team, with the tacit permission of the newly formed Athletics Council, squatted on this piece of land following the 1895 season, in which it won all five games and did not give up a single point. In fact, after three seasons, Varsity had played 17 games and won 16 of them. Texas football was off to a good start and already, the students, faculty and townspeople were beginning to take pride in the program.

UT's new football field belonged to an absentee owner, a Mr. de Cordova, who would permit the students use of it for three years and then demand that they either buy or vacate. Responding to de Cordova's ultimatum, Dean of Engineering T. U. Taylor (later known as "the Grand Old Man of the University") and Judge R. L. Batts negotiated a price of $3,000, to be paid in three installments. Refunded student library deposits paid for the first, Taylor solicited money from faculty and alumni for the second, and the Board of Regents finished it up in 1901. Thus was the campus first expanded and Texas football gradually institutionalized.

The renaming of Varsity Athletic Field in 1904 was the work of D. A. Frank, editor of the *Texan* (the student newspaper was then published bi-weekly). A year earlier, Frank had pinned the nickname "Longhorns" on the school athletic teams. In what would today be considered a questionable journalistic ploy, Frank himself wrote and printed anonymous letters, signed "A Senior Law," "A Senior Engineer," and "A Football Player," urging that the athletic grounds be named in honor of university proctor James B. Clark. The *Texan* soon began using the term "Clark Field," which gradually gained acceptance.

Frank could hardly have made a better choice. Clark, a Harvard University law graduate, was a member of UT's first Board of Regents, but became proctor in 1885 and kept that post until his death in 1908. Yet he did much more than preside over student examinations. "Judge" Clark was also auditor, librarian, registrar, superintendent of buildings and grounds, secretary to both the regents and the faculty and, some said, the father confessor to everyone on campus. A vigorous supporter of the school's athletic teams, he seems to have been the most beloved person in early UT history.

Few Longhorn fans today even know of the original Clark Field, which began as a rather uneven area lined with chalk. Modest bleachers were later added, and yet as it got bigger, it was less able to handle the growing crowds. In November 1907, the *Texan* opined that "it is disgraceful that students are forced . . . to stand four and five deep at every big game." Soon a fundraising drive (again, students were hit up for their library deposits) enabled the Athletics Council to expand Clark Field to a seating capacity of 2,000. Engineering and law students, aided by black laborers, went to work with hammers and saws, finishing the job in less than a week.

FOOTBALL BOOMING AT UT

With undue optimism, the *Texan* then envisioned "no more shoving and contending for elbow room." But the expanded Clark Field was still too small because the team kept drawing more and more fans. The 1907 UT-Texas A&M game drew 6,000, three times the number of seats available.

Football teams in those years did battle on a weed-choked field laid out north-south between tilted wooden goalposts. A hand-operated scoreboard gave spectators only the score of the game. Young boys walked about with baskets full of apples, selling them for five cents apiece, and many a visiting team got pelted by apple cores. Yell leaders and their megaphones were the sole system of public address; organized yells and cheers formed a much bigger part of the spectacle than they do today. A pistol shot usually signalled game's end.

But football alone did not attract people to Clark Field. The place teemed with students participating in various intramural and intercollegiate sports. UT's popular "Field Day," forerunner to track and field, was first held in 1896, while baseball and even outdoor basketball vied for space. Other events took place there, like the "Varsity Circus" and the annual March 2 pushball contest between freshmen, known derisively as "slime," and upperclassmen. At the University Interscholastic League (UIL) track meet held every spring, as many as 800 high school athletes took part.

Track men ran on a rectangle rather than an oval, disappearing from the fans' view once per lap behind the football scoreboard. Before football games, the student manager did his best to line the field and then level it with dirt and sawdust.

The goalposts and basketball courts were pretty crude. UT played intercollegiate basketball outdoors at Clark Field until 1912, when the Men's Gym was constructed next door on Speedway. This building would play a key role in the 1924 Memorial Stadium fundraising drive.

Clark Field's new covered west-side grandstand had a rudimentary press box. It blocked the view of students accustomed to watching the games from the upper floors of nearby B Hall, the well-known "Citadel of Jeffersonian Democracy." The creaking wooden facility contained just 20 rows, west and east, and temporary end-zone bleachers were usually assembled for the bigger football games.

Lots of people paid admission or scampered over the wooden fence surrounding the grounds, with the understanding that all seats were occupied, so they had to stand throughout the game. Seeking the best possible view, these fans perched on the roof of the grandstand, assembled in passageways and within a few feet of the field itself. Photographs of the time show people observing from trees, fences, telephone poles and the roofs of nearby houses.

Occasionally, the Longhorns made a show-biz entrance, being driven onto the field in a caravan of Ford convertibles.

CHARMING, BUT OUTDATED

Decked out in orange and white bunting for a big game, Clark Field had a certain charm, as the years lent an air of tradition. After 20 seasons as the Longhorns' home, it had become a special place, the site of countless exciting, hard-fought games. The 1914 UT team, with stars like Clyde Littlefield, K. L. Berry and Louis Jordan, went undefeated, scoring 358 points and allowing just 21.

Students sat on the east side of the field, and coeds got instructions in ladylike behavior from Helen Marr Kirby, dean of women. Typical halftime shows included a performance by the all-male Longhorn Band, the congregation of former lettermen (called "T Men"), and even cowboy stunts by students riding horses. After a victory, these exuberant young Texans would perform a large snake dance while the band played "The Eyes of Texas."

If Clark Field did not rival the more imposing stadiums of Harvard, Yale or Princeton, for example, it was no worse than that found at any other Southern state university of the time. Still, it proved inadequate for the big crowds, which were becoming more common, partly due to improved roads throughout Texas. In 1913, Notre Dame visited and spanked UT, 30-7, before an estimated 7,000 fans. Two years later, the Ramblers—not yet known as the Fighting Irish—were back, again beating the Longhorns in front of an equally large gathering.

The 1916 Texas A&M game, which marked the introduction of a steer named "Bevo" as the UT mascot, drew heavy interest because it was the first time the Longhorns and Aggies met in Austin since 1909. Fifteen thousand people, more than half of whom did not have an actual seat, jammed the friendly confines of Clark Field to see Texas pull an upset, 21-7. And it would only get worse: The 1920 and 1922 UT-Texas A&M games both drew around 20,000 fans.

With time, complaints grew, especially from people unable to get inside on game day. But even those lucky enough to gain admittance to Clark Field found it unbecoming of a major university. The *Daily Texan* featured many cartoons bemoaning the cramped quarters and called the press box "a rickety disgrace."

Even in its prime, Clark Field was basically an ad hoc, temporary structure. By the early 1920s, some people entered with trepidation, afraid that the bleachers might collapse. Its location, so near the center of campus, and its very material, lumber and nails, assured that Clark Field would not always be the home of University of Texas athletics.

It was clear that the Longhorns would eventually need an honest-to-God stadium. The idea had been bandied about for years in the *Daily Texan* and *Alcalde*, the magazine of the Ex-Students' Association. Two vigorous men would be most responsible for bringing it to fruition. One was a native Texan, heir to a huge fortune, and the other was a Northerner, a Yankee who had to scrape through college. Yet this unlikely pair became close, life-long friends, backing each other through many a storm. While both have now been dead for a quarter of a century, they still have their staunch defenders and vociferous critics. Their friendship—call it a partnership—led to the construction of Texas Memorial Stadium in 1924.

ENTER LUTCHER STARK

Some might think it prophetic that Henry Jacob Lutcher Stark would be born and raised in a town by the name of Orange. William and Miriam Stark, their wealth deriving from lumber, steel, oil and rice-farming interests, pampered their only son, and would not allow him to take part in the rough-and-tumble games of most boys.

Matriculating at the University of Texas in 1905, "Lutch" was no natural athlete, although he would eventually learn to play a mean game of handball. Most of his sports thrills were of a vicarious nature, and nothing meant more to him than seeing the Longhorns play football. As the 1910 team manager, Stark arranged the schedule (six of the eight games that year were at Clark

Field) and took care of the team as no one had ever done before. In 1911, Stark became the first UT student to own a car, an orange roadster.

While a freshman, he met, courted and later married Nita Hill, daughter of Dr. Homer Hill, voluntary physician of the football team. Nita's mother, Ella "Granny" Hill, ran a west-campus boarding house that catered to UT athletes. Stark thus had entree to the most socially esteemed group on campus, the football squad. At this time, he began his long practice of sitting on the Texas bench, rather than in the stands.

After graduating, he took a stronger hand in running the family's businesses, especially while his father served on the UT Board of Regents from 1911-1915. Stark himself became a regent in 1919, and except for a two-year hiatus from 1931-1933, would remain on the board continuously until 1945.

During much of his 40 years on the UT campus, Lutcher Stark was the dominant figure, a man who made decisions, sometimes unilaterally. Not even his best friends and strongest admirers would deny that Stark used his financial and political clout freely.

Several years after his death, Stark was characterized by Ronnie Dugger in *Our Invaded Universities*, a somewhat polemical book about the use and abuse of power at UT. Dugger cryptically wrote "There was a Texan of power then named Lutcher Stark. When I went to the university that was all I heard about him, 'Lutcher Stark,' his name. Evidently the words had a meaning by themselves, because no one ever described him or told you anything about him. You gathered he had been an enemy back in the history of the school somewhere. 'Lutcher Stark'—that told the whole story."

Perhaps not. If some people regarded him as an enemy, others thought of him as a generous man who loved his school. Even before graduation, Stark had begun to loan or give money outright to struggling fellow students. And far from seeking applause for these and other actions, he insisted that the fortunate recipients keep it quiet. While much has been made of Stark's financial involvement with UT sports, he once estimated that for every athlete he helped, there were seven ordinary students.

Even so, Stark took a strong interest in Texas athletics. Team equipment, band uniforms and instruments, watches, trophies, first-class travel, summer jobs—there was hardly anything he was not willing to provide for the greater glory of his alma mater. It is also true that Stark helped subsidize many a talented athlete choosing to pursue higher education at the University of Texas. Clyde Littlefield, George "Hook" McCullough, Bohn Hilliard and many others benefited from his largess. While the practice raised some eyebrows in a time before athletic scholarships, Stark was not entirely unique, and there was nothing illegal about proffering such gifts.

Willful, powerful men had attempted to mold the university to their vision before (George Brackenridge, George Littlefield and Will C. Hogg come to mind), and would do so in the future (Frank Erwin). But no one, of whatever era, has wielded more actual power than H. J. Lutcher Stark did in the 1920s.

BELLMONT, THE MOVER AND SHAKER

The exact date of the first meeting of Stark and L. Theo Bellmont is uncertain. When the latter was hired to fill UT's newly created post of athletic director in the summer of 1913, Stark was just two years out of college, working on expansion of the family fortune in Orange. Since his father was then a regent, we can safely assume that Stark arranged to meet and interview Bellmont, soon giving his approval.

A native of Rochester, New York, Bellmont entered the University of Tennessee when he was 22 years old. His student days in Knoxville were full, as he worked his way through school, sometimes even using a pick and shovel to earn money. But he left an impressive record, including stints on the football, baseball and basketball teams, and found time for a plethora of non-athletic endeavors. Graduating with a law degree in 1908, the handsome and self-confident Bellmont had the unmistakable look of a young man going places.

In just four years, 1909-1913, Bellmont had a big impact on the Young Men's Christian Association in Houston. In April 1913, a *Houston Post* article contained this glowing praise: "The extensive widening of the scope of the YMCA physical department must be largely attributed to L. Theo Bellmont, whose insatiable energy has been expended in achieving the result. . . . Bellmont has worked wonders, and Houston can bear faithful witness that he stands high in the ranks of the big figures of Texas sport."

But he loved the academic environment and when the UT job came open, he jumped at it. In announcing Bellmont's hiring, Athletics Council chairman T. W. Mather said "The University of Texas has reached that stage when the services of an athletic director are imperatively needed. The day of larger things is at hand."

Bellmont would prove up to the task and then some. One of his stated goals upon accepting the duties of AD and professor of physical training was the construction of a new stadium. But Bellmont, a do-it-now type, had no idea it would take 11 years to see that long-deferred dream come true.

He took over an athletic program that had been largely run by well-meaning but inexperienced students with some faculty supervision. He soon had it out of debt and operating on a much sounder basis. The 1913 and 1915 UT-Notre Dame football games in Austin were his doing. Besides Bellmont's work in the high-profile world of intercollegiate sports—he also coached basketball for four seasons—he took seriously the physical condition of the average male student. (Anna Hiss was in charge of the women.) He introduced a system of compulsory medical examinations and an intramural sports program that would become the envy of every other college in the United States.

Along with Mather, Bellmont formed the Southwest Conference in late 1914. The first-ever SWC event was a track meet at Clark Field, which he had worked to improve almost from the day he arrived in Austin.

"Order came slowly to college football in the Southwest," wrote Lou Maysel in *Here Come the Texas Longhorns*. "Teams had their own eligibility rules and some had no qualms about using players who were not enrolled in school. A few even imported players from other regions of the country." UT had not been immune to such pressures, and Bellmont, a stickler for high-minded amateur sport, was determined to clean it up.

THE WAR COMES TO UT

In the spring of 1917, World War I boldly intruded into the quietude of the University of Texas, draining it of around 500 male students (fully a fifth of the total student population) and 40 faculty members. The government set up a school of Military Aeronautics and one of Automobile Mechanics, and erected along Speedway several supposedly temporary wooden barracks. Now Clark Field was more than just an athletic park, as thousands of soldiers-to-be marched and trained there.

Lettermen Louis Jordan, Pete Edmond, Bothwell Kane, Mahlon Wallace, James Greer and James Higginbotham were among the 91 students, alumni and faculty of the university who died in the war effort, and many others returned with impaired health. If the pages of the *Daily Texan*, *Alcalde* and *Cactus* yearbook are indicative, patriotism ran high, and people were aware of the sacrifices Texans had made in the muddy trenches of France. Bellmont himself attained the rank of major while serving in a stateside reserve role.

By 1923, UT's only memorial to the fallen soldiers of World War I was a plaque in the Education Building (now Sutton Hall). There was no shortage of discussion and ideas, only of action. Three reasons may be suggested for this situation.

First, the university had a lethargic air, stretching back two decades. Rare was the person with both the means and desire to improve the campus, student culture or the low pay for professors and administrators. With a few exceptions, alumni did not maintain strong bonds to the school, as class reunions were at a low ebb in the early 1920s. Such lethargy was embodied in the dreary pinewood shacks dotting the campus. A student could hear three lectures at the same time in one of the shacks, and was well advised to bring an umbrella *inside* on a rainy day.

Second, the veritable war that Governor James Ferguson waged on the university in 1917 sent a chill through many an otherwise-progressive person. A large memorial project would be quickly relegated to secondary status when the very existence of the institution came under attack. Furthermore, Ferguson's depiction of UT as a rich man's school may have pleased those in College Station, but it was laughable to the residents of B Hall or the many self-styled "PWGs" (poor working girls).

And finally, in 1921, the University of Texas came close to moving four miles southwest to the 500-acre Brackenridge Tract on the Colorado River. The possibility of such a cross-town shift had been around for several years, because the university felt hemmed in on the south, west and north. But for various economic and political reasons, the move was voted down, and instead, Governor Pat Neff signed the University Expansion Bill, annexing 135 acres of land east of the campus.

This long-running uncertainty about the geographical location of the school probably hindered it in erecting permanent buildings. After all, why replace the weatherbeaten shacks and other obsolete structures (such as Clark Field) if such a move were in the offing? Although the regents, Stark included, had gone on record as backing the move, only in April 1921 did it become clear that the university would remain in its familiar spot, less than a mile north of the Capitol.

Among the many political twists and turns this story took was one that pertains to our topic. A bill introduced in the Texas Legislature would have acquired 60 acres east of UT and appropriated $500,000 for a memorial building, of indeterminate nature, dedicated to Texans who had died in the World War. While the bill failed, things were moving along.

Later in 1921, the UT Board of Regents received a proposal to build a "Memorial Dormitory," but it hardly got off the ground. Undeterred, the students tried again in 1922, but this time it was for a "Memorial Union" to honor the veterans. Expected to cost $1 million, this building would hold the Ex-Students' Association headquarters, a hotel, student government offices, a large auditorium, a dining facility and a swimming pool.

Considerable organizing was done preparatory to a fundraising drive, but this ambitious project did not get much farther than the dormitory idea. It is no wonder some students, faculty and alumni were skeptical when the subject of a "Memorial Stadium" came up in late 1923.

STADIUM OR GYM?

And yet perhaps the university needed a gymnasium more urgently than a stadium. Since 1907, former regent Thomas W. Gregory had sought to get a good gym built on the UT campus. Four years later, he started a subscription drive for that purpose. Somewhat successful (nearly $50,000 was raised), the campaign still faltered when Gregory was called to Washington, D.C. to serve as attorney general to President Woodrow Wilson. Of course, Gregory Gymnasium would be built in 1930, but in the meantime, Texas students had to make do with the Men's Gym, a delapidated firetrap.

Evidence of the raging debate could be seen in the November 1923 issue of *Alcalde*: "The question of the respective merits of a stadium and a gymnasium is one that will always be before us until something definite is done toward building the one or the other. Arguments pro and con may be advanced, the adherents of outdoor athletics favoring the stadium, while hundreds of others, equally honest, believe that a gymnasium ought first to be provided."

The outdoor contingent prevailed. As has been mentioned, by 1923 anyone remotely connected to UT athletics knew that Clark Field was outdated and would need to be replaced soon. Although the Athletics Council had set aside $10,000 to shore up the sagging stands at Clark Field, Bellmont feared it would be wasted money. If the Longhorns did not get out of Clark Field and into a decent stadium, some people thought UT was headed for athletic oblivion. Even the head football coach got into the act. E. J. "Doc" Stewart said "The present athletic field at Texas University [sic] is an eyesore and we should be ashamed of it." Talk about a new stadium had been going on for over a decade, but it got more frequent and heated in the early 1920s.

More often than not, Bellmont was the object of the "knockers," as he called them. Although he had expanded Clark Field and made it as attractive and comfortable as possible, the situation was hopeless. People also bemoaned UT's weak 1923 home schedule, featuring such non-conference opponents as Austin College, Phillips and Southwestern, whom the Longhorns outscored 126-0. But given the limitations of Clark Field, what could Bellmont do?

He and Stark had many private discussions, agreeing that a modern facility was imperative. But before anything was done or said publicly, Bellmont began researching new stadiums at other schools.

Since the war, the popularity of college football had skyrocketed. The best football was no longer being played in the Ivy League schools that had given birth to the sport, but in the Midwest, on the west coast, and to a lesser extent, in the South and Southwest. But as other schools built massive new steel-and-concrete stadiums, Bellmont saw UT falling behind. Clark Field was looking more quaint every year.

He set up four long wooden boards in his Men's Gym office, and soon filled them with information about what other colleges had done and their methods of funding and construction. Bellmont learned that Stanford, California, Iowa, Wisconsin, Indiana, Illinois, Minnesota and Ohio State—among many others—had in recent years staged public fundraising drives to erect large, modern football stadiums, costing as much as $2 million. In fact, more than a dozen facilities named "Memorial Stadium" had been built and dedicated to veterans of the World War. Stark was impressed with these findings.

It has long been supposed that the sequence of events soon to transpire was coincidental, but with two shrewd go-getters like Stark and Bellmont, that seems improbable. In mid-November 1923, Stark spoke to a Houston gathering of Texas Exes, stressing the need for a big new stadium. The speech received an enthusiastic response, and was followed a week later by a conversation between Bellmont and George T. Kirksey, sports editor of the *Daily Texan.* (Forty years hence, Kirksey would play a part in getting the Houston Astrodome built.)

As the two sat in the Clark Field stands on the afternoon of November 22 watching the team practice, Bellmont reputedly uttered the words "If we win the A&M game, I'm thinking seriously of launching a drive to build an athletic stadium for Texas." Bellmont had planted a bug in the right person's ear, because in the November 23 *Daily Texan,* readers found a front-page article entitled "A Victory Thanksgiving Day May Mean [a] New Stadium."

Regardless of earlier disappointments, the UT student body showed instant and overwhelming support for the idea. Seizing the moment, Bellmont invited 30 student leaders to a meeting on November 25 in the University Commons (the cafeteria) to discuss that possibility. This group would later be known as "the Original 30."

Actually, two of the invitees did not come, but the other 28 deserve mention by name. They were: Ira J. Allen, James R. Beverly, Rosalie Biggio, Richard C. Blalock, Ben Brown, Cecil Chamberlin, Moulton "Ty"

Cobb, Charles Dean, Russell Dunbar, Dorothy Fisher, Henry C. Fulcher, Johnnye Gilkerson, Read Granberry, Lloyd Gregory, James Hamilton, George T. Kirksey, Ray E. Lee, F. F. "Rube" Leissner, Kathryn Lemly, Lloyd Martin, B. F. "Shorty" Mayer, John Mayfield, William L. McGill, Richard McNatt, Arno "Shorty" Nowotny, E. D. Smith, W. Robert Smith and Murray Smythe.

Some did little more than attend the meeting, others took a more active role, and a few did yeoman duty on a project that would become a watershed event in University of Texas history—the funding and construction of Memorial Stadium.

Funding and Building
"The Giant Athletic Amphitheatre"

Leo Bellmont, H. J. Lutcher Stark, Doc Stewart, Anna Hiss and Longhorn baseball coach "Uncle" Billy Disch extended a warm greeting to the 28 students who came to the University Commons at 6 P.M. to enjoy a turkey dinner. All but Hiss spoke of the need for a new stadium, and the message was well received—for the most part. While the 1923-1924 student body, faculty, administration and alumni were solidly in favor of building a stadium, true unanimity on the matter never existed.

"That date [November 25, 1923] . . . should certainly be designated a campus holiday for years to come," wrote Nowlin Randolph in the November 1924 issue of *Alcalde*. "At the time there was a heavy drag on Varsity enthusiasm. A number of prominent persons about the campus were up in arms at the idea of Texas attempting such an undertaking. . . . But the majority preached to the minority until the minority began to get enthusiastic also."

Perhaps the main spark came from Stewart, whose UT football team had a 7-0-1 record heading into the season finale against Texas A&M. He introduced the motto "For Texas, I Will," appealing to state pride and the willingness to sacrifice. Actually, Stewart borrowed and modified the words of a University of Chicago athlete who, some years earlier, had played despite injury. This saying would be heavily relied upon in speeches, posters

13

and editorials throughout the fundraising drive and construction of the stadium.

Before the meeting concluded, Rube Leissner, president of the Student Assembly, appointed William L. McGill to head a six-member stadium committee. McGill had already distinguished himself by co-founding the Texas Cowboys, a student service organization. He would later help initiate the spring Round-Up celebration, teach journalism, serve as president of the Ex-Students' Association, be a right-hand man to five Texas governors and run the state Civil Defense office. But from 1923-1928, while manager of Texas Student Publications, McGill would prove to be one of the most valuable of all stadium workers.

The day after the meeting, four trainloads of students and other fans traveled to College Station to see the Longhorns and Aggies go at it. But first, another meeting was held in Guion Hall, graciously provided by the Texas A&M administration. At this recently built 3,000-seat auditorium, UT students and alumni held a big rally, with much animated talk about a new stadium on their own campus. They went Bellmont one better, wearing armbands that stated "Win or lose, a stadium by Thanksgiving 1924."

Playing on a muddy field that day and not allowing a single Aggie first down, Texas won by a score of 6-0. It was the first such football victory ever at Kyle Field (a forerunner to the current Texas A&M stadium of the same name) and a big win; the game ball still sits in a trophy case in the foyer of Gregory Gym. Immediately afterward, delirious UT fans returned to Guion Hall and reaffirmed their desire for a stadium by making the first pledges in what would become an arduous fundraising project.

Back in Austin, the movement picked up steam as McGill and others held meetings, collected data and stirred interest. UT's acting president, W. S. Sutton, received dozens of letters and telegrams showing support for the proposed athletic facility.

The exciting news quickly spread all over the state. Witness the following headlines: "Huge Stadium Being Planned for Texas U." (*Beaumont Journal*), "Drive Starts to Give University of Texas Huge Sport Stadium" (*San Antonio Express*), "'East Woods' Chosen Site of Stadium" (*Houston Post*) and "University Plans Memorial Stadium" (*Dallas Morning News*).

During the first week of December, some students hardly prepared for final exams, choosing instead to talk and dream about the great project before them. The Student Assembly and Faculty Senate went on record as earnestly backing the stadium, and on December 11, President Sutton called the first mid-semester convocation in two years.

CONVOCATION

Approximately 1,000 students, along with several professors and Austin citizens, arrived at the Men's Gym at 10 A.M. Awaiting them was probably the most impressive convocation ever held on the campus to that time. A 60-foot banner proclaiming "For Texas, I Will" hung behind the stage, while songs, yells and speeches went on for two hours.

Shorty Nowotny, a former yell leader then attending law school (and later dean of students), presented the plan to the assembled group. Doc Stewart, a gifted speaker, said "Standing here this morning I see a vision. While the sun is setting on the western horizon next Thanksgiving Day, I can see 30,000 people leaving the new and commodious stadium exuberant over the Longhorns' victory over A&M."

Naturally, that drew a cheer, but Stark added a note of caution, warning against any bickering. "The surest way to kill the stadium is to fight over the material, the cost or the location. The remainder of the details will be worked out by the experts and engineers," he said, and then proceeded to clear up another point. "Lutcher Stark of Orange is not going to build this stadium. I recently saw in the *Texan* a statement that made me ashamed of the paper. It stated that many ex-students were still hoping that some prominent alumnus would give the major part of the funds needed to construct the stadium and name it after his family."

Stark said that while he planned to give his share, he would emphatically not pay for any "Stark Stadium." Toward the end of the meeting, the Texas Cowboys and the Orange Jackets (a women's student service organization) distributed pledge cards which were signed for a total of $3,000. This was more than two months before the actual fundraising drive would commence. Well-attended meetings were held, as students volunteered their time and pledged money. The residents of Scottish Rite Dormitory and numerous fraternities and sororities also jumped the gun in pledging for the stadium.

And why not? As Bellmont said, "A new athletic stadium for the University of Texas is absolutely essential. . . . Our seating capacity is now the poorest of any state university athletic park in the South. This will bring the faculty, student body and alumni closer together."

Considerable work was done during the Christmas holidays, led by Stark and Bellmont. The Athletics Council put up $5,000 to cover preliminary expenses, and on December 18, the Board of Regents, meeting in Galveston, gave its approval of the stadium project. Of course, this was something of a *pro forma* act, since the powerful Stark served as chairman.

Stark also headed the central committee. Other members included William T. Caswell and Dave C. Reed representing Austin's business community; Ed C. Connor of Dallas, W. H. Richardson, Jr. of Austin and Frost Woodhull of San Antonio representing UT alumni; Bellmont and Ira Hildebrand representing the faculty; and McGill of Corsicana, Cecil Chamberlin of Stephenville and Lucy T. Harding of Fort Worth representing the student body. (The following people later served: J. A. Kemp of Wichita Falls, E. C. H. Bantel of Austin, S. Eldon Dyer of San Antonio and Richard T. Fleming of Houston.) The organization was then divided into executive, finance and construction committees.

The regents authorized Dallas architect Herbert M. Greene to draw up plans for the stadium. He received input from James M. White, who had designed the stadium then under construction at the University of Illinois, UT civil engineering professor A. T. Granger and Stark, who was himself trained as a civil engineer.

BRACKENRIDGE FIELD

Another important decision was made on the location of the proposed stadium, although most people already knew where it would be: Brackenridge Field, also called "East Woods." Three blocks east of the campus, on the far side of Waller Creek, this hilly area must have seemed a bit remote at the time. But Stark and the others foresaw the university's eastward growth and made a wise choice. Actually, this spot had been envisioned as the future home of UT athletics for almost 30 years.

The yet-unnamed stadium would lie between 21st and 23rd streets, and between Red River Street and Waller Creek. (San Jacinto Boulevard, even as a dirt road, waited five years in the future.) The university planned to build a bridge over the creek at 22nd Street to connect the campus and stadium.

What was the history of this land that would come to hold UT's Memorial Stadium? Native Americans, primarily the Comanche, Tonkawa, Waco and Lipan tribes, had long lived in or traversed the area, and Waller Creek had served as a watering spot for cattle drives going north.

After the founding of the university in 1883, this lightly populated, rustic area attracted adventurous students. Presumably named after UT benefactor and regent George Brackenridge, it gave field practice to civil engineering, forestry and geology students. The site of many sandlot baseball games, tug-of-wars and hair-raising freshman initiations, Brackenridge Field also provided a measure of privacy for romantic couples. But it would serve a new and bigger purpose in the development of the University of Texas.

The central committee first met on January 3, 1924, at which time Stark emphasized the need to rush all aspects of the work; he took seriously the goal of having a stadium ready by Thanksgiving Day. Former assistant registrar Max Fichtenbaum was appointed as executive secretary, one of the few paid positions in the whole stadium drive. Fichtenbaum, a quiet and cautious man, had graduated from the university a few years earlier and had recently been employed by the Ex-Students' Association in compiling an alumni directory. While that job ended in a salary dispute, the mostly finished directory would prove helpful when it came time to contact alumni for stadium pledges.

The *Daily Texan* had previously followed an all-news policy, eschewing publicity campaigns. But editor Henry Fulcher, perhaps with the subtle guidance of McGill, changed that. In 1924, the *Daily Texan*, reflecting the sentiments of most students, made no secret of its ardent support for the stadium. It did this with editorials, photographs, cartoons, allocation of space and discount advertising rates. The UT campus had entered a hectic, stressful, but ultimately exhilarating time.

Bellmont, ever aware that some people were alarmed at the growing focus on athletics, tried to calm them. But his assurances did not stop the critics, who regarded him and Stark as leaders of the campus "athletic oligarchy." An editorial in the *Hillsboro Mirror* expressed this view: "The drive for a $500,000 athletic stadium at the University of Texas is on. Meanwhile, shacks adorn the campus. . . . But instead of a drive for shack destruction comes a drive, not for the glorification and securer housing of scholarship, but for the glorification of athletics."

By coincidence, J. Frank Dobie was not on campus during the stadium excitement. The famed folklorist, author and savant, never too keen on organized team sports, would surely have doubted the validity of the whole business. But at the time, he was on sabbatical from UT, teaching English at Oklahoma A&M (now Oklahoma State).

By mid-January, Greene had completed his blueprints and presented a drawing of the football/track stadium, with touches of the Spanish-Mediterranean architecture then common on the Texas campus. The east and west stands, both 118' × 437', would seat 26,000 people. Greene's vision of the stadium went far beyond what could be done in 1924, however. It was not until after World War II that the twice-enlarged stadium would approximate his drawing, but the ornate towers he wanted set at its four corners were never built. Even so, this proposed facility eclipsed Clark Field and would be the first actual stadium in the South. Greene's plans were received with great fervor.

EXPERT ADVICE

That same week, Bellmont wired a telegram to the San Francisco-based Lyman Pierce Company, asking it to send a representative to Austin. From his 1923 research, Bellmont knew that the Pierce organization had the greatest expertise on fundraising to build college athletic stadiums. A reputation for fairness and ethical conduct did not hurt, either. In recent years, Pierce had helped Stanford, California, Illinois and Minnesota raise money for big new stadiums.

This would be the company's first foray into the South and by far the most difficult fundraising job. Working on a flat-fee basis paid by the Athletics Council, Pierce representative Harry D. Cross provided crucial advice during the long drive. A contract, signed in late January 1924, stated that the company would help get at least $500,000 in pledges, a goal Cross hoped to achieve by June 15.

At a meeting in President Sutton's office, Stark offered a motion that the stadium be dedicated to Texans who had served in the World War. Again, this had the appearance of a *fait accompli*, since the university had been attempting to erect a suitable memorial structure for some time. Patriotic feeling about the war and its attendant sacrifices still ran strong, which would make a public fundraising drive much more palatable.

Ira Hildebrand, dean of the UT School of Law, saw several legal hurdles facing the board, so he filed appropriate papers with the Secretary of State, thus forming the Texas Memorial Stadium Association. With this structure in place, the dream of UT sports fans came closer to realization.

Austin's John D. Miller, president of Miller Blueprint Company, donated a new multigraph machine to the stadium drive, a gift that would save hundreds of dollars in printing and labor costs. The Students Memorial Fund, consisting of $300, was transferred to stadium coffers in early February.

At this time, the primary topic of conversation among UT students was the stadium. Just where on Brackenridge Field would it sit? How many fans would it hold? How would it be financed? And when would it be ready? Whether it was a roundtable discussion at a fraternity or sorority house, a couple chatting over lunch at Scholz's Garten or Martin's Kum-Bak hamburger stand on Guadalupe Street (a.k.a. "the Drag"), or students walking along a corridor in one of the shacks—most had the stadium on their minds.

They were kept informed by the *Daily Texan* and the ever-active Bill McGill, who spoke at dozens of classes and organizational meetings. Students Rob Murphree and Genevieve Aron put on a number of stunts to arouse further interest in the stadium. More than 500 students signed up to take part in the campus fundraising drive, set for the week of February 25-March 1, 1924. These students comprised 68 teams, each with a captain.

Despite all that had been done, the organizing and rallies, and the sense that a great and historic time had come for UT, the students did not know how much work it would take to finance and erect Memorial Stadium. They had heard tales of the ease with which some Northern schools had raised money for their stadiums. A drive at the University of Minnesota allegedly produced $665,000 in just six days, and even more amazing, Illinois was said to have raised $330,000, Purdue $460,000 and Indiana $500,000, each in a single day. Most of these institutions had larger, more affluent student bodies than UT, but in each case, a handful of alumni made sizable pledges. It would not be that way in Austin.

THE CROSSROADS

During a February 20 meeting at stadium headquarters in the YMCA building on Guadalupe Street, Stark told the workers "Texas students cannot—they dare not—fail on this proposition. It means more than anything they ever attempted or ever will attempt again. . . . You will never build this stadium with pocket change. You've got to shuffle up and come across with real money."

Dean Taylor put it even more bluntly: "Texas University is standing at the crossroads. Down the right fork is the stadium, symbolizing good luck, success and prosperity. Down the other fork lies dismal failure. Which do you choose?"

A few skeptical exes, looking past all the hoopla, doubted that the students would make more than a small dent in the $500,000 goal. Perhaps as little as $20,000 would be pledged on campus, an amount unlikely to inspire alumni generosity. Stark, Bellmont, McGill and every student leader constantly preached the need for starting the stadium campaign with a bang. So they chose the optimistic figure of $100,000 as a campus goal.

Finally the big day arrived—February 25, 1924, the beginning of the Memorial Stadium fundraising drive, divided into three parts: the campus, Austin and then the dispersed alumni. Those looking for a bad omen found one in the weather as a blizzard hit, dumping snow and freezing rain all over town. Nevertheless, 2,500 students (out of an enrollment of 4,465) trudged to the Men's Gym for another convocation.

Keeping their coats on inside the frigid, barn-like gym, the students witnessed a hot show. First, the Longhorn Band played, followed by Jimmie's Joys, a jazz band made up of recent UT grads which had lately won national fame. Fifteen minutes of organized yells preceded vigorous speeches by Stark, Stewart, McGill and Taylor.

Before the meeting adjourned, Stark announced that for every $10 in pledges the students collected, he would give one. This evoked a big cheer from the bundled audience, providing yet another point any campaign worker could make in asking for donations. With good humor, Stark urged them to make him dig deep in fulfilling his promise.

As the drive began, the students were aware of just what they were doing and why. The inadequacy of Clark Field as a home for UT athletics was painfully evident to all. And since by law the Texas Legislature could only fund buildings for educational purposes, money for the stadium had to be raised in another way. Student workers were to remind people that Memorial Stadium would honor all Texans who had served and fought in the war, not just those with a UT connection. According to the manual given to each worker in the campaign, "No finer tribute could be paid to these men and women than to erect upon the campus of the state university a great memorial of concrete which will stand through the ages."

The students learned to drop the names of other colleges that had raised much larger sums for athletic stadiums. Emphasis was given to the lifetime benefits accruing to a person with a University of Texas degree and the need to reciprocate. They said it was the first time in the 41-year history of the school that students and alumni were called upon to build "a greater Varsity." That was not quite true, since Thomas W. Gregory had launched a drive for a modern gymnasium in 1907, but no one quibbled.

HOW PUSHY?

These 500 volunteers were urged to make their own pledges before asking another person to give. And when solicitation began, they faced the eternal fundraising dilemma: How pushy should they be? Obviously, a passive, apologetic approach would not get it done, but neither did they want to be so aggressive as to turn off prospective givers.

Harry Cross, experienced in these matters, stressed that there should be no "evangelistic, pressure-type tactics" used to get pledges. He taught the workers how to parry objections and give assurance that all of the money would go to the construction of Memorial Stadium. Overhead expenses were paid by the Athletics Council and the Stadium Association's Board of Directors. Much of this money probably came from H. J. Lutcher Stark, generalissimo of the whole effort.

Team captains met for lunch at the gym every day of the drive. They reported results (written on a giant chalkboard), gave cheers, heard speeches and learned to be more effective at the fine art of extracting money. Competition among teams was encouraged as a way to boost pledges.

After the first two days, $27,000 had been pledged, which exceeded the doubters' predictions, yet left McGill slightly disappointed. As he told the *Daily Texan*, "We are up against a big game. If you think $10, $15, or $25 pledges will build this stadium, the game is lost before we begin. The students must think in terms of $100, $200, and $1,000."

Such statements may have been intended for the wealthy fraction of the UT student body, but they risked alienating many others. Still, the students were not being asked for so much. A $100 pledge, stretched out over two years, came to a daily sacrifice of just fifteen cents. To help "build that stadium for fighting Texans" (the winning entry in a slogan contest), Taylor urged male students to forego cigars and suggested that most coeds could have their hair bobbed less often.

Everyone on campus got a chance to pledge. "Carrie," a black janitor, signed on for a donation of five dollars, regretting that she could not give more. And some students, such as Ann Caswell, gave $1,000 to balance it out.

One of the most colorful stories about the 1924 campus fundraising drive involved five-foot firebrand Shorty Nowotny, co-founder, along with McGill, of the Texas Cowboys. He borrowed a cannon from the Capitol lawn and placed it beside the west entrance to the old Main Building. For every $10,000 pledged, Nowotny fired the cannon, once in the early morning hours, drawing the interest of the Austin police.

And mention must be made of the "stadiumeter," which stood near the cannon. This large drawing of a thermometer kept count of the money pledged to date, with the campus goal of $100,000 at the top. It featured a message of "Let's Bust the Darn Thing!"

Late February found the UT campus cluttered with messages pertaining to the stadium. The *Daily Texan*, the primary medium of information in those basically pre-electronic days, was loaded with stories, advertisements and editorials. Posters adorned nearly every tree and the walls of classrooms and dorms. The walls of the library (now Battle Hall) held four huge signs stating "For Texas, We Will," "Don't Delay, Pay Today," "Build That Stadium," and "We Cannot Fail."

Note the repeated use of the first-person plural—"we." There was, in those days, a tangible sense of community among the University of Texas student body, then roughly one-twelfth its current size. Not only was it smaller, but more cohesive in terms of age, ethnicity and geographical derivation. Multiculturalism had not yet come to the Forty Acres.

The vast majority of students in the early 1920s were undergraduates, between the ages of 16 and 22. Many had grown up on farms or ranches. Non-Caucasians and those from outside of Texas were rare, so most adhered to a common identity. This made it easier to appeal to the loyalty of individual students and also left them susceptible to peer pressure, regardless of the pronouncements of Cross and others.

DON'T BE "LEFT OUT"

Not everyone pledged. Some students and faculty never attended football games and did not care if the Longhorns won or lost, much less whether they had a modern stadium in which to play. Still, these people were not vocal in expressing such views. While the word "pariah" is a bit strong, those who refused to pledge were made to feel excluded from the great movement to build Memorial Stadium. As one *Daily Texan* editorial surmised, "It seems that a fellow who didn't give would feel strangely 'left out.'"

As the pledge drive went on and the totals rose, so did enthusiasm. One of the students most responsible for this success was Mineral Wells native Carl Webb, a good-looking young man with a knack for extemporaneous speaking. He captained team number 27, which pulled in $6,157 in pledges (nearly twice as much as the second-place team), and took part in the other fundraising drives that would follow. Webb was truly one of the unsung heroes in the effort to build Memorial Stadium.

On Friday, February 29, campus pledges went over the $100,000 mark. The cannon boomed, and the "stadiumeter" was altered to give it a shattered look. While the drive was scheduled to end the next day, the stadium Board of Directors extended it through Tuesday, March 4 in hopes of raising more money.

Spirits were further boosted by a telegram from Fayetteville, Arkansas, where the undefeated UT basketball team was playing the Razorbacks. Signed by team captain Ivan "Bobby" Robertson and Stewart, who coached basketball as well as football, the telegram applauded the students' generosity.

March 2, Texas Independence Day, was the traditional gathering time for UT alumni. Whether in El Paso, Wichita Falls, Beaumont or elsewhere, they discussed the campus stadium drive, which was now approaching $150,000. A feeling of euphoria had taken hold because of what the *Daily Texan* called "the biggest thing in the history of the school." In the first tangible sign that a stadium would be built, some students did preliminary clearing and surveying of Brackenridge Field, and engineering professor E. C. H. Bantel performed soundings of the base rock in the area. The stadium would lie on a grid with the campus, 7° east of due north.

"The game is over and the victory is ours," proclaimed the student committee on Wednesday, March 5. "The campus has responded to the call for stadium funds in a way that has astonished the entire state of Texas."

Here, compiled by UT auditor W. L. Long, are the final numbers from the first campus drive: 3,322 students pledged $120,724; 289 faculty and staff pledged $11,209; and various UT organizations pledged $19,376, coming to roughly $151,000.

CELEBRATION TIME

Student leaders presented Stark with an oversized check for $15,000 to be drawn on the "Bank of Campus Loyalty," and he promptly paid it, bringing the total to $166,000. With the campus fundraising drive over and a major success, the students had an evening of revelry that would become part of UT lore. First a 7 P.M. rally shook the rafters of the Men's Gym, then the students paraded through downtown, stopping briefly at Sixth Street and Congress Avenue. Then it was off to the circus grounds south of the Colorado River, where a huge stack of wood had been prepared.

An estimated 3,000 students, plus another 7,000 Austinites, watched a giant bonfire, whooped, shrieked and joined in a series of snake dances. Traffic over the Congress Avenue bridge came to a halt as the celebration went into the night. All in all, it was a joyous gathering, and few people noticed when, in a brief speech, Stark reminded them of the crucial difference between a pledge and money in hand.

March 10-15 was designated "Stadium Pay-Up Week" on the UT campus, when students were asked to make first installments on pledges. Yet by March 20, only half of those had actually been paid, a fact that worried Stark and Bellmont, who knew that large bills were coming due soon. To Max Fichtenbaum fell the unpleasant task of politely dunning the laggards. He presented a brave public face, saying "We are satisfied with the way the students and others are paying up. . . . The percentage of those who have allowed their pledges to go unpaid is very small and in most cases, is due to the pledge falling at an inconvenient time."

Some people buckled down and gave, ever willing to do their small part. All 323 female students at Scottish Rite Dormitory twice went without meals to help pay their pledges. One girl cut her hair and sold it, another gave blood to cover her pledge, and tennis player Marshall Bell bet Stark $50 that he could lose 10 pounds, which he did, donating the money to the stadium fund. The Women's Athletic Association held a block party to fulfill its $500 pledge. Several students would seek stadium construction jobs in the summer of 1924, using the money to pay pledges as well as help finance their education. Funds were also raised by such diverse means as a wrestling match, a watermelon party and the sale of a bicycle.

Other than Stark's big payment capping the campus drive, only $15,000 had been collected by March 30, so all the backslapping and declarations that the stadium was now a reality seemed premature. All of this made stadium officials more conscious of the need to succeed big in the two remaining portions of the fundraising drive: first in the city of Austin and then among the alumni.

THE AUSTIN DRIVE

In 1924, the population of Austin hovered around 55,000 (including 2,000 UT graduates), and it was estimated that the university pumped $5,000,000 into the local economy per year. A new football stadium for Texas would mean even more people coming to town, filling hotel rooms and spending money. And such a big construction project would be an economic boost in itself. Bellmont had long stressed these points in his discussions with Austin's government, business and civic leaders. For the local segment of the stadium drive, scheduled to last from April 4-11, the goal was set at $166,000, the amount pledged on campus. Three streamers spanned Congress Avenue from Third Street to the Capitol, reminding people to give generously.

Sam Sparks, president of the Texas Bank and Trust Company, was not a UT alumnus, but he offered to head the Austin drive. Seeking to enlist help, Sparks affirmed the importance of the proposed stadium, saying with confidence "Texas needs but to call, and her sons and daughters will answer."

Adhering to the advice of Cross, Sparks put together a 30-member executive committee and arranged the cooperation of Austin's five major civic organizations: Rotary Club, Lions Club, Exchange Club, Kiwanis Club and the Young Men's Business League. Headquarters of the Austin fundraising drive was the Driskill Hotel, which followed the campus pattern by hosting daily luncheons for the 375 volunteers, divided into 53 teams, who would canvass the capital city.

Take a look at some of the names involved in the Austin fundraising drive: Caswell, Long, Covert, Pennybacker, McCallum, Wooten, Koen, Reed, Scarbrough, Woodward and Mueller. We still recognize them because of the streets, schools, companies, a bridge, a dormitory, a lake and even an airport bearing their names.

The beginning of the Austin drive was set to coincide with ground-breaking ceremonies on Brackenridge Field. At 4:45 P.M. on Friday, April 4, the Longhorn Band marched from Clark Field to the future site of Memorial Stadium, where a crowd of perhaps 300 waited. Interestingly enough, it did not include Stark or Bellmont, who were in Dallas, consulting with architects and engineers.

Standing atop a makeshift wooden platform, Bill McGill gave a brief history of the stadium movement and then introduced the day's four speakers: Governor Pat Neff, UT President W. S. Sutton, D. K. Woodward representing the Ex-Students' Association, and Col. Alvin Owsley, Jr., former national commander of the American Legion and a Texas graduate himself. They extolled the stadium and its location on the UT campus, the scene of training for many soldiers during the war. One of the speakers read supportive letters from Rice football coach John W. Heisman and Texas A&M coach Dana X. Bible, who was later to lead the Longhorns in Memorial Stadium.

After each man spoke, he set off a blast of dynamite in what would become the four corners of the stadium. But the high decorum was shattered when Owsley pressed the lever for the final explosion, which caused the platform to collapse. Neff landed on his back amid the falling planks, a flagpole struck a young girl on the head, and one woman fainted. It was nothing too serious though, and Neff made light of the accident.

The List & Gifford Company of Dallas had made the lowest bid for the stadium excavation work, which began with these four blasts. The $28,944 contract called for the company to prepare the area for construction and to move some 15,000 cubic yards of rock and topsoil from east to west, partially eliminating a big slope.

R. M. Brooks, superintendent for List & Gifford, set up a camp for 40 workers and brought in two steam shovels, an elevator, grader, tractor and 25 teams of mules. While dozens of trees were cut down, the record contains no word of protest by UT students.

As had happened on campus, the Austin drive got off to a slow start, raising just $34,000 in pledges the first two days. McGill and others had expected this bigger and more affluent group to give freely, for both noble and selfish reasons.

UT students had planned a "monster stadium parade" from the campus, around the Capitol and then downtown. And they were not happy. The night before, 25 student workers (including McGill, Nowotny, Mayer and Webb, all of whom took part in the Austin drive) issued a statement through the *Daily Texan*, concluding this way: "Regardless of the small total to date, regardless of the alarming reports which we receive from downtown, we still have faith and confidence in the citizenship of this city. We know that they will not, cannot, fail us in this crucial hour."

The parade, which was supposed to be an elaborate event with floats and big-name officials, turned out to be impressive, but in a different sort of way. While a heavy rainstorm impinged on the colorful and orderly procession planned, nearly 2,500 students gathered at the intersection of Sixth Street and Congress Avenue to show the downtowners how they felt. Not until the Longhorn Band led the drenched students in "The Eyes of Texas" did they head back to campus.

The stadium drive in Austin, extended through April 15, picked up steam after that, although it never got the really big donations. Stadium workers accepted pledges ranging from the W. A. Achilles Company to Hubert Zimmpleman and even one from the local chapter of the Ku Klux Klan.

Totals for the Austin drive came to $115,103, as 2,393 individuals and organizations pledged. Dr. A. W. Griffith's team was most successful, pulling in $9,221, while the team led by Hallie Maud Neff, the governor's daughter, raised $4,280, tops among women. If some campus people grumbled that Austin's better-off citizens could have come up with larger donations, they also knew that a total of $281,000 had been pledged toward the stadium. All things considered, it was a very good start. With the excavation work well under way, with the alumni excited, and with men like Stark and Bellmont at the helm, it seemed that Varsity really would have a stadium by Thanksgiving Day, 1924.

THE ALUMNI'S TURN

While the campus and Austin fundraising drives went on, the exes had been preparing for their own. UT had an estimated 30,000 living alumni at the time, and nearly all would get an opportunity to make a stadium pledge. Many of them showed signs of awakening from a long period of indifference to the school's progress. The reason lies in the nature of this project. Constructing a new dormitory or classroom building would get few people's attention, but a big, modern football stadium for the Longhorns? That was another matter. The alumni had taken note of this from the beginning and watched with interest as the students and people of Austin did their part.

Every city in the state (and a few beyond its borders) with more than 50 UT alumni formed a fundraising committee, or at least one person took charge. A 60-day drive ending in late June was expected to bring pledge totals over the half-million dollar mark and up to the new goal of $600,000.

The alumni may have been inspired by the tremendous showing of Longhorn athletes during the 1923-1924 school year. Doc Stewart's football team won eight games and tied one; his basketball team, probably the best in Southwest Conference history to that time, went undefeated in 23 games; Daniel Penick's tennis team won every match, including a national doubles title by Louis Thalheimer and Lewis White; Clyde Littlefield's track team won every meet it entered, and the quartet of Richard McNatt, George Ritchie, Kenneth Hackler and Jim Reese set a world record in the medley relay; and Billy Disch's baseball team proved victorious in every game but one. All told, UT teams posted a gaudy 88-1-1 record that year. The time was right for raising funds.

Texas students were not shy in telling the alumni that they needed to come through, as one *Daily Texan* ad stated in large letters, "There Are 30,000 of You." An *Alcalde* editorial fully acknowledged it: "The students have challenged us. . . . And on our answers hangs the future of our school. If we fail in this, the whole state will point the finger of scorn at Texas."

All prospective donors were informed of the stadium seating options, good for 10 years. While tickets still had to be paid for, a $50 donation reserved two seats, a $100 donation got four seats, and every succeeding $100 merited another seat, up to a limit of 10. Those who gave the most sat nearest to the 50-yard line. Fair enough.

The alumni drive had to succeed, because the Stadium Association was in financial trouble, with pledge payments coming in much more slowly than bills. For this reason, the redoubtable Stark loaned it $25,000, and Dave Reed another $15,000, to meet expenses. As Stark and McGill had made clear, the stadium would not be built from the proceeds of bake sales, nor from poor folks' penny jars.

The first of the "Flying Squadrons" got underway with an April 24 trip to meet students, teachers and administrators at the UT Medical School in Galveston. For these junkets, Stark, Bellmont, Stewart, McGill and a few others would travel to a town, make speeches and give advice and best wishes for a bountiful fund drive. They would make nearly 200 such trips before the campaign ended, with varying results.

In what should have been a boost to the statewide alumni drive, on May 7 the general contracting company of Walsh & Burney was chosen to build Memorial Stadium. This San Antonio firm had submitted a bid of $201,091 to put up the east and west stands according to specifications, with an option for a north-end horseshoe. The bid was $20,000 less than any of the other five construction companies and something of a bargain to stadium officials. Company directors Edward Walsh and R. L. Burney (a Texas A&M graduate) understood the need to expedite construction, with Thanksgiving Day as the firm goal.

Using Fichtenbaum's alumni directory, Stark sent copies of a form letter to thousands of ex-students, beginning with the words "We wish you could have participated in the stirring events recently enacted on the campus in connection with the Memorial Stadium campaign. We wish that it were possible to sit down with you and tell you of these events and of the new day which has dawned for Texas."

POLITICAL BROUHAHA

Stark detailed the pledges made so far and the need for "this permanent memorial to those splendid men and women who served in the World War," and enclosed a subscription card. But the alumni drive got off to an even worse start than the campus or Austin drives. Some exes had begun to show apathy or outright hostility to the stadium effort.

Here is why. By May 1924, the University of Texas had been without a permanent president for over a year, as W. S. Sutton performed the duties of the office on a "temporary" basis. Many people on and off campus were alarmed when Stark floated Governor Pat Neff as a possible replacement. Neff, who had lost a re-election bid a few months earlier, was said to be interested in the UT position. Since he had appointed a majority of the Board of Regents and was close to Stark, it appeared he would get the nod.

Both friends and foes warned Stark not to pick Neff because he was unqualified, and the deal reeked of politics. But the chairman of the board could be quite bullheaded, and if he wanted Neff as president of the university, then he would have him.

Stark got his wish, and on May 16 the Board of Regents, by a 7-2 vote, elected Neff as president. But there were immediate repercussions, as Frank Jones and Sam Cochran resigned in protest. Although the outrage vented on Stark and the six pliant board members was ferocious, it would have faded if not for Will C. Hogg of Houston, who had the economic and political power, combined with deep indignation, to fight Stark on this issue.

Hogg, the son of former Governor James S. Hogg, had become wealthy by exploiting Brazoria County oil fields. He cared passionately about the University of Texas, from which he had graduated in 1897. The founder of *Alcalde*, Hogg also steadied the Ex-Students' Association in hard times, and as a regent, defended the university against Governor Jim Ferguson in 1917. Like Stark, Hogg had helped countless students through school and had long maintained that UT could actually fulfill that haunting phrase, "a university of the first class."

While there would appear to be no connection whatsoever between the stadium fundraising drive and the regents' choice for president, Hogg insisted that there was. He sought to use the stadium issue to bring down Stark, calling him "a rampant young ass with a rush of money to the head." Hogg had no legal standing in this matter, apart from chairing the executive committee of the Ex-Students' Association, a purely advisory position. But that did not deter him.

Although Neff soon declined the UT presidency offer, Hogg would not stop until he had Stark's scalp. In the next two weeks, he would send many letters and telegrams to alumni around the state, urging them not to give to the stadium drive until Stark resigned from both it and the Board of Regents. Stark, quite naturally, responded with defiance.

On May 21, the *Daily Texan* printed a lengthy statement signed by 25 students. They finessed the issue of the university presidency, but came down firmly on the side of Stark and especially the stadium: "The dynamic fact that concerns the student body of the University of Texas is that the STADIUM MUST AND WILL BE BUILT and that Lutch is our friend and has proven it with his timeless endeavors in our behalf." Without naming Hogg, they expressed contempt for those who would "throw a wrench into the wheels of the greatest project that the University of Texas has ever attempted."

With all the charges and countercharges issued via speeches, mail, telegrams and newspapers, stadium pledges and payments on those pledges nearly came to a standstill. An architect's drawing and a torn-up hillside were then the extent of UT's great new football stadium. It was suddenly unclear whether the stadium would be built in time for the Texas A&M game, or built at all, for that matter. Maybe the Longhorns would continue using old Clark Field, a depressing thought to those who had worked so hard in the stadium drive. In light of the Stark-Hogg feud, a committee of Waco citizens traveled to Austin with the suggestion that the November 8 UT-Baylor game be played 100 miles up the road. Bellmont sternly refused.

Many exes stood solidly behind Hogg, believing that principle—a university free of political control—was more important than any football stadium. Their interests may have resembled Hogg's, in that he merely tolerated athletics in a collegiate setting, while Stark and others positively thrived on it. For the latter group, the building of Memorial Stadium was of paramount importance.

For a few days in late May, it appeared that Memorial Stadium had gone the same sad way as the Memorial Dormitory and the Memorial Union. The mood among students and many alumni was gloomy, as expressed in a letter to Hogg from John B. Pope: "It looks to me now as if you and Stark between you, had killed the stadium, which cannot but be regretted by every citizen of Austin, as we have already raised our part of the fund, and to fail now will be keenly resented by all of us."

Hogg showed courage by meeting with 35 students in the YMCA auditorium on the night of May 29. He explained his actions vis-a-vis Stark and the stadium drive and heard an impassioned plea by Bill McGill. Carl Webb quoted Hogg's speech in Dallas a week earlier, in which he denigrated the stadium drive and promised to fight it to the last breath in his body.

"It is all a lie!" shouted Hogg, taken back by the students' unmitigated impudence. "You are trying to make a dunce out of me." He then left the building, peppered by students' questions and vows to see the stadium built, regardless of what he might do.

THE BIG BOYS MAKE UP

Stark and Hogg both felt pressure to compromise and finally they did. They met with McGill and David C. Bland, president of the Ex-Students' Association, in a three-hour conference in San Antonio's Gunter Hotel. Hogg agreed to halt his anti-Stark, anti-stadium campaign and even pledged $10,000. Stark, for his part, gave up leadership of the stadium fundraising drive (which was turned over to McGill). But he did not resign as president of the Stadium Association and certainly not from the Board of Regents. Although Hogg and his friends privately claimed victory, he had been outgeneraled by Stark.

Hogg offered to take responsibility for the stadium drive in Houston, which he had caused to stagnate. But in fact, it was his younger brother, Mike, who got that task. The expectation that both Houston and Dallas would soon raise $100,000 proved much too rosy.

As for the UT presidency, following Neff's refusal, it was next offered to Guy Stanton Ford of the University of Minnesota and then to Herbert Eugene Bolton of the University of California, both of whom also turned it down. Finally, Walter Splawn of the Texas Railroad Commission was chosen and accepted. One of the first things Splawn did was to inquire about the progress of Memorial Stadium.

While it had been hoped that the fundraising drive might conclude by mid-June 1924, the Stark-Hogg schism put a severe handicap on its success. The larger cities—Houston, Dallas, San Antonio, Fort Worth and El Paso—had hardly raised a dime at that point.

Following all the upheaval, the stadium campaign was quite fortunate to have a hardworking, inoffensive man like Bill McGill, who was unanimously endorsed by both the Texas Exes and the Stadium Association's other officials. Stark, while keeping some distance from fundraising efforts, remained deeply involved in all other aspects of erecting Memorial Stadium.

But the fundraising effort never recaptured the momentum of the days before Stark and Hogg battled. Only 2,500 alumni pledged, and the total came to around $152,000, far short of what Bellmont, Stark and McGill had hoped. Some $54,000 came from Houston, a disappointing $22,000 from Dallas, $11,000 from Wichita Falls, $8,500 from Fort Worth, and $8,000 from San Antonio. Smaller towns and rural areas were canvassed as well, with Corsicana having the best per-capita average of all.

Back on campus, the students were a bit disturbed that the alumni had not given more liberally. Did the exes not understand the importance of building this great memorial to honor Varsity's military heroes? Not that $152,000 was so bad after all, especially if it were *paid*. And perhaps the alums would have a better record of paying pledges than the students.

Still well short of the original half-million dollar goal, McGill expanded the focus of the stadium drive. "It is our intention to give every man and woman in Texas a chance to get in on this first statewide memorial to our fighters," he declared, "because we think a statewide memorial should be democratic. We do not want anyone to feel that this is strictly a University of Texas proposition; it is broader than any school, and it is as broad as our state."

BUILDING THE STADIUM

Seeking pledges and collecting on them would continue for more than four years, but in the meantime, the infrastructure of Memorial Stadium was being laid. List & Gifford had completed most of the excavation work by early June. In some places, they had to blast and dig through more than 20 feet of limestone to reach solid rock, upon which pillars would be placed.

Almost as soon as the contract was signed, Walsh & Burney began hauling equipment, material and workers to Austin. The lumber they would use in building the stands was provided at cost by the Lutcher Moore Lumber Company of Orange, one of the Stark family's many operations. The reinforcing steel came from the Concrete Steel Company of Kansas City.

Before hitting a lick on the stadium per se, superintendent A. A. Hasbrook's men started preparing the field, possibly with a sense of the historic work they were doing. Walsh & Burney had originally planned to use a central mixer and tower, chuting concrete to both east and west stands. But the need to rush construction prevented such a setup on the field, so it proved necessary to erect a mixer and tower behind each set of stands. To have a fertile base for growing grass, they brought three feet of black dirt from nearby Waller Creek and covered that with an inch of sandy loam from the flood plains of the Colorado River. The field, sloping 16 inches from the center to each sideline, was later planted with Bermuda grass, fertilized and encircled by a menacing barbed-wire fence.

Even as early as May, Hasbrook was bothered by all the sightseers coming to watch the changes to Brackenridge Field. As many as 50 people at a time, some of whom had traveled a great distance, would stand and view the workers, mules, equipment and mountains of material needed to build the stadium.

The *Daily Texan, Alcalde,* the *Austin American-Statesman* and the *Longhorn T* (an athletic department publication) all contained articles expressing amazement at the size of the project, which if placed downtown, would have more than covered the area from the Scarbrough Building to the Majestic Theater. By the standards of the day, UT's Memorial Stadium would be immense. It required roughly 24,000 sacks of cement mixed with 2,000 cubic yards of sand and 4,000 cubic yards of gravel. Some 320 tons of structural steel and 500,000 feet of lumber were used in building what the *Daily Texan* confidently called "the South's greatest athletic field."

A team of inspectors, headed by UT civil engineering professor A. T. Granger, checked all material coming onto the construction site. Although

Stark kept an eye on things, Granger was his man in the field. He and his assistants had a small office, where they reviewed every aspect of the stadium's progress. Granger, who helped design the stadium, worked closely, and for the most part cooperatively, with Hasbrook in implementing those plans.

In the summer of 1924, many students returned to their hometowns to carry on the fundraising drive. A few though, stayed in Austin and labored among 150 to 200 men, most of them black and Hispanic. They handled picks, shovels, wheelbarrows and sledgehammers, and poured concrete into wooden forms. The non-union labor crew generally consisted of 60 carpenters, 100 day laborers, 12 steel workers, two painters and five foremen. Quite a few of the workers actually lived on the grounds during construction, while others stayed in nearby boarding houses. The payroll came to $4,000 per week.

Most students found the work too hard and tedious, and soon sought easier jobs or quit. Two lasted the entire summer, and we know the identity of just one. C. D. Bedford came to Austin from west Texas in 1923 as a poor, yet determined freshman. Bedford had lived with his brother and two other students, first in an army tent and then in an abandoned shack in the woods east of campus, close to where he was now helping build the stadium. The money Bedford earned that summer enabled him to pay his stadium pledge and, presumably, to live in more comfort his sophomore year.

The presence of ground water delayed pouring concrete for the more than 300 subterranean pillars until solid rock was reached in every hole. When the first concrete went into the ground on June 20, the students in town for summer school hailed it as a milestone, another indication that, yes, Varsity would have its long dreamed-of stadium.

Since the east stands would lie on a hill and be easier to erect, they went up first. Memorial Stadium was constructed in equal-sized "sections," ten of them in both stands. Once the perimeter of the east stands was determined and all the pillars firmly embedded, Hasbrook's workers started on the first section in the north end. They erected a web of structural steel, then set wooden forms to mold concrete for the 52 rows, 13 aisles and seven portals.

At Granger's suggestion, the builders used a concrete mixture of one part sand, two and 2/3 parts gravel, plus three and 1/3 parts cement. When everything was ready, on July 14 the first section was poured, the concrete flowing from a long chute. Beginning at the top and working their way down, several men with rakes and shovels prodded the concrete into place, then smoothed it over with trowels. The gray mush settled and dried while they moved on to the next section immediately south, starting the whole process over again.

As the stadium took shape, UT track coach Clyde Littlefield (also an assistant football coach) expressed hope that a new dawn had arrived for college athletics throughout the state. Perhaps he was spurred by the fact that Austinite Mack Keeble had recently set a world record in the 75-yard high hurdles while competing for the University of Missouri. For years, poor facilities in Texas and a desire to go against the best had caused many fine high school track and football stars to leave the state. Besides Keeble, Littlefield named Texas expatriates who were then competing at such colleges as Dartmouth, Cornell, Yale, Vanderbilt, California, Southern California and Stanford.

In July, Littlefield was delighted to see work begin on the track enclosing the stadium's football field. The track at Clark Field, with its bumps and tight corners, had not been conducive to top performances and was thought to have caused many injuries over the years. So while some workers built forms and poured concrete in the stands, a group of them prepared the track under Littlefield's watchful eye. Since those were pre-metric days, the men laid out a quarter-mile track, 25 feet wide on the east and turns, and 30 feet wide on the west, to accommodate sprints. An added feature was the 220-yard straightaway extending southwest.

Workers first removed one foot of dirt throughout the entire track. Then eight inches of broken rock was laid for a foundation, followed by three inches of coarse cinders and a one-inch topping of fine black cinders. A drainage system was installed so that the track would not become soggy after a rain. And finally, several months later, a concrete curb was put in, separating the track from the football field.

BASEBALL IN MEMORIAL STADIUM?

From the beginning, there was confusion about many aspects of the stadium. Some reports had it as a horseshoe or a bowl, and people did not know if it would hold 26,000, 40,000 or even 60,000 seats. But the biggest question concerned baseball. If Clark Field was to become so much firewood after 1924, where were Billy Disch's Longhorn baseball teams to play? No other segment of UT sports had been as successful as Disch's boys, who won the SWC title nearly every season.

While baseball did not draw 20,000-plus people to Clark Field like some football games, it was a popular sport, and Disch was a revered figure, halfway into his 28-year tenure as the UT coach. Would there be baseball at Memorial Stadium, too? Some people were under that impression. Disch had surely done his part as an advocate for the stadium, overcoming an aversion to public speaking. There is some indication he hoped his teams would join Stewart's footballers and Littlefield's track men there.

The issue was settled on July 10, 1924 when Bellmont announced that Memorial Stadium would not host baseball games. Disch would remain at Clark Field (which was already partially dismantled) through the 1927 season, and then move to the new Clark Field just north of the stadium. Incidentally, there was much sentiment to name the new baseball park after Disch, but the Athletics Council declined to do that. Not until 1975, with Disch-Falk Field across Interstate 35, would Billy Disch be so honored by UT.

In the midsummer heat, more sections of the east stands got their load of concrete, work on the west stands began, and the football field and track took form. Ed C. Connor, who headed the Stadium Association's construction committee, returned to Austin from a long trip to view other college stadiums. Not ordinarily given to gushing, Connor nevertheless said "This stadium will be as fine as anything I saw anywhere in the East. . . . I am immensely pleased with the way the construction is going forward and the quality of work being done. The people of Texas have every right to be proud of themselves for the way their dream is being realized. The greatness of this thing astounds me."

Connor's enthusiasm was typical, yet stadium officials may have wondered how they would pay for the work done. While more than $400,000 had been pledged to the stadium fund by early July, less than a quarter of the money had actually come in, and the contractors had to be paid. Bills amounted to $49,000 in July alone, and the Stadium Association was nearly out of money.

A month earlier, the Ex-Students' Association (perhaps smarting under the criticism of current students) had voted to loan the entire amount of the Gymnasium Fund, roughly $45,000, to the Stadium Association at 6 percent interest. This was done with the blessing of Thomas W. Gregory, who had raised most of the money. But soon even that was gone, and until the pledges were more fully paid, UT's stadium was in fiscal trouble.

The *Daily Texan* reported this matter and that the Stadium Association had received a loan from an unspecified source. It is not hard to believe that the money came from the ever-generous chairman of the Board of Regents. That H. J. Lutcher Stark had already donated $15,000 and loaned another $25,000 to the stadium fund is well known. Though he was disappointed that other wealthy alumni had not contributed more, in all likelihood, Stark gave quiet assurances that he would take care of this eventuality. Including his donations, the lumber sold at cost and unpaid "loans," Stark may have given as much as $100,000 to the stadium drive.

Following the dictates of the Stadium Association's construction committee, architect Herbert M. Greene had designed a facility that could be added onto over the years. This was called the "unit system," the first units consisting of the east and west stands. While not everyone agreed on which unit would come next, the consensus was that it should be the north-end horseshoe and four memorial towers, augmented later by more rows to both east and west stands.

People had been informed that Memorial Stadium would seat 26,000, but that number inexplicably grew to 27,000 during the summer. While the stadium did not get any bigger, the seats—not yet installed—got smaller. It had been advertised that each seat in the stadium would be a spacious 20 inches, certainly a welcome relief from the 16 inches afforded at Clark Field.

Evidently, Bellmont decided that was a little too much room and reduced it to 18 inches, thereby expanding seating capacity by 1,000. Sound businessman that he was, Bellmont knew this move would enhance the athletic department's financial picture. Perhaps by this time, in view of the somewhat disappointing fundraising results, he realized that football revenues would be required to finish paying off stadium contractors.

In late August, several old houses on Trinity, Neches and Red River streets were removed by power of eminent domain, to make room for a large park that would eventually surround the stadium. However, one house northeast of the stadium remained, to serve for 43 years as the chief groundskeeper's home and a shed for the tractor and tools.

By September 1, as students were returning for the fall semester, the football goalposts were set in concrete at opposite ends of the now-green field, and tickets to the November 27 stadium dedication game against Texas A&M went on sale to the general public for $2.00 and $2.50. If Memorial Stadium was still far from finished, most students who had been away for the summer were thrilled with what they saw. The feeling was exemplified in a large *Daily Texan* ad featuring a picture of the Roman Coliseum and these words: "Our Memorial Stadium will be a modern coliseum of concrete and steel, capable of resisting the erosion of countless centuries. This massive edifice will command the admiration of generations unborn. Like a mantel of ivy, time will weave o'er its beloved walls a soft halo of tradition."

BELLMONT'S DECREE

The students' original goal was to have a stadium by Thanksgiving Day. It now seemed certain that they would, though the stadium might still have a few rough edges. A grand celebration and homecoming were planned for the Texas A&M game, but Bellmont surprised some people by announcing that the game against Baylor on November 8 would not be Clark Field's football swan song. The game would be staged at the new stadium.

Bellmont stated that UT would save $5,000 by not having to add bleachers to Clark Field for that final game. But his logic seems specious for three reasons: (1) Baylor was not really a big-draw opponent; (2) bleachers were not erected and taken down for every game at a cost of $5,000; and (3) Memorial Stadium would be nowhere near completion on November 8.

The decision to hold the Longhorn-Bear game in the new stadium, 19 days before its actual dedication, met with quiet protest from students and former lettermen, but Bellmont would not change his mind. He and athletic business manager Wiley Glaze evidently felt that more people would attend the game in a half-finished Memorial Stadium than in old, decrepit, though historic, Clark Field. Bellmont and Glaze had begun kicking around possible attendance and revenue figures that made them dizzy, especially from the 1924 UT-Texas A&M game. They already knew that Memorial Stadium would be a profitable investment for the university.

Texas teams had practiced and battled at Clark Field for nearly 30 years, so it was a big moment when the Longhorn players first ran onto the turf at Memorial Stadium. On the afternoon of October 3, 1924, Doc Stewart and his young men took the field for the first time. It undoubtedly gave stadium workers (still toiling 10-12 hours daily, sometimes even at night under faint lights) a refreshing pause to see them.

The primary purpose of this visit to the new stadium was to allow UT photographer Dan McCaskill to shoot pictures and a film which would be distributed to alumni clubs around the state. He first took a team picture, and then filmed a kickoff, an end run, an off-tackle play and captain Jim Marley bucking the line for a score.

By the time of this initial workout, all of the concrete had been poured for the east stands and the northern part of the west stands. Both ends of the east stands had been enclosed with a brick wall stuccoed on the outside. For seats, hundreds of wooden planks treated with boiled oil were ready to be bolted onto the inverted-U-shaped steel standards. Thirteen aisles were spaced just 30 feet apart, allowing easy access to the seven portals on each side.

Rising 40 feet in 52 rows, the stadium's stands were not very steep. And the first, lowest row was set so that the fans' sightline would be level with the athletes' knees. This feature, considered an advantage at the time, would later become a headache to stadium officials. Because of the hill the stadium was built upon, the top row on the east was only 25 feet above ground, while that on the west stood 60 feet high.

Superintendent Hasbrook's men erected a 3/4-mile length fence, made of extra heavy woven wire, around the stadium park. The fence stood seven feet high and had seven entrance and exit gates, each with an ornamental sign reading "Texas Memorial Stadium."

Austin electrician John Martin won the stadium lighting contract with a bid of $2,985, agreeing to use only underground conduits, not poles. The firm of Donnelly and White won the plumbing contract for $5,305 and got busy installing two men's and two women's restrooms under both stands.

Fundraising efforts did not stop. The summer school students had held a moderately successful drive, and the alumni were then doing cleanup work in the big cities and starting less-intensive drives in the smaller towns and rural areas. Exes and various friends of the university would eventually make pledges totaling $180,000.

The UT campus geared up for another fundraising drive in the fall, ostensibly directed toward new students (freshmen and transfers), although older students were encouraged to enlarge their previous pledges. In this campaign, Tom Pickett of Palestine directed 175 workers, divided among 25 teams. Those new to the school were virtually inundated with stories of what had happened in the spring. A *Daily Texan* editorial called the campus stadium drive "one of the most remarkable accomplishments in the history of the university. . . . Students in future years will reap the benefits from the unselfish spirit of the student body of 1923-24."

This somewhat boastful statement was entirely true. The new students met the challenge by garnering pledges of $37,000 (including Stark's 10 percent), thus raising the campus total to more than $200,000.

CLARK FIELD BIDS ADIEU

As Memorial Stadium hurtled toward completion, the Texas football team had beaten three lightweights in Southwestern, Phillips and Howard Payne, before they lost a close one to Southern Methodist University in Dallas. On October 25, 1924, the Longhorns met Florida in the last UT varsity football game ever staged at Clark Field. Although the Gators had a stronger team, they could only manage a 7-7 tie. The game's highlight took place in the final minutes when Florida had the ball at the Texas three-yard line. Four straight times, 205-pound running back Bill Middlekauff pounded up the middle but failed to score.

With a loss the next week to Rice, Texas took a 3-2-1 record into the Baylor game, the unofficial stadium opener. Only a year earlier, Doc Stewart had been showered with praise, since his football team went 8-0-1, and his basketball team won every game. But now people were griping and finding fault with every imaginable thing.

The fans could not be too unhappy though, since the new stadium was almost ready for use. The *Houston Chronicle* called it "The Giant Athletic Amphitheatre," and everyone else seemed to have similar comments. Throwing restraint to the wind, Lloyd Gregory wrote in the *Longhorn T* "The stadium is stupendous, gigantic, astounding. It is inconceivable that so mammoth a structure could spring into being within so short a time. The stadium is a mighty monument to the faith of L. Theo Bellmont, the man who first said 'It could be done,' to Bill McGill, Lutcher Stark, Max Fichtenbaum, and to the hundreds of others who labored and gave that the stadium might be."

While Memorial Stadium's dedication would wait until November 27, UT students were getting excited about the Baylor game, despite the lack of pageantry. In the week before the game, pep rallies were held on three different nights.

According to the *Daily Texan*, "the whole student body" met at Clark Field on Monday, November 3, practiced yells and listened to sentimental speeches about the old athletic park. Then, following the Longhorn Band, they marched south on Speedway, turned east at 22nd Street and headed down the hill to the new stadium, which still had the appearance of a construction site. While workers built a press box on the west side, on the east, the students did a few more yells and sang "The Eyes of Texas" for the first time in Memorial Stadium.

Three

Let the Games Begin!

Open That Stadium Right" was the latest slogan adopted on the University of Texas campus a week before the first Memorial Stadium football game, against Baylor on November 8, 1924. But students at the Waco school took the same slogan and gave it an entirely different meaning.

The Bears were heavy favorites to win. Southwest Conference champions in 1922, in the following year, they had provided the only blemish on the Longhorns' record—a 7-7 tie.

To place the opening of Texas Memorial Stadium in some context, it is helpful to consider what was happening to the north and east. On October 18, 1924, Memorial Stadium at the University of Illinois was dedicated. In front of 67,000 fans, the Illini's Red Grange scored four long touchdowns against Michigan in the first 12 minutes. And on the same day in New York's Polo Grounds, Notre Dame beat Army before a crowd of 55,000. Grantland Rice of the *New York Herald Tribune* was moved to write: "Outlined against a blue-gray October sky, the Four Horsemen rode again. In dramatic lore they are known as Famine, Pestilence, Destruction and Death. . . ."

While Clark Field had seen its last big football contest, UT students still played there in its final three years of existence. Physical training classes continued, the freshman football team (coached by Clyde Littlefield) practiced and played there, the varsity sometimes practiced there, and a few non-UT

39

games were held. In fact, on Friday afternoon, November 7, St. Edward's and Tulsa met on Clark Field's well-worn grass.

That very day, an estimated 1,000 Baylor students and fans traveled south to Austin via car and train. And there was nothing meek about this set of Baptists, as they did the "Bear Prance" up Congress Avenue to the recently opened Stephen F. Austin Hotel. BU had defeated Texas A&M the previous week and was on its way to another conference championship in 1924. (But this would be the Bears' last SWC title for 50 years.)

"Fight—fight, inspired by a desperate determination to open the gigantic Varsity stadium with an orange and white victory—is the hope of the Longhorns Saturday," wrote Lloyd Gregory in the *Austin American-Statesman*. They were not going to do it on talent, because even UT fans agreed that Baylor had bigger and faster athletes.

Twenty-four Baylor players made the trip, nine of whom had played at Waco High School under legendary coach Paul Tyson. Waco, then home to 39,000 people, took considerable pride in both Tyson's teams and Frank Bridges' Bears. Bridges, the Harvard-educated coach of the Baylor team since 1920, had earned the nickname "Little Napoleon." He was a high-strung man who savored doing things differently, sometimes just to unnerve an opponent.

The game was set for 2 P.M. Saturday, and since Memorial Stadium would not be formally dedicated until Thanksgiving Day, there were no ceremonies of any kind. Players, coaches and fans knew it was a historic day, yet Bellmont insisted on no acknowledgement thereof. The pomp and circumstance would have to wait.

Despite the feverish work of A. A. Hasbrook's men in recent weeks, Memorial Stadium was hardly ready to host a football game. The east stands, with seats in place, were largely complete, and brick trimming along the upper and outer edges gave a nice look. But most people approached the stadium from the west, and what they saw was rather messy—such as scaffolding, discarded lumber and other debris. The west stands (which were begun later and were harder to build due to topography) still had a long way to go. While most of the concrete had been poured, there were no seats, and the seven western portals were not prepared to furnish entry and exit to fans. At least the field was in shape, though. Planted several months earlier, fertilized and watered, it gave the teams a lush bed of green on which to play.

THE FIRST GAME

In chilly weather, 13,500 fans entered the gates of Memorial Stadium for that first game. They were requested not to sit in the west stands, but this was not enforced, and perhaps 2,000 of them sat there on the rough concrete. Since the stadium had no locker rooms, the Baylor players dressed at their hotel and drove to the game in automobiles. Texas players suited up in a shack at the corner of Speedway and 22nd Street, crossing Waller Creek via Stadium Bridge.

The Bears, wearing green jerseys with gold numbers on the back, arrived first, but Bridges would not allow them to take the field. His players reposed on boulders strewn south of the stadium until Stewart's Texas team, in orange jerseys with white numbers, went through one of the western gates and entered the field. Then as now, UT took the west sideline, and the visitors were on the east.

Bridges' gamesmanship was also seen on the first play in Memorial Stadium history, when he had Ralph Pittman take the opening kickoff and punt the ball right back to the Longhorns. As he had done at Clark Field and elsewhere, Stewart sat high in the stands with binoculars to get a better view of the action. He then relayed his instructions to assistant coaches and players on the field.

The *Dallas Morning News'* game story began: "Texas University opened its new million-dollar [sic] stadium with the most crushing defeat on its home grounds in years, the Longhorns bowing to Baylor University by a 28 to 10 score." Bill Coffey, the Bears' 138-pound sophomore quarterback, was the star of the game, scoring on touchdowns of 39, 3 and 25 yards and doing an excellent job of returning kicks. Four of UT's 10 points came on intentional Baylor safeties, while the first Longhorn touchdown in the new stadium was captain Jim Marley's one-yard plunge late in the fourth quarter, after Bridges had pulled most of his starters.

Marley's score was attributed in part to Shorty Nowotny, the former yell leader who had been involved in stadium affairs from the start. Getting drubbed at home had a dampening effect on the Texas fans until Nowotny, serving as an usher that day, jumped on the concrete ledge between the field and east stands. He soon reinvigorated the rooting section as the team moved toward its only offensive score of the game.

Line captain Cotton Dayvault's injured shoulder kept him on the sideline, but Stewart's other veterans—Marley, K. L. Berry and Bud Sprague—played well, while a couple of relative unknowns, Ben Dave "Stookie" Allen and Maurice Stallter, made strong showings. The latter two would earn a place in UT football annals against Texas A&M 19 days later.

The statistics for the game show that Baylor outrushed Texas 214 yards to 99; BU's Coffey completed all three of his passes for 95 yards, while UT threw 27 times, completing nine, for 85 yards; the Longhorns gained 13 first downs to 10 for Baylor; and the Bears' Bennie Strickland punted 15 times for a 47-yard average, while Texas' Swampy Thompson and Stuart Wright combined on nine punts for a 41-yard average.

The superstitious Bridges spent much of the game rubbing the head of a young boy, the team mascot who, according to one account, "mumbled queer incantations." The *Daily Texan* reported on "the informal opening of Texas' mammoth stadium, the South's greatest athletic field and war memorial."

Baylor fans, meanwhile, did the "Bear Prance" up and down Congress Avenue for two hours, delaying the Austin-to-Waco train. Jinx Tucker of the *Waco Tribune-Herald* wrote "Thus we say all honor to the football warriors of Baylor University, all honor to each and every one of them, as all contributed their part in the sensational victory. For this afternoon they 'opened that stadium right'—they got Texas."

They sure did, and quite a few orangebloods were displeased with Stewart's team, winless in its last four games. Those with the time and inclination to complain did so, again questioning Bellmont's decision to hold the Baylor game in the new stadium. Others were peeved by the option plan giving the best seats to those who had made the largest donations to the fundraising drive. In response to this criticism, Bellmont said "The stadium fund has been going on for a year now. Some of the Texas alumni have sidestepped the issue, and now they're howling."

If that were not enough, Bellmont had trouble lining up big-name opponents to visit Memorial Stadium. The 1925 season still had two open slots, and the Texas AD tried unsuccessfully to get Notre Dame or Michigan to come. The distance to Austin and the need for a sizable guarantee prevented such dream matchups, as Bellmont realized that making the Longhorns a national power would take more than just a new stadium.

THE FINANCIAL STRUGGLE CONTINUES

November 10-15 on the UT campus was designated the second "Pay Your Pledge" week. By this time, $470,000 had been pledged, $30,000 short of the goal, which was regarded with utmost seriousness. The very notion of deficit financing was unthinkable to stadium officials, who spoke of the campaign "crisis." Truly critical, however, was the widespread failure to pay pledges, whether on the part of students, alumni or others. McGill knew that he did not need more empty pledges, yet that figure of $500,000 impelled him and others onward.

As they had done before, the students laid most of the blame on UT alumni. A November 14 *Daily Texan* article featured this self-righteous headline: "Students to Rescue Stadium Drive/Campus Refuses to Let Alumni Lethargy Defeat First Varsity Project," and began with the declaration "The ex-students have failed."

McGill then introduced the "Each One Get One" campaign. The idea was that every student could find one more pledge from whatever source—a shopkeeper, landlord, parent, friend back home, or even a person who had already subscribed and was willing to give more. While this week-long drive was the subject of many McGill speeches, not to mention articles and ads in the *Daily Texan*, it proved disappointing, raising pledges of only $2,295.

To compound matters, the Stadium Association still sought four "godfathers," each of whom would donate $30,000 to pay for memorial towers at the stadium's corners. Architect Herbert M. Greene had wanted the towers built to relieve the row-upon-row monotony of the east and west stands. They were all to have a winding staircase, a copper top and an emblem symbolic of Texas, such as a cowboy, the state flag or the UT seal. The two towers on the west would stand 120 feet above ground.

For months, prospective donors were told of this opportunity to keep their families' name prominent for generations to come, and yet nothing seemed to work. Nobody stepped forward to pay for a single tower, and eventually the whole idea was dropped. It never made any sense; McGill and his volunteers had battled for enough donations to build a functional, unpretentious stadium, yet they sought $120,000 to add these towers for purely aesthetic reasons. And where would the money for additional construction come from?

A week before the dedication game against Texas A&M, $485,000 had been pledged toward Memorial Stadium, now much closer to completion than it had been for the Baylor game. Walsh & Burney's contract stipulated that the job was to be completed by Thanksgiving Day, and the crew toiled furiously as the deadline approached. The stadium would almost be finished in time, as a concrete tower and half of the scaffolding under the west stands remained, and a good bit of touch-up work still had to be done.

On November 15, UT raised its record to 4-3-1, defeating Texas Christian University in Fort Worth. That improved people's spirits somewhat, yet those with a sense of perspective knew that the 1924 Longhorn season hardly mattered compared to the overriding fact that a huge new stadium had been erected. Memorial Stadium was such a departure from the norm for football fans in the Southwest that pride and amazement were the order of the day.

Some people looking at the stadium from the west had doubts about its safety. When Stark asked a team of engineers to test the stadium's structural integrity, they declared it not only sound, but a marvel of engineering.

Bellmont had hoped that John J. Pershing, commanding general of American Expeditionary Forces in the World War, would serve as guest of honor on November 27. Pershing declined the invitation, and since time was short, no one else was asked.

Clark Field was the scene of an unusual contest the Sunday before the game. Fans paid 50 cents apiece to see line coach Ed Bluestein's "Ragnots" (varsity substitutes) play Clyde Littlefield's freshmen. What made it unique was that Bluestein and coaches Tom Dennis (like Bluestein, a former all-SWC tackle) and Alex Waite took part. The frosh got help from Littlefield, who at age 31 could still run and throw. The Ragnots won the game, 12-7, and raised $262 for the stadium fund.

As the Thanksgiving Day game approached, Austin took on a festive air with shops downtown and near campus decorated in both orange and maroon. An exact replica of Memorial Stadium, carved from Palmolive soap, was on display at a grocery store on Guadalupe Street. The city, university and Chamber of Commerce cooperated on what was regarded as one of the biggest days in Austin history.

Sandwiched between two rallies and a bonfire was a lively dinner party at the University Commons on November 25. Exactly one year after the Original 30 met to discuss plans for a new stadium, they met again in the same place. McGill sent invitations with the promise of "fewer speeches and more groceries." Due to attrition, only 13 students could attend, along with Cross, Stark, Bellmont and their respective wives. Max Fichtenbaum was invited, and so was Carl Webb, the most diligent of all the student stadium workers, although not one of the Original 30.

Cross, who was leaving to begin a similar project at Oregon State, received a farewell tribute and a silver loving cup. Fichtenbaum, his work far from over, was given a butterfly net to aid in catching pledged money. All in all, it was a highly convivial evening.

Though both the Longhorns and Aggies were out of the SWC title chase, Stewart expected his team to be ready to play, telling the *Austin American-Statesman* "My men will draw inspiration Thursday from the fact that they will be formally dedicating the huge Memorial Stadium. They feel they just can't lose, that they must not lose to the Aggies on such an occasion. . . . Too, my men will draw inspiration from the fact that they will be playing before 35,000 fans, the largest crowd ever to witness an athletic event in the South. I believe that every man will play the game of his life."

They might have to, especially in light of some statistics turned up by the *Wichita Falls News-Record*. It determined that 39 college football stadiums had been built in the previous five years, and that the home team had lost the dedication game 34 times.

Despite student criticism of UT alumni during the Stark-Hogg fight and throughout the fundraising drive, all was forgiven during the two-day homecoming that marked the stadium's dedication. Many exes had never even been back to campus after graduating, but they drove and took trains to Austin for this occasion. The Ex-Students' Association building at 2300 San Antonio Street bustled with activity on both days. The Main Building and all professors' offices stayed open to greet the returning alumni.

A front-page headline in the *Austin American-Statesman* read "Football Hosts Gather/Austin Thronged as Never Before for Grid Battle." Most Texas A&M faculty and exes stayed at the Driskill Hotel, while the Stephen F. Austin Hotel served as UT headquarters. Restaurants and streetcars did a booming business as people spent freely. Quite a few Texas alums took their first look at the stadium, uttered a string of superlatives and enlarged their pledges, thus gladdening the heart of Fichtenbaum.

THE JORDAN FLAGPOLE

A Wednesday night Longhorn Band concert and rally at the Main Building was followed by more partying, with two dances on campus and another at the roof garden of the Stephen F. Austin Hotel, but the real hoopla took place the next day. While campus buildings and offices were again open, the focus at 10 A.M. was on the 100-foot flagpole in the south end of the stadium. At its base was a bronze tablet inscribed "In memory of First Lieutenant Louis J. Jordan, University of Texas, 1911-1915, who died in the service of his country in the great World War, 1914-1918. Erected by the citizens of Fredericksburg. Dedicated Nov. 27, 1924, A. D."

Louis Jordan (sometimes spelled "Jourdan") may have been the most popular athlete UT had produced to that time. The 205-pound Fredericksburg native won three letters in track and four in football, earning second-team all-American recognition by Walter Camp in 1914. Jordan's gentlemanly manner won admiration during his life, and his death in battle at Luneville, France on March 6, 1918 caused deep mourning on the Texas campus.

Jordan would be among the first group of men admitted to the Longhorn Hall of Honor when it opened in 1957, and the flagpole erected in his honor stood until 1971. Fredericksburg's American Legion post still carries his name.

The somber ceremony had barely concluded when 2,400 Aggie cadets left the train depot and marched in military fashion up Congress Avenue. "The coming of the opposition team added a further quickening of interest that was already lively," wrote an *Austin American-Statesman* reporter. "With confident faces, high hearts and flying banners the Aggies bravely marched up the Avenue, bringing a stab of pity or a premonition of defeat to Texas supporters." The khaki-clad contingent was reviewed from the balcony of the Stephen F. Austin Hotel by Governor Pat Neff, Governor-elect Miriam "Ma" Ferguson, UT President Walter Splawn, Texas A&M President W. B. Bizzell and other dignitaries. After demobilizing at the Capitol, the cadets ate a turkey dinner with Aggie alumni, then headed to the stadium.

The gates opened at 12:30 P.M., and under cool, cloudless skies the fans began entering Memorial Stadium. Now-silent Clark Field, the scene of so many big games since 1896, was used as a parking lot that day. While some sentimental people paused on their way to the stadium, few tears were shed for Clark Field. It had served long and well, but everyone seemed to realize that UT was moving from a shotgun shack to a veritable mansion. Why bother to even look back?

The game program, on sale for 25 cents, presented an overview of the stadium's history that included the meeting of the Original 30, List & Gifford's excavation of Brackenridge Field, Walsh & Burney's months of construction, the fundraising efforts, and the names of the students and alumni of the university who had died in the war. President Splawn wrote "For forty years we have waited for a rallying place and for some unifying, vital movement. The great Horse-shoe Stadium is the goal of the united student body, of generous support from the faculty, the ex-students and the citizens of the state. It is an omen of good luck for university ideals, whether in defeat or in victory."

Since he would have such a major influence on events at the stadium in later years, Aggie coach Dana X. Bible's words are of interest. "My message today is one of congratulations to the University of Texas," he wrote in the program. "Congratulations to those who conceived the Memorial Stadium idea, to those who fostered the campaign for its construction and to those who shared in its completion. It reflects credit not only upon the University of Texas, but upon the Southwest as well. We are happy to have a part in its formal dedication."

Nowotny was again among the ushers directing between 33,000 and 37,000 people—accounts vary—to their seats in the east and west stands, as well as bleachers erected in the north and south ends. Atop each set of bleachers stood a large billboard with the words "Remember! Walsh &

Burney Built This Stadium On Time," and the company logo. Before sitting down, every non-cadet adult received an envelope containing both a hearty welcome and an open palm; the stadium fundraising drive was not over yet. They were asked to sign a pledge or place currency or a check in the envelope and return it to the usher standing in the aisle. Just like in church.

SHOW TIME

Almost every seat was filled at 1:45 P.M. when a well-organized procession formed south of the stadium and began to move, even though Ma Ferguson had yet to arrive. The 82-member Aggie band was given the honor of entering the field first, followed by the Freshman and Longhorn bands behind drum major Robert Levy, the Texas Cowboys, Orange Jackets, Governor Neff, Bishop G. H. Kinsolving, Bizzell and Splawn. Then came Stark and the UT Board of Regents, the academic deans of both Texas and Texas A&M, along with representatives of the other Southwest Conference schools. The Athletics Council and coaches entered, then student leaders and officers of the Ex-Students' Association. The remnants of the Original 30 got a big hand, followed by Bellmont and the Stadium Association Board of Directors, architect Herbert M. Greene, contractors and both schools' yell leaders. It was a huge group, covering much of the field.

From a platform in the north end, UT engineering professor and stadium official E. C. H. Bantel served as master of ceremonies. Kinsolving (who would later have a campus women's dormitory named after him) gave the invocation, and Neff made a five-minute speech that concluded this way: "In dedicating this stadium, may we indulge the hope that its service to humanity will be as pure, as loyal and patriotic as was the service of our soldiers to the course to which they risked their all."

Then, as the crowd stood at attention, the United States and Texas flags were raised aloft on the flagpole dedicated that morning to Louis Jordan. The combined bands played "The Star Spangled Banner" and "The Eyes of Texas," and the Orange Jackets released 500 balloons, only half of which took to the air, although one was found the next day tangled in a tree 200 miles to the southeast.

One thousand co-eds dressed in white formed a giant "T," performed a snake dance around the field, then took their seats in one section. Before the teams came out for the game, a football with orange and white streamers was dropped several hundred feet from a Ford tri-motor airplane, piloted by Grace McClellan. It was from this plane that a photographer for the *Fort Worth Record* took aerial pictures of the gathering.

This would be the 30th meeting of the Longhorns and Aggies, dating back to 1894. UT led in the series with 19 victories, 8 defeats and 2 ties, but Texas A&M, with a 15-pound per man weight advantage, hoped to avenge the previous year's loss in College Station. Those wagering had the Aggies (sometimes called the "Farmers") as seven-point favorites.

The Longhorns had their own reasons to want the game, most obviously the desire to christen the stadium with a victory. Stewart undoubtedly reminded his players of Louis Jordan, Pete Edmond and other T Men who had died in battle some six years earlier. One person with special incentive was K. L. Berry, the 32-year old lineman who had lettered in 1912, 1913 and 1915, served in the army during the war, and returned to complete his education and play football. Many had doubted that Berry could make such a comeback, but he had, and won all-SWC honors despite a lingering knee problem.

Since the pre-game ceremonies ran a bit long, the game was late in starting. The Aggie cadets, sitting in the south portion of the east stands (a visitors' arrangement that is still used today), cheered and waved their caps as the Texas A&M team came onto the field. But it was an unusual entrance as the 40 players followed their captain, Louie "Silent" Miller, who walked with crutches due to a broken leg suffered early in the season. Reaching midfield, Miller made a rousing plea to his teammates, urging them to destroy "t.u.," "the Teasippers," "the Yellowbellies," and other such derogatory names used for Texas teams.

Moments later, the home fans made some noise of their own, as the Longhorns raced through the south goalposts and onto the field. As the players warmed up, Stewart and Bible chatted and conferred with game officials, who would keep score and time, since the stadium still lacked a scoreboard or clock.

The public address announcer then read a statement evoking cheers from Longhorns and Aggies alike. He announced that the UT Athletics Council had donated $15,000 to the stadium fund which, combined with money collected that day in the stands, put the drive over the top with $503,000. The council had met two days earlier to discuss stadium finances, and in all likelihood this decision was made then.

KICKOFF, AT LAST

Captain Jim Marley of Texas and acting captain Charlie Waugh of Texas A&M met at midfield for the coin toss. The Aggies won it and chose to defend the north goal, with a slight wind at their backs. It was nearly 3 P.M. when UT's Swampy Thompson teed the ball up for the opening kickoff. The announcer on radio station WCM set the stage for listeners in the Austin area. That moment, frozen in time, must have been one of the proudest in the lives of Stark, Bellmont and many other people.

Finally, boot met ball, and it landed in the hands of Taro Kishi near the Aggie goal line. Kishi, almost certainly the first person of Japanese ancestry to play in the Southwest Conference, ran the ball out to the 45-yard line. Despite good field position, the Aggies could not move in three downs, and Fay Wilson kicked the first of his 17 punts of the day. Thompson and Stuart Wright of Texas combined for 14 punts themselves, in a game dominated by defense.

The lack of offense came despite vigorous rooting by partisans of both teams. Nearly every time "The Eyes of Texas" was played, the Texas A&M band struck up "The Aggie War Hymn." UT yell leaders and students used the "Fight Yell," "Hullaballoo," the "Whistle Yell," "Fight, Fight," the "Locomotive Yell," and the "Cannon Ball Yell," among others.

Former UT and Texas A&M lettermen stood near their respective benches, exhorting and advising the players. On the west side between the 40-yard lines were eight boxes arranged for various state and institutional dignitaries. Governor-elect Ferguson finally arrived, but she showed more interest in socializing and gladhanding than in the game.

After recovering Marley's fumble midway through the first quarter, Texas A&M had a chance to score, reaching the UT two-yard line. But Berry, Sprague, Dayvault, Heinie Pfannkuche and the rest of the Longhorn defense held. Field goal attempts of 29 and 38 yards by Wright failed, and though Texas seemed to have the upper hand, the first half ended in a scoreless tie.

Halftime saw performances by the Longhorn and Aggie bands, stunts by the Texas Cowboys and Orange Jackets and a truckload of feminine beauty. At one end of a tractor-trailer, a dozen UT coeds in fetching attire smiled and waved, while several representing Texas A&M (which would not fully admit women until 1968) were at the other end.

Pop Boone, covering the event for the *Fort Worth Record*, was pleased with the semi-enclosed Memorial Stadium press box which sat 50 reporters and seven Western Union telegraph operators. He praised Bellmont for ". . . the very complete press box that has been built. It conforms in modernity to the rest of the great structure, which is the best compliment I can pay it."

While Boone and others were served turkey sandwiches and hot coffee at halftime, they got an unexpected scoop when an angry Bellmont appeared in the press box. He informed them that 27 people had already been arrested for possession of alcohol (including a UT student, Percy Foreman, who would later become a famous lawyer). Despite warnings before the game against Prohibition violators, many people had smuggled flasks into the stadium, filled with either "prescription" whiskey or the bootleg variety. Texas Rangers, Travis County sheriffs and Austin police officers did their best to enforce the law.

"They've filled up the city jail, and the game's not over yet. Now they're moving the prisoners over to the county jail, and they'll probably have that full by the end of the game. We're going to make this a clean place," fumed Bellmont. A total of 35 inebriated fans were removed from the stadium.

GAME'S CLIMAX

The second half began, and if the huge crowd had come to see offensive fireworks, they were sorely disappointed. Stewart's and Bible's teams gained a total of just 11 first downs, playing conservative though generally error-free football, as they waited for the game to break the right way. Only once in the third quarter did the Aggies get into Texas territory, although the threat soon fizzled. Yet three times Longhorn receivers, open for a touchdown, dropped passes, as the deadlock continued.

Late in the fourth quarter, when most fans had reconciled themselves to a scoreless tie, the game turned. On third down, with less than four minutes remaining and the ball on the Aggie 45-yard line, UT's Maurice "Rosy" Stallter faded back to pass. He zinged the ball across the line of scrimmage, where Marley had come out of the backfield, and Stookie Allen was running a crossing pattern. The pass appeared to have no chance of completion since two Texas A&M players, Bob Berry and Mitt Dansby, awaited it. But instead of knocking the ball down, they went for the interception, and it ricocheted off both of them straight to Allen.

A gangly player and one of the slowest on the Longhorn team, Allen gathered in the ball at the 25-yard line and began running toward the south goal. The now-awakened fans came to their feet and screamed as Allen raced an Aggie defender to the goal line. Different reports have it as Berry, Dansby, Kishi or Wilson, but whatever his identity, the Texas A&M player made a flying leap at the two-yard line, just touching Allen's heels. He scored, and Thompson kicked the extra point, as UT took a 7-0 lead.

The score stood, and what had looked like a dismal season two weeks earlier was now capped with honor and glory. Somewhere, the ghost of Louis Jordan was smiling. In contrast to the pushing and shoving long customary after games at Clark Field, within 20 minutes the crowd easily filed out of

Memorial Stadium. UT students wasted no time in forming a "shirt tail" parade on Congress Avenue to show their glee.

The December 1924 issue of *Alcalde* stated "That 7-0 victory is already written down in history as a spectacular climax for the grand opening of the half-million dollar Memorial Stadium on its first anniversary. It was a dedication that chimed in well with the successful stadium campaign, one that pleased the bulk of the largest crowd ever gathered for a football contest in the South."

The students had barely concluded their downtown parade when it was time for a more sedate Thanksgiving reception at the Main Building. The day's events concluded with a 10 P.M.-2 A.M. dance at the Driskill Hotel even if most of the Texas A&M guests had already left. With the stadium built and dedicated, and with the stirring victory, most of the UT community was in high spirits.

But a sour note was soon sounded when Maury Maverick, a state legislator from San Antonio, made a speech accusing UT students of an overindulgence of "booze, society and athletics." It was not the first time these charges had been leveled, nor would it be the last. Yet such curmudgeonly voices were few and seldom heard.

Much more representative were newspaper articles and editorials praising the stadium, the people who built it and what it meant to the University of Texas. In "Texas Stadium Dream Realized," the *Fort Worth Record* called it "the turning of another page in the colorful history of the state's leading institution of higher learning. What the stadium stands for is noble, [and] how it was achieved is a remarkable tribute to the loyalty of Texas students, alumni and 'Exes.' . . . probably no other school in the Southwest could have achieved such a vast undertaking."

In "The Stadium Fulfills Its Promise," the *Austin American-Statesman* editorialized: "A brief glance cast backward shows how thoroughly the game had been prepared and the two contending football teams inspired by the to-be newly dedicated stadium, standing like a mystic shrine on its white hill in the far distance. . . . Thus, the Memorial Stadium has given that touch to intercollegiate sport that makes it a genuine stimulus to higher education, so earnestly desired."

Four

The Stadium in Infancy: 1924-1948

William McGill resigned as chairman of the fundraising campaign on November 27, 1924, Memorial Stadium dedication day. Having given so much of himself—without payment—to the stadium drive, the indefatigable McGill needed to devote more time to his job as manager of Texas Student Publications. And yet for another four years, he continued attending meetings and doing other stadium work. Aware of the stadium's importance to the development of the University of Texas, he could not bear to walk away.

In his resignation letter, McGill pointed with pride to the campaign that had, for the first time, brought together UT students, faculty, administration, alumni and the city of Austin. He made no mention of the Lutcher Stark-Will Hogg power struggle that had threatened the erection of the stadium, commented obliquely on the difficulty of collecting all funds pledged and lamented the lack of large donors.

Although no successor to McGill was named, executive secretary Max Fichtenbaum became the de facto head of the stadium drive. Everyone agreed that it would be cheaper and more efficient to keep the Walsh & Burney equipment and crew on site and enlarge the stadium immediately, but that is not what happened. No decision had yet been made on whether to build the north-end horseshoe next, to extend both sets of stands or perhaps just to enlarge the west side and build two ornamental towers.

But the money simply was not there, with indebtedness reaching almost $100,000. Walsh & Burney fulfilled its contractual duties, staying long enough to complete the west stands, do touchup work and dismantle the scaffolding and remaining concrete tower. The equipment was taken back to San Antonio, and the crew dispersed.

In the weeks following the 1924 football season, there was plenty of work yet to be done, especially on the still-rustic stadium grounds. Removal of boulders, landscaping and finishing the track were the three main tasks.

The caretaker of Memorial Stadium until his retirement in 1948 was Jacob "Jake" Bleymaier. A janitor at the university since 1909 and hired by the Athletics Council to maintain Clark Field in 1921, Bleymaier now had a much bigger job, and he did it with a vengeance. He, his wife and five children (a son, Joe, would play football at UT in the mid-1930s) moved into a cottage on the northeast corner of the stadium grounds. This house, which doubled as a tractor and tool shed, remained an integral part of the stadium complex before it was torn down in 1967. The mostly German-speaking Bleymaier ruled the roost at Memorial Stadium and was especially protective of the football field.

In anticipation of track season, Bleymaier and some helpers dug high jump and broad jump pits on the west side of the field and a pole vault pit on the east. On January 10, 1925, Clyde Littlefield's Longhorn track team had its first workout at Memorial Stadium. And in March, the football team was back, for spring practice. There were few problems between the two groups since they had always shared space on Clark Field, several men played both sports, and Littlefield was an assistant football coach himself.

Actually, one clash *did* arise—that between athletic director L. Theo Bellmont and baseball coach Billy Disch. Disch's baseball acumen was beyond reproach, as can be seen in his UT career won-loss record of 465-115. But he chafed under Bellmont's close supervision, and did not like playing in run-down Clark Field while the football and track teams had a spanking new stadium in which to cavort. Disch tentatively agreed to become the new coach at SMU, but that was canceled when he and Bellmont papered over their differences. Yet problems between them would erupt again two years later.

STADIUM USE ABOUNDS

Until the Intramural Fields and Freshman Field were set up west of Waller Creek in 1928, Memorial Stadium got heavy use. UT commencement ceremonies were held there in June 1925, as a record 510 students received diplomas. A July 4th fireworks display was attended by a crowd of 12,000, and the Varsity Circus and countless intramural and interfraternity football games and track meets took place at the stadium. Until a gravel floor was installed under the west stands in 1926, the football team practiced there on rainy days.

The stadium was occasionally used at night, as Bleymaier strung 500-watt floodlights along its base. Students played pickup baseball games at "Stadium Field," a cleared plot of ground just north of the stands. Some of these events might have easily been held at Clark Field, but given a choice, who would not prefer to use the stadium? After all, as the students often claimed, they had been most responsible for construction of the facility.

In the 1925 football season, Southwestern, Mississippi, Rice, Baylor (when student-section flash cards were used for the first time) and Arizona visited Austin. Physics professor Leroy Brown had built a speech amplifier system for Memorial Stadium. It was a major improvement, since in late 1924, fans could scarcely hear stadium announcements.

As they would for the next several years, T Men sat behind the Longhorn players' bench on the west side of the field. This had been arranged by Jim Hart, a turn-of-the-century letterman who remained involved in Texas football.

Interestingly enough, a 1925 *Daily Texan* ad for the Walter Wilcox clothing store featured a drawing of Bevo with the words "Hook 'em." That term got sporadic use over the next 30 years before some inspired students invented the "Hook 'em, Horns" hand sign. Also in 1925, Doc Stewart made a slight change in the team's uniform; the jerseys would be somewhat darker, introducing another new term into the Longhorn lexicon, "burnt orange." While few students expressed opinions about the new color at the time, it was the beginning of a long-running debate about the proper school color, one that has not entirely ended today.

More serious matters dogged Max Fichtenbaum, such as money. In April 1925, a total of just $222,000 had been paid to the stadium fund, $260,000 by July and $271,000 by October. Most people paid on time, occasionally exceeding what they had pledged, but some dallied and others gave only excuses. It was part of Fichtenbaum's job to relentlessly ask and remind. For example, in a July 25 letter to H. V. Alexander of Austin, he wrote "Despite the fact that you have consistently refused to answer our letters and notices concerning your stadium pledge, I still have faith in your subscription. I honestly believe that you intend to pay this pledge; otherwise I do not think you would have made it. . . . We are willing to make almost any arrangement you desire concerning your pledge. If you have had a run of hard luck, tell us; if you want to defer payment until a later date, say so; if you want to send a check now (large or small), do so—but regardless of what you want to do, write us something. It is this terrific silence that is getting on our nerves."

Alexander owed the Stadium Association $15.

UT STUDENTS RESUME FUNDRAISING

Without waiting to learn when and how the stadium would be expanded, a second "new students" campaign got started in early November. Gordon Greenwood of Austin served as chairman, setting a goal of $35,000. With guidance from such stadium veterans as Carl Webb, Nowlin Randolph and Joyce Cox, 200 people were divided into teams and set to work.

The extraordinary spirit of 1924 was not easily renewed, as *Daily Texan* editor Stewart Harkrider wrote "The great wave of enthusiasm for stadium fundraising has long since died away." But the editorials, ads, slogans, posters, speeches and even use of the "stadiumeter" still helped enlist pledges.

The Stark family again offered to give 10 percent of whatever the students raised, which came to roughly $24,500, for a total of $27,000. By far the most successful teams were the men's and women's Flying Squadrons, which got out-of-town pledges. The new students wanted to be part of the great movement; according to the *Daily Texan*, "[the stadium] can be seen across the valley. There it stands, the first product of the united effort of Varsity's students, past and present."

Shortly after this campaign ended, stadium officials met and decided that a horseshoe with 49 rows (three fewer than the east and west stands) would be added to the structure's north end in time for the 1926 Texas A&M game. Fichtenbaum estimated construction costs at $125,000 and that seating would be boosted by 11,000-13,000.

A. T. Granger, the UT civil engineering professor who had been closely involved with Memorial Stadium's construction in 1924, drew up plans for the horseshoe, which would have 13 arches, each about 33 feet wide, varying in height from 30-40 feet. Granger put a nice touch on the large central arch and surrounding area, giving it an Alamo-esque look.

Before bids were received and construction commenced, the Stadium Association got a report from the Dallas accounting firm of Rankin & McAlpine. It determined that as of January 31, 1926, $531,655.65 had been pledged to the stadium drive, of which $306,789.38 had been collected. The cost of raising this money (such as office maintenance, salaries and other collection expenses) came to 9.62 percent of funds collected. Rankin & McAlpine concluded its report by stating "We found the records of the association to be in exceptionally good condition considering the volume of work handled through the office."

Donations varied from Stark's $18,808.50 (not to mention his several loans) and the Hogg brothers' $10,000 apiece, down to 153 pledges of a dollar or less. The largest group, 2,744, gave $50 each, the minimum needed for inclusion in the Memorial Stadium seating option.

On May 25, 1926, the Stadium Association board of directors met. Present were Stark, Bellmont, McGill, Hildebrand, Bantel, Fichtenbaum, W. H. Richardson, Granger and secretary Stella Peden. They opened bids from six companies hoping to erect the stadium horseshoe. One of them was Walsh & Burney, builder of the east and west stands in 1924. But the contract went to the Kroeger-Brooks Construction Company, also of San Antonio, with a low bid of $116,766.

And how to pay for it? While over $200,000 in pledges remained outstanding, stadium officials had begun taking an increasingly realistic view of the matter, with "less conservative allowance for shrinkage," as Fichtenbaum carefully put it. Yet they trusted that whether because of loyalty, guilt or persistent reminders, most of the foot-draggers would eventually come across. In the meantime, the Ex-Students' Association, which had only recently been repaid its $45,000 loan to the stadium fund, offered the money back, again at 6 percent interest, and it was gratefully accepted.

BUILDING THE HORSESHOE

Without the fanfare of two years earlier, ground at the north end was broken on June 7, and Kroeger-Brooks wasted no time in beginning work. The Thanksgiving Day game—as in 1924—was a clear goal, and the company's contract promised a bonus if it were met. Soon an outline of the "U" shape could be seen, along with holes for dozens of columns.

A crew of 74 workers (including Heinie Pfannkuche, the 1925 Longhorn line captain, and track star C.B. Smith) had all the columns up and the structural steel in place by August 17. Setting of wooden forms and pouring of concrete started on the east side and went west. Expected groundwater problems did not arise, so construction proceeded quickly.

In the *Austin American-Statesman*, Duby DuBose wrote "Out at the stadium one will find improvements underway and nearing completion that are nothing short of startling in magnitude. One will find Memorial Stadium . . . now taking on the form of a gigantic horseshoe, with a capacity of 40,500—enabling 13,500 more people to witness future Longhorn gridiron classics."

DuBose described the new concrete driveway and sidewalks approaching and surrounding Memorial Stadium, the terraced parking area for 600 cars ($2.50 for season-parking privileges) and other changes. At the south end of the field, just in front of the Louis Jordan flagpole, the Flury Advertising Company built a large scoreboard perched 10 feet above ground. Costing $350, it was painted green and white, and featured the words MEMORIAL STADIUM at the top. It had a 15-minute electric clock, showed the score of TEXAS and VISITORS, gave the down, quarter, yards to go, penalty information and updates on other games. Hand-operated by three people in telephone communication with the press box, the scoreboard also carried a sizable plug for the University Co-op.

The Athletics Council appropriated $8,000 to build three clay tennis courts, with a grandstand for 600 spectators, just northwest of the stadium. Originally called Varsity Athletic Courts and soon renamed in honor of longtime tennis coach Dr. Daniel Penick, these were reserved for intercollegiate play. When finished in early 1927, they provided UT with another excellent facility. Here, such Longhorn tennis players as Wilmer Allison (the future Texas coach), Berkeley Bell, Bruce Barnes, Karl Kamrath, Sr., Bill Blalock, Bobby Goldfarb, Johnny Hernandez, Sammy Giammalva and Richard Keeton competed over the years. Sometimes, when the stands were full, people would observe the action from atop the northwest portion of the nearby stadium.

Rank-and-file students were provided with 10 grass courts southeast of the stadium. Naturally, these 13 tennis courts expanded the duties of Jake Bleymaier and his assistants. The ever-ambitious Bellmont also spoke of building a nine-hole golf course north of Memorial Stadium, but this plan fell through.

Another pending project was the construction of a new baseball park replacing the soon-to-be-razed Clark Field. In mid-1926, the Athletics Council announced tentative plans to build "Disch Field" north of the stadium, across 23rd Street. Bellmont expected to spend $15,000 for excavation, $15,000 to build the park and another $15,000 to prepare the diamond. Despite the simmering feud between him and Billy Disch, Bellmont agreed that the park should be named in honor of the veteran Texas baseball coach.

The *Daily Texan* questioned the use of $45,000 for a baseball stadium and suggested that the university needed an auditorium more urgently. But the addition to Memorial Stadium had to be completed first, so the matter was shelved, and Disch's team played one last season, 1927, in old Clark Field.

Work proceeded on the stadium. A flagpole was erected between two curving driveways outside of the new north end. A large steer head had been placed above both the north and south entrances of the west stands in 1924. While the steer head on the south end remained, the one on the north end was taken and set above the central arch of the horseshoe. Under it, in 18-inch bronze capital letters matching the curve of the arch, workers installed the words TEXAS MEMORIAL STADIUM.

Although "Texas" was officially part of the stadium's name, it soon disappeared from common usage.

IN MEMORIAM

"What criticism has been directed at the Memorial Stadium, the outstanding instance of unselfish and almost unanimous giving by the great mass of students and ex-students of the University of Texas," editorialized *Alcalde* in 1926, "has been concerned with the fact that as the huge monument exists today, it is a memorial in name only." Other than the Louis Jordan flagpole, there was no actual recognition of the Texans who had fought and died during the World War. But that situation was finally changing.

In an arrangement between UT and the J. W. Davis Company of Dallas, the families of those who had made the supreme sacrifice could, for $5.75, have an 8" × 12" bronze plaque erected in their honor in the stadium. President Walter Splawn wrote a letter to each such family, notifying them of this opportunity. The original expectation of some 3,000 responses, however, proved much too optimistic. Robert Gragg of Austin, whose son had died in the war, offered to pay the fee for any other family unable to afford it. Even with Gragg's generous help, only 223 plaques were bought, manufactured and bolted onto the walls of the stadium's 22 portals.

The horseshoe, with its concrete and brick exterior, received a white stucco coating and an additional memorial feature. The six Southwest Conference schools in Texas—excluding the University of Arkansas—each had a bronze tablet erected on alternating columns of the stadium's north wall, listing all of their students or alumni who had died in the war. For the record, going from east to west, SMU's tablet contains 11 names, Baylor's 24, Texas A&M's 54, UT's 91, Rice's 16, and TCU's 3.

Six years earlier, Stark had presented the university with a large plaque, "erected to honor the 'T' Men of the University of Texas who gave their lives for freedom's cause": Jordan, Pete Edmond, Bothwell Kane, Mahlon Wallace, James Greer and James Higginbotham. This plaque stood in the

Education Building (now Sutton Hall) until the university transferred it to the east wall of the stadium's new main entrance.

Directly across from it, on the west wall, was placed another large plaque with the state seal, followed by the words "The Texas Memorial Stadium/Erected by Popular Subscription As a Memorial to Those Texans Who Served in the World War/Dedicated November 27, 1924." It listed the Stadium Association's board of directors, credited Herbert M. Greene and Walsh & Burney for the east and west stands, and Granger and Kroeger-Brooks for the north stands. A wrought-iron gate was placed at the entrance, close to the two plaques. At the same time, workers installed a thick steel bar one foot above the stadium's retaining wall, which remains in use today.

As the horseshoe neared completion, so did work around the stadium. Red River, 22nd and 23rd streets all were improved, and the 21st Street bridge spanning Waller Creek greatly enhanced approach and exit on game days. No longer was Memorial Stadium, the seemingly perpetual construction site, "a reproach to the university in its unfinished state," as one person claimed. UT had built a huge and graceful, if utilitarian, stadium engendering an immense feeling of pride in Texans of the 1920s.

Stark called it "a concrete emblem of beauty standing out there on the hill, commemorative of the deeds of valor by Texas heroes and the sacrifices of over 11,000 students and ex-students. It marks a new era that is just opening for the University of Texas."

Stadium official William T. Caswell said "I have noticed in traveling recently that people always associate Austin with the stadium. Even in Maine, I heard several people commend the building of this structure. They seemed to have heard of the stadium and then learned that there was such a place as Austin, where there was a state university. It is one of the biggest advertisements for the University of Texas and one of the best assets of Austin."

Since contractors were due $25,000 in October, and the Stadium Association had only $2,000 on hand, the third and final "new students" campaign began, with Bob Smith of Houston as chairman. The goal this time was to match the $27,000 pledged in 1925. Stark's 10 percent offer remained in effect, and the students went to work, making sure that new faculty members also got the chance to pledge. The *Daily Texan* compared Memorial Stadium to St. Peter's Cathedral, which was built gradually by peasants sending money to Rome. Just over $22,000 was pledged in this drive, and if some students who had spent most of their college years being harangued for money were tired of it, that was understandable.

"ARCHITECTURALLY COMPLETE"

Rather surprisingly, some people favored building the east and west extensions immediately, regardless of the lack of money or need. But in an editorial entitled "Architecturally Complete," the *Daily Texan* stated "until the day arrives when more than 50,000 seats are needed, the *Texan* believes that the board of directors of the stadium should halt construction work after the completion of the 'horseshoe.' It would be neither a wise policy nor sound business to build something which would stand for years before it is actually used."

The *Daily Texan* editors were quite right—it would be a long time before UT needed to enlarge Memorial Stadium. In fact, it came nowhere near selling out except for the Texas A&M game on even-numbered years. Early-season non-conference games against weak teams drew poorly, with some "crowds" as small as 2,000 sprinkled in the cavernous stadium. So it was unnecessary, during the 1926 football season, to ask fans not to sit in the end-zone seats then under construction.

En route to a 5-4 record, the Longhorns ripped Southwest Oklahoma Teachers College in Austin by a score of 31-7. Bedlam erupted in the east stands during the fourth quarter when students, evidently bored by the mismatch, began throwing apple cores at each other. Head yell leader John Jackson later said "This affair ought to go down in history as one of the most disgusting demonstrations of poor sportsmanship ever given by Texas students at home or abroad."

But that was nothing compared to what happened in Waco a few weeks later when Baylor and Texas A&M played. At halftime of the game, a free-for-all broke out (not an unusual occurrence of the time), and an Aggie cadet, Charles M. Sessums, was killed. Student comportment at SWC football games improved considerably after that.

In preparation for the 1926 Thanksgiving Day game against Texas A&M, Bellmont purchased a shipment of American flags. They would be flown from the 24 poles erected around the perimeter of the stadium, which was in much better shape than it had been for the 1924 dedication game. The completed horseshoe, the landscaping around the stadium and the various memorial plaques added the final touches to the game between old rivals.

Not quite filling the stadium, 35,000 people came to see offensive stars like Mack Saxon of Texas and Joel Hunt of Texas A&M, as the Longhorns won the game, 14-5. Gate receipts amounted to $76,194, and even after deducting $33,931 for the Aggies, a hefty chunk remained to help pay off stadium debts and subsidize other sports and intramurals. According to *Alcalde,* "Football may be the spoiled child of the college family, but there are times when he proves unquestionably that he's the sturdy wage earner and sole support of a large and ailing list of hungry relatives."

Such ambivalence about college football was common at UT in the late 1920s and early 1930s. There had always been quiet opposition to the financing and construction of Memorial Stadium, especially given the university's more pressing needs, like brick dormitories and classrooms. In addition, the huge pro contract signed by Red Grange of Illinois and the tragedy at the 1926 Baylor-Texas A&M game led to a long period of soul-searching in Austin and elsewhere.

In the *Daily Texan*, Dick McMurray wrote a 12-part series on issues concerning UT athletics. If not investigative journalism by modern standards, it nevertheless provided students a chance to look at the $100,000 budget presided over by L. Theo Bellmont. An article by Harvard professor Morton Prince, "Hand Back the Game to the Boys," struck a chord, as did "Vale, Football!" reprinted by *Alcalde* from the *Columbia Alumni News*, containing this view: "College football, in large measure, has been an attitude of mind. Wrapped up in it has been whatever of romance and chivalry and glorious combat remains from the days when college knighthood was in flower."

To the writer of the article, commercialism, meaning pro football, was a menace threatening the pristine nature of the college game. University Interscholastic League president Roy Bedichek echoed this in a speech entitled "Shall We Have Athletics for Pay or Athletics for Play?" delivered over radio station KUT on January 19, 1927. When the Athenaeum Literary Society debated whether the *Daily Texan* gave too much coverage to athletics, the judges voted in the affirmative.

One more example was an *Alcalde* article, "Is Intercollegiate Athletics Wrong?" by Daniel Penick, UT Greek and Latin professor, tennis coach, president of the Southwest Conference and a proponent of the ideals of amateur athletics. While not urging abolition of intercollegiate sports, as some of his academic colleagues did, Penick suggested serious reforms, and we can assume he directed them toward his own institution. If college football was in fact on the decline, then Texas had gone through a tremendous effort and sacrifice to build a stadium destined for white-elephant status.

BELLMONT OUSTED

There were other forms of trouble brewing on the UT campus. Doc Stewart's football teams had begun to slip from the lofty positions they once held. A 5-4 record in 1926 and too much attention to outside interests doomed him. The Athletics Council replaced Stewart with Clyde Littlefield, who had over the years turned down offers from Texas Tech, Baylor and

SMU to stay at Texas. But Stewart did not take his firing gracefully, vowing to bring down Bellmont, and with the help of Billy Disch, he eventually succeeded.

While the story of how a couple of coaches engineered the ouster of athletic director L. Theo Bellmont could take up a chapter, if not an entire book, an overview will do here. By almost any standard, Bellmont (known to his admirers as "the Chief") was an extraordinary man, and his accomplishments since coming to Texas in 1913 spoke for themselves. He was largely responsible for the formation of the Southwest Conference, bringing Longhorn athletics into the big time, construction of Memorial Stadium and helping Littlefield start the Texas Relays. In 1937, UT students would dedicate the *Cactus* to Bellmont.

Yet some people regarded him as haughty, dictatorial and abrasive, and he had earned a few enemies over the course of 14 years. The personality clash between Bellmont and Disch got further fuel with the firing of Stewart. He and Disch encouraged T Men to write letters to the administration, criticizing Bellmont. Placed on probation by President Harry Benedict in 1927, Bellmont could surely see the writing on the wall.

You might think that anti-Bellmont feeling would be strongest among the UT faculty, resentful toward the athletic czar from the east side of campus, but that was not the case. Most professors supported Bellmont, who had tried to keep athletics subservient to academics. His election as president of the Faculty Club in January 1928 is indicative of how they viewed him.

If anyone opposed him more than Disch and Stewart, it was regent Robert Holliday of El Paso, who kept the issue alive after the Texas AD had been exonerated by both the faculty and regents. Holliday wanted to sever all connections between Bellmont and the university. But Bellmont, adroitly using the legal training he had received at Tennessee 20 years earlier, put up a spirited yet dignified self-defense, asking why Thomas W. Gregory and Bill McGill had not been called for their opinions. It was not enough though, as the regents voted 8-1 (only Stark remained in his corner) to depose him. President Benedict concurred, saying Bellmont was "too deeply involved in personal controversies" to restore harmony to the UT athletic department.

Contrary to Holliday's wishes, Bellmont was retained as professor—and later, dean—of physical training, working in that post until his retirement in 1952. Though deeply hurt, Bellmont admitted he had made mistakes, refused to criticize the people who brought him down and pledged cooperation. In charge now were Dr. H. J. Ettlinger (an assistant football coach from 1913-1919) and W. E. Metzinthin (head coach in 1907 and 1908). Actually, the Athletics Council as a whole took over Bellmont's manifold duties and tried to run things by committee. It is unlikely that Bellmont took any pleasure in seeing the Texas athletic department slide into chaos over the next eight years.

Stewart, by the way, coached two seasons at Texas College of Mines (now UT-El Paso) and met an untimely death in a 1929 hunting accident. His successor in Austin, Littlefield, coached the team to a 6-2-1 record in 1927 with a new emphasis on passing. He also started a tradition that remains strong today. When the Longhorn Band played "The Eyes of Texas" before and after games, the players stood and faced the band.

The UT Athletics Council occasionally allowed other schools to use Memorial Stadium. St. Edward's football teams played some "home" games there, as they had done at Clark Field. More surprising, perhaps, is that several black colleges like Paul Quinn, Samuel Huston (a precursor of Huston-Tillotson) and Prairie View A&M played at the stadium. In keeping with the racial segregation then prevalent, a special section was erected for white patrons. And vice versa when the Longhorns played, as black fans were relegated to an area at the southeast edge of the stadium. Provided with separate restrooms and water fountains, blacks endured the Jim Crow arrangement until the late 1950s, when it was quietly dropped. By that time, the UT student body was at least nominally integrated, although it was 1970 before Julius Whittier became the first black football letterman.

When Max Fichtenbaum resigned as executive secretary of the Stadium Association in 1927, he offered advice on how to handle outstanding pledges. Roughly $185,000 remained uncollected, and some people believed that lawsuits should be brought to enforce payment. Fichtenbaum discouraged that notion, referring to the University of Missouri, which had attempted to sue for funds pledged to its own Memorial Stadium. This caused much ill will on the Columbia campus, and UT wisely decided not to do the same. Yet letters asking for payment were still being sent out as late as 1929.

The stadium grounds took another step forward with the construction of East Campus Boulevard (later renamed San Jacinto Boulevard) in 1928. The city and the university spent several months arguing over which side of Waller Creek it should be built along, eventually choosing the east. This street connected the main entrances to the stadium, eased traffic congestion on game days and provided access to the new baseball park.

CLARK FIELD II

Clark Field was literally in tatters its last few years. With Memorial Stadium now hosting Longhorn football games and track meets, the old park no longer drew the big crowds and got little maintenance. The grandstand roof had been torn off during a storm and replaced with a canvas covering, and the bleachers creaked as never before. Excavation for the university power plant was already underway as the last baseball games were played.

On May 14, 1927, Disch's team won a doubleheader from Texas A&M, clinching another SWC title. Four days later, the Texas Senate, with help from Governor Dan Moody, beat the House of Representatives there by a score of 17-11. And the last athletic event ever held in old Clark Field was a high school baseball game in October 1927. Within a month, it had been entirely dismantled; the stands were sold for $351 and the fixtures and fences for $119, although some people took weatherbeaten boards as souvenirs.

The power plant and the Mechanical Engineering Building were soon erected on the site of old Clark Field, and its memory to UT sports fans began to fade. A new baseball park of the same name (the Athletics Council vetoed "Disch Field" over some objection) was built north of Memorial Stadium, across 23rd Street. Some 20 houses were removed before construction, performed by the J. F. Taylor Company of Fort Worth for $54,838, not including excavation costs. The flagpole from the old park was transferred to the new one and set in center field above the unique rock bank later known as "Billy Goat Hill." Seating 2,400, the new Clark Field was an attractive structure, better than many professional parks.

No fundraising drive was necessary to build it. Athletic department surplus, deriving mainly from the sale of football tickets, paid for the new Clark Field.

On March 24, 1928, before an overflow crowd, the Longhorns played an exhibition game against the Detroit Tigers to dedicate the park. "Benny," as President Benedict was affectionately called, threw out the first ball. A year later, in an exhibition game against the New York Yankees, Lou Gehrig hit a monster home run that some people claimed landed near the stadium. Just as they did for tennis at nearby Penick Courts, fans often stood on the top row of the Memorial Stadium horseshoe and gazed over 23rd Street as players like Bibb Falk, Pete Layden, Tom Hamilton, Bobby Layne, Bill Bethea, Burt Hooten and Keith Moreland maintained the strong Texas baseball tradition.

By now, UT had first-class facilities for four of the five so-called major sports: Memorial Stadium for football and track, Penick Courts for tennis and the new Clark Field for baseball, leaving only basketball. Fred Walker, who took over Stewart's hardcourt duties, still had to use the drafty, bat-infested Men's Gym, which doubled as an auditorium.

For years, Austin's fire marshal had been alarmed at the condition of the gym, which was highly flammable, had no fire extinguisher and only four exits. Smoking was permitted. In late March 1928, Bill McGill gave a speech lambasting the Men's Gym. "That old building is going to burn down one of these days," he said, "and it ought to."

Early the next morning, that is exactly what happened, as a fire of unknown origin reduced it to a pile of ashes. Some people joked that McGill had indulged in arson, but the prevailing sentiment was relief that the fire occurred while the building was empty.

The University of Texas lost more than another Speedway shack when the Men's Gym burned. Since his arrival in 1913, Bellmont had compiled a virtual museum of Longhorn sports, with trophies, game balls and more than 120 photographs. These were located in the Men's Gym basement, which the *Daily Texan* described as "the inner confines of the sanctum sanctorum," reputedly never seen by female eyes.

GREGORY GYMNASIUM

The fire caused Walker's basketball team to play two seasons of "home" games at the State School for the Deaf and at Austin High School. It also energized the Union Project, an ambitious building program first espoused by the Ex-Students' Association in 1927. With fundraising experience garnered from the various stadium drives, many of the same people worked on the Union Project: Thomas W. Gregory, McGill, Nowotny, Bellmont, Stark and even Hogg. This led to the construction of Gregory Gymnasium in 1930, the Women's Gymnasium (later renamed Anna Hiss Gym) in 1931, and the Texas Union and Will C. Hogg Auditorium in 1933. These buildings went a long way toward improving the UT campus and many facets of student life. Over a period of five years, the Athletics Council gave $50,000 to the Union Project.

Ground was broken on May 10, 1929 for Gregory Gym at the northeast corner of Speedway and 21st Street, a stone's throw west of Memorial Stadium. And while Gregory did not seek the honor, it was appropriate that the building, which cost $510,000, should be named after the man who devoted almost a quarter of a century to seeing that the university had a good gymnasium. Like its predecessor, Gregory Gym was a multi-purpose facility, hosting literally thousands of intercollegiate, intramural and high school sporting events, as well as speeches, dances, commencement ceremonies and musical performances. It was also the site of UT course registration for four decades.

Although Gregory Gym would become cramped and outmoded by the mid-1940s, it was a veritable basketball palace early on. Around 50 highly skilled carpenters employed during those Depression years had crafted the court out of bird's-eye maplewood. Seating 7,500 fans quite close to the court, the gym served as a friendly home to Longhorn teams and a classic snakepit to visitors until the 16,000-seat Frank Erwin Special Events Center was built in 1977.

Attempting to pick the best players over Gregory Gym's 46 years as the home of UT basketball is a dangerous endeavor, but you might choose Jack Gray, who was also an outstanding football player, in the 1930s; Slater Martin in the 1940s (he sparked the Horns to a 26-2 record and third place in the 1947 NCAA tournament); high-scoring Raymond Downs in the 1950s; Olympian Jay Arnette in the 1960s; and Larry Robinson, Texas' first black basketball star, in the 1970s—although you could make a case for Johnny Moore, who led the Longhorns to the 1978 NIT title. Moore would go on to a fine career with the San Antonio Spurs.

Gregory Gym held the offices of various coaches and officials, as the Athletics Council met for years in a room above the main entrance. This became known as the "T Room," which served the same function as the basement of the Men's Gym, with an assortment of UT athletic photos and trophies. A second T Room would open at the stadium in 1960.

Gregory Gym featured handball courts, a weightlifting room, an abundance of lockers and showers for physical training classes and a 50-meter tile pool that was, again, the very best you could find in Texas at the time. Curtis "Shorty" Alderson started a UT swimming program, vying for recognition as a major sport. Gregory Gym filled such a crying need at the university, so many of them, in fact, that in May 1931 *Alcalde* remarked on how it had elevated campus spirit in just one year.

The Union Project benefited greatly from a 1930 amendment to the Texas Constitution allowing interest on oil money from university-owned lands in west Texas to be made available for erection of campus buildings. Construction began on several new buildings in 1932, and by the Texas Centennial in 1936 (when work on the Tower started), UT had a solid physical plant for the first time in its existence.

The Permanent University Fund and the huge wealth accruing from the two million-plus acres of oil-laden land UT owns in west Texas would change its destiny. Ever since May 1923, when Santa Rita Rig No. 1 blew in, the university's petroleum money was bound to change the campus sooner or later. But it happened sooner, primarily because of Memorial Stadium.

As described earlier, until the stadium was built in 1924, the shack-ridden Texas campus was downright ugly, relieved mainly by the appearance of bluebonnets each spring. Alumni seldom returned to their alma mater, and the notion of giving money to the university was rarer still. But the stadium drive galvanized the exes, gave them a focus for their energies and funds and made them look toward UT's future. Membership in the Ex-Students' Association multiplied, and when the stadium was completed, it gave enormous pride to most students, alumni, faculty, administration and Texans not even remotely connected to the school. If such a huge project as Memorial Stadium could be achieved, maybe some other things were possible, too.

THE STADIUM ASSOCIATION ADJOURNS

L. Theo Bellmont's firing as the Texas athletic director would take effect on December 1, 1928. It was no coincidence that the day before, at the Driskill Hotel, the stadium association officers held their final meeting. Bellmont's friends in the group did not want to complete their business without him. Seven men were present that day at the Driskill: Bellmont, Stark, McGill, Ira Hildebrand, Dave Reed, W. H. Richardson and E. C. H. Bantel. It was a brief meeting.

Reed moved that the officers transfer all of the association's assets to the UT Athletics Council if the council would assume the remaining obligations. Pending the Board of Regents' agreement, the stadium was deeded to the University of Texas. Since that was the only order of business, the meeting adjourned, although undoubtedly the ex-officers lingered over cigars and refreshments to savor their massive accomplishment one last time.

They took this action because stadium construction was complete in every sense, and the association's assets outweighed liabilities. Approximately $162,000 in pledges remained to be paid, while indebtedness came to $45,000. They cancelled the 10-year contract by which the association leased the stadium to the Athletics Council for $10,000 annually. Everything considered, the university got a good deal, and the Board of Regents accepted the offer.

The stadium's fiscal deficit had been seriously reduced the previous week when UT and Texas A&M played. Just as Texas fans had boasted in 1924 and again in 1926, it was the largest crowd ever to witness an athletic event in the South, as 42,571 overflowed Memorial Stadium to watch the Longhorns capture the SWC title. Their country cousins had apparently seen enough, because soon Texas A&M began work on its own large stadium, Kyle Field. Costing $350,000 and seating 33,000, it had an uncanny resemblance to the horseshoe in Austin. Kyle Field was dedicated on Thanksgiving Day 1929, as the Aggies returned the favor, 13-0.

It may seem strange to people today, but Memorial Stadium lacked any form of locker and shower facilities during its first six years of operation.

Both the Longhorns and their visitors dressed and showered away from the stadium, and at halftime, players and coaches left the field to huddle casually under the stands. In October 1929, the Athletics Council engaged UT architecture professor R. L. White to design a 57′ × 28′ west-side locker room.

Costing around $25,000, this long-overdue component of the stadium was finished in the summer of 1930. Centrally located under the west stands, most of the locker room was given over to varsity football and track, with a smaller area for visitors and freshmen at the north end. Far from plush, and poorly ventilated, the locker room was nevertheless a welcome relief.

Also in 1930, the stadium received its last major memorial feature, a 47′ × 7′ bronze tablet above the north-end horseshoe. The Texas Legislature had appropriated $10,000 for such a monument in 1927, but nearly two years passed before construction began. Roughly 100 seats were lost in making room for this tablet, which was designed by S. C. P. Vosper and sculpted by Hugo Villa. It listed the 5,246 Texans known to have died in the World War, and in its center, a draped female figure (representing democracy) held aloft an olive branch. The tablet enumerated 14 of the military battles in which American forces took part.

On January 14, 1931, it was unveiled by Governor Dan Moody—a World War I vet himself—and accepted on behalf of UT by R. L. Batts, chairman of the Board of Regents. Since the war had ended 12 years earlier and the stadium was by then more than six years old, this was a rather belated gesture. But the university still appreciated the tablet, connoting governmental sanction of Memorial Stadium.

You can find some duplication of names among the six SWC plaques on the stadium's north wall, individual plaques on the portal walls and the huge end-zone tablet. A few of the deceased soldiers listed three times at Memorial Stadium are Thomas W. "Hutt" Crouch and Boyd McCutcheon Williams of Baylor, Walter Tips Scherding and Dan Chiles Leeper of UT, Thomas Lee Coates of Rice, and William F. Bourland and Benjamin Howard Gardner, Jr., of Texas A&M.

FURTHER ALTERATIONS

Additional toilet facilities were built at the stadium in the early 1930s, along with storage rooms under the stands. Fans noted the recently planted shrubs along the edge of the field, at the base of every vertical aisle. Another pleasing touch came when Bleymaier and his helpers painted the stadium's retaining walls orange and white all the way around. Within a decade though, the shrubs were gone, and the retaining walls were a solid white, as they are today.

The question of installing lights at Memorial Stadium first arose in 1931, but it was tabled because of the expense and the well-voiced fear that night-time football would be a further capitulation to crass commercialism. While an estimated 100 stadiums across the country did have lights, and other factors besides revenue made the idea attractive, it would be another 24 years before the Longhorns played a home game at night.

We may presume that the Athletics Council determined the location of the stadium scoreboard, which had been in the south end zone since the 1926 season. Yet in 1932, it was placed in the north end, above the main entrance, just in front of the horizontal aisle. *Cactus* photographs show the scoreboard back in the south end in 1933, north from 1934-1936 and finally back in its original south position in 1937. Just why the scoreboard kept going back and forth is anybody's guess, but it did not block the view of many spectators while perched in the north-end stands. During the entire decade of the 1930s, Memorial Stadium was never sold out.

Big crowds in the 40,500-seat stadium were uncommon except for the biennial Texas A&M game. Five Texas home games in the 1933 season (Clyde Littlefield's last as head football coach) drew a total of just 34,000 fans—not enough to fill the stadium once. Having little to lose, the university earned some good will and future fans by giving free end-zone admission to the "Knothole Gang," originally a group of 100 children aged 7-13 sponsored by the Austin Optimists Club. Even after the freebies were rescinded and 25 cents charged for admission, kids continued to gather in the wide-open spaces of the horseshoe. Some watched the games and others engaged in youthful hijinks.

It was as much a part of the Memorial Stadium scene as the bands, the affluent alumni and administrators on the west side or raucous student sections on the east side. Even now, people refer to end-zone seats as "the knothole section."

Billy Disch's baseball teams kept winning conference championships in the 1930s, and his status on campus seemed to grow with the years. And yet even he could not prevent the UT football program from impinging on his domain at Clark Field. The football team often practiced in the outfield of the adjacent baseball park, where temporary goalposts were erected. This offended Disch, who did not hesitate to make his feelings known. But even worse, for years Clark Field was used as a parking lot during Longhorn football games.

Memorial Stadium served another purpose beginning in 1934. Bricks from the old Main Building (then under demolition) were stored below the stadium's stands. A year later, the Athletics Council paid $4,575 for a tarpaulin to cover the field. It was actually 12 sections of canvas, each 33' × 175', that could be rolled onto the turf or up against the retaining walls by a crew of workmen in 30 minutes. This tarp was a smart investment since it protected the stadium grass from heavy rain when not in use. Despite all of Bleymaier's efforts, the field eroded during the course of a football season. And something like the 1927 Texas-TCU contest, a scoreless tie played in a downpour, could turn the field into a quagmire, leaving it in poor shape for subsequent games.

Consumption of alcohol at Memorial Stadium was officially forbidden, even after the repeal of Prohibition in 1933. That does not mean it never happened; witness the arrests on the stadium's dedication day. Some students considered it great fun to smuggle a flask of liquor into the stadium, drink and get boisterous. This trend reached rock bottom in the 1935 UT-Rice game, when some members of the Longhorn Band were visibly drunk while doing their halftime routine.

The incident prompted Dean of Students V. I. Moore to make an appeal for better behavior from those in the east stands (although non-students imbibed, too). The *Daily Texan* editorialized "Students do not have the right to make football games uncomfortable for spectators. . . . They have no right to encourage the use of the stadium as a bar for outsiders who are ashamed to drink at home where their respectable friends and associates might see them."

Drunkenness was greatly reduced in the ensuing games, as faculty, Austin police and state highway police became more vigilant in enforcement and students more discreet. According to the December 1935 *Alcalde*, "There were fewer bottles on display and fewer students making themselves ridiculous."

Former UT athletes John "Tiny" Gooch and Joseph "Potsy" Allen had served as the Memorial Stadium public address announcers since the late 1920s. But in 1941, Shorty Alderson took over the microphone and held it for 17 years. He had, at various times, coached football, basketball, swimming and track on the Forty Acres and was possibly the most knowledgeable person in the state about sports rules.

THE BIBLE ERA BEGINS

Jack Chevigny's time as head coach at Texas (1934-1936) was characterized by a downhill slide only interrupted by the arrival of Dana X. Bible, who had coached winners at Texas A&M and Nebraska. Short and bald, but blessed with an impressive manner of speaking, Bible was described by one of his former players this way: "He was confident as a banker, astute as a schoolmaster, poised as a preacher and expressive as a salesman." Not averse to using allusions to the Alamo, reciting poetry or other forms of psychology to rouse his teams, Bible would be the dominant figure in UT athletics for the next two decades. A pursuit pilot during the war, Bible may have known some of the very people whose names were on the walls of the stadium.

Taking over as head football coach and athletic director for the then-staggering salary of $15,000, Bible made the recruitment of players a top priority. What was called the "Bible Plan" divided the state into 15 districts and encouraged alumni to point promising athletes toward Austin. In a move that surprised some, he chose to openly pay Longhorn players—at 50 cents per hour—for work done, which most often consisted of janitorial duties at Gregory Gym or the stadium. This evolved into the practice of offering athletic scholarships, as we know it today.

The 1937 season began with Lutcher Stark in an unfamiliar position: up in the stands. His power and money had earned Stark the privilege of sitting on the Longhorn bench for almost 30 years, but Bible ended that. This oft-told tale has Stark (who was instrumental in bringing Bible to UT) willingly, almost jovially relinquishing his spot on the sideline. But in truth, he was hurt and slowly began to pull away from such deep involvement with Longhorn athletics. By 1940, Stark and Bellmont, the two men most responsible for the creation of the stadium, though they remained on campus, were essentially out of the picture.

The recently constructed 27-story Main Building, known as the Tower, became the focus of Longhorn football fans' attention in 1937. When the team won, "victory lights" turned the Tower orange. This would become perhaps the most visible and lasting tradition on the Forty Acres.

After Bible got to Texas, Memorial Stadium underwent some minor changes. Based on a study of the strength of the stadium's concrete, steel braces were put up along the inside walls. The old open-air press box was replaced by one 70 feet long, with two floors, room for reporters, photographers, radio broadcasters and a public address system. In 1938, a lecture and film room was built adjacent to the home locker room, and visitors finally got a locker room of their own, under the east-side stands.

In 1939, the stadium witnessed its largest crowd yet, 45,000, although not for a football game. It was the gubernatorial inauguration of "Pappy" Lee O'Daniel, a former radio announcer, band leader and flour salesman from

Fort Worth. Nearly 40 high school and college bands paraded into the stadium for a gaudy program that merited five pages in *Life* magazine.

Four years later, while World War II raged, 30,000 people gathered in Memorial Stadium for a patriotic show aimed at earning scholarship money for returning veterans. Pilots from nearby Bergstrom Field performed aerial maneuvers and held a mock battle between "Allied" and "Axis" forces. Among the social byproducts of the war was the inclusion of women in the depleted Longhorn Band in 1944, although they were prohibited from wearing uniforms or marching until 1957. Glenn Appling and Doris Billings were the first female cheerleaders at UT in 1939.

While Bible's Longhorns won just three games in his first two seasons, things were improving. Some quality players had come to Texas, and just as important, the acrimony of previous years had been replaced by cooperation and optimism. *Alcalde* editorialized "Not visible on sports pages or to those who view intercollegiate sport only in terms of championships is the changed attitude of the campus toward . . . football and the lack of criticism of [Bible]."

After the team managed a 5-4 record in 1939, the corner had been turned. The University of Texas football program, that sleeping giant, had begun to awaken. And as the team started winning, attendance picked up. In contrast to the 1930s, when Memorial Stadium yawned half or two-thirds empty for most games, tickets were much harder to come by, some being scalped for as much as $50. In 1946, Bible's last year as coach, home games against Missouri, Colorado, Oklahoma A&M, Arkansas, SMU and Texas A&M produced some of the biggest crowds in the Southwest.

At such times, the fraternity brothers of Kappa Alpha were perfectly situated. Their elegant three-story house sat on a hill northeast of the stadium, allowing a decent view of both football games and Clark Field baseball games.

During the years after World War II, student enrollment boomed, and the university scrambled just to keep up. In 1946, Bible and Athletics Council chairman Byron Short declined the opportunity to play a post-season game at Memorial Stadium to raise money for a veterans' fund. Many vets had taken advantage of the GI Bill and enrolled at UT, but they were housed in crude "hutments," an updated version of the detested shacks.

A NEW HOME FOR TEXAS HOOPS?

The demand placed on UT athletic facilities was tremendous, as Gregory Gym, the Women's Gym, the Intramural Fields and tennis courts were overrun with students. One option discussed in Athletics Council meetings and in the press was to replace Gregory Gym, though less than 20 years old, with a bigger, modern fieldhouse. Longhorn basketball really took off in the mid-1940s. Assistant football coach-turned-head basketball coach Bully Gilstrap led the team deep into the NCAA tournament in 1943, and four years later, Jack Gray—back from his war duties—took the Horns to the NCAA semifinals. His 26-2 "mighty mites" were considered the best basketball team the Southwest Conference had then seen. Gregory Gym was woefully insufficient to handle the numbers of people wanting to watch UT basketball. It held just 7,500, about half of the student body at the time.

A 20,000-seat coliseum honoring those who served in World War II was proposed, but the idea never got very far. Bible made clear that the athletic department would not fund such a facility. In any event, UT's surge to the top of college basketball was brief, attendance subsided, and venerable Gregory Gym continued as home for the Longhorns through the 1976 season.

Criticism of Dana X. Bible as athletic director was rare and generally muted, but what little there was tended to accuse him of fiscal conservatism and an overemphasis on football to the detriment of other sports. He probably should have been more open to the notion of replacing Gregory Gym and giving basketball a chance to earn revenue as well.

It was obvious to Bible and anyone else that Memorial Stadium needed work. In 1941, he had remarked on the paucity of restrooms and sidewalks at the stadium, and in 1944, the Athletics Council discussed—and delayed—resurfacing concrete in the north-end horseshoe. The call to add lights was growing, and the stadium had to expand to hold the crowds coming to see winning Texas teams with players like Hub Bechtol, Ralph "Peppy" Blount, Dick Harris, Tom Landry and Bobby Layne.

For a while, it appeared that lighting would come first. In 1946, Bible's final season as coach, the Athletics Council accepted bids for lighting the stadium, but quickly vetoed the idea when projected costs neared $200,000. While the need remained, nighttime football at Memorial Stadium then stood nine years in the future.

Perhaps Bible realized that it made more sense to expand the stadium before installing lights. In April 1947, after getting the Athletics Council's recommendation and seeing the plans of architect George Dahl, the Board of Regents voted to enlarge the stadium. The east and west stands would both get 26 more rows (for a total of 78 rows), plus a section to the south. The two L-shaped configurations brought permanent seating to 60,130. Plans also called for new restrooms, drinking fountains, paving under the stadium, a new press box and other repairs. Dahl, who later designed several other campus buildings, had originally estimated the cost at $600,000. But when the

R. P. Farnsworth Company of Houston submitted a low bid of $1,402,636, Bible reportedly threw a fit.

The days of student fundraisers were long over. The Athletics Council had $300,000 on hand and another $300,000 secured in loans, but now it was forced to issue $950,000 in stadium bonds, at 2 1/2 percent interest, to three local banks. The fact that UT was spending almost five times as much as it had cost to build Memorial Stadium in 1924 was lost on few people.

Work did not begin until after the 1947 season, Blair Cherry's first as Texas head coach. At the Texas Tech game, some fans got a minor scare when a fire started underneath the east stands. Those in section 39 were calmly evacuated while the fire was put out, and the game continued. It was similar to a fire that had occurred during the 1938 Texas A&M game; no serious damage was done to the stadium, and no one was hurt.

Plans were well in place to expand Memorial Stadium in 1948. But the *Daily Texan* offered a radical proposal in an October 12, 1947 editorial, "Enlarged Stadium Will Not Fit Future Campus." Citing traffic, parking and academic space concerns, it stated "Long-range planning for the university's campus of the future runs smack up against this obstacle: Memorial Stadium is located in the worst possible place. . . . The stadium should be torn down and rebuilt five miles from town."

This shocking suggestion drew no letters—whether pro or con—in the newspaper's "Firing Line," but it foreshadowed a controversy that would arise two decades later. If the UT Athletics Council was about to put another $1.4 million into the stadium, that would seem to be a clear indication of its permanence.

A BIGGER AND BETTER STADIUM

Two weeks after Texas beat Alabama in the Sugar Bowl on New Year's Day, 1948, work began on the expansion of Memorial Stadium. The first thing to go was a group of stately oak trees that had stood near the west stands. The old press box was removed, walls were ripped out and piles of debris littered the grounds. Nearly 200 men worked on the job, as bulldozers, steam shovels, compressors, jackhammers, buzz saws and a diesel crane made quite a racket.

As with Walsh & Burney in 1924 and Kroeger-Brooks in 1926, Farnsworth, under superintendent H. A. Lott, had a financial incentive to complete the work in time for the 1948 season. Bad weather impeded progress at first and in March, a group of union ironworkers struck, claiming that Farnsworth favored lower-paid non-union men. The dispute was quickly settled, and work resumed.

The pouring of concrete began at the south end of the east stands and went north. Again, as in 1924 and 1926, topography dictated the order of work: The east stands, resting on a hill, were easier to build upon than the west.

The new double-decked press box would serve as a model for those at other stadiums. Appreciative sportswriters dubbed it "Bill Sansing's Penthouse" in honor of the UT sports information director who played a big part in its design and operation. Sansing adamantly insisted that only working media and coaches should gain admittance. Legislators, generals, wealthy businessmen and various hangers-on were kept out. A heated and air-conditioned soundproof radio booth was built specifically for Kern Tips, the incomparable announcer for the Humble Oil & Refinery Company's broadcasts. The press box roof, reserved for photographers and later for television cameras, would be enclosed in 1952. Sansing was responsible for installing a ditto machine that provided sportswriters with statistics much faster than before.

Other work done to the stadium and its grounds included electrifying the scoreboard and moving it back against the Louis Jordan flagpole. For football games, new public address speakers were stationed at the press box, while those at the scoreboard continued to be used for track meets. Parts of Trinity, 23rd and 24th streets were widened, and a wooden building for the Longhorn Band was brought from off campus and placed between the stadium and Clark Field.

During the previous 24 years, many stadiums had gone up, some of them larger than Memorial Stadium. But with the addition of almost 20,000 seats, UT had the third biggest facility in the South, trailing only Tulane Stadium (the Sugar Bowl) in New Orleans and the Cotton Bowl in Dallas.

Five

The Stadium in Adolescence: 1948-1968

The University of Texas lost many people in World War II, including former football coach Jack Chevigny and these ex-players: Shelby Buck, Chal Daniel, Red Goodwin, Ralph Greear, Bachman Greer, Glenn Morries, Jack Seale and Mike Sweeney. So the Athletics Council decided to rededicate the newly enlarged stadium. On September 18, 1948, a ceremony was held before the UT-Louisiana State game honoring Texas men and women who had died in the war. University President T. S. Painter gave the address, saying "This stadium will always stand as a lasting memorial to those who so gallantly gave their lives that we might be free."

After Texas Sweetheart Ann Tynan and LSU representative Betty Pfeffer were escorted on and off the field, the Longhorn Band played "The Eyes of Texas," and the game began at 2 P.M. Some of the 47,500 sweltering fans undoubtedly wondered when the stadium would get lights and avoid more early-season afternoon games. It was coming, because George Dahl designed and R. P. Farnsworth built for the eventual installation of lights at the stadium. Texas won the game, 33-0.

The 1948 season saw the Longhorns' 16-game home winning streak come to an end against SMU before 66,000 people. (For overflow crowds, Jake Bleymaier and his crew placed temporary bleachers in the south end and ground-level chairs on the track.) The Mustangs' Doak Walker, who had graced the covers of several national magazines, was on his way to winning the Heisman Trophy. One month later, another packed house saw a 14-14 tie between the Horns and Aggies. At halftime of that game, the retiring Bleymaier was honored for 40 years of devoted service to the university.

Across 23rd Street, Bibb Falk's 1949 UT baseball team embarked on the first of two straight national championships. In a 6-4 football season, the most exciting thing to happen was when Bevo IV threatened to stampede during the Baylor game before 57,000 people. Considered the most ornery of the 13 steers to serve as UT mascot, Bevo IV lasted just one season before retiring.

Blair Cherry's final year as coach before turning it over to Ed Price was 1950, when the football team began wearing orange jerseys at home and white pants at all games. Some Aggie students evidently pulled a good trick early in the season by planting wild oats that spelled "A&M" on the stadium grass. The name of UT's archrival remained quite visible for the rest of the season. However, the real culprit was assistant coach Bully Gilstrap, who sought to motivate the Texas players. It did not hurt, because the team went 9-2 (including a 17-0 win over Texas A&M) and reached the Cotton Bowl.

By the early 1950s, the track straightaway at the southwest corner of the stadium had been eliminated. Since the straightaway was seldom used in competition, no one missed it. And southeast of the stadium, the intramural tennis courts were turned into a parking lot. The first football game ever televised from Memorial Stadium was between UT and Texas A&M on November 27, 1952. With that game, Austin station KTBC signed on the air.

Visiting teams got a new locker room in 1953 at the south end of the west stands. It was more modern and slightly larger than the old one under the east stands, which was converted into a restroom. Also that year, a first-aid station was built in the north end of the west stands.

Early in the 1953 season, the Memorial Stadium press box was integrated in terms of gender. As in virtually every other stadium then, the press box was a male bastion, off-limits to women; its door once had a sign, "No Women Allowed." But Western Union sent Mallie Coker there to transmit reporters' copy onto a teletype machine. UT sports information director Wilbur Evans hesitated before letting Coker in, relented, and instructed her to go to the upper level and be inconspicuous. Coker was later joined by other female teletype operators and finally by female sportswriters. The identity of the first woman to cover an athletic event at the stadium is uncertain, but it may have been Norma Mills, a *Daily Texan* sportswriter in 1955.

That was the year of the famous brawl outside of Clark Field. For the first time in 14 seasons, Texas did not win the SWC baseball title. Texas A&M had already clinched it when the Horns and Aggies met for a late-season game in Austin on May 17, 1955. Some 3,700 students came from College Station to cheer their team and rag the "poor Teasippers." Although Clark Field supposedly held just 2,400, more than 6,000 people got in that day, and there was trouble from the start. The game, dedicated to the late Billy Disch, was won by the Aggies, 7-4.

The jousting was loud, and a number of fights broke out in the stands, as campus police were unable to stop it. When the game ended, the fisticuffs continued outside of Clark Field and escalated to a free-for-all with "hundreds" of combatants, according to some witnesses. For several minutes, the entire area between Clark Field and the north end of Memorial Stadium was filled with students fighting. The main event involved a pair of football stars: Buck Lansford of UT and Jack Pardee of Texas A&M. Austin police finally ended the fun and games, and no arrests were made.

LIGHTING THE STADIUM

The matter of night football at Memorial Stadium, first broached in 1931, would not go away. In 1947, the Athletics Council had paid most of the $40,000 needed to light the nearby Intramural Fields. Thirty light towers enabled students to play softball, touch football, soccer and tennis after sunset, and it was a very popular move. So why not the stadium?

The technology required to adequately illuminate a large facility like Memorial Stadium had been available for years, and by the early 1950s, UT's home field was rather anomalous in this regard. Austin had earned a reputation as a place where the September sun could be brutal. At the 1947 Texas Tech game, the temperature was a blistering 98°; the 1948 New Mexico game was 90°; the 1950 Purdue game was 87°, as was the 1951 North Carolina game. In 1952, under 90° skies, Notre Dame coach Frank Leahy made a show of equipping his players with jungle helmets and oxygen tanks, and insisting that his team share the west sideline with Texas. The 1953 Villanova game was played in 96° heat, and for LSU the next year, it was 93°.

Such oven-like temperatures were hard enough on fans, but they could be dangerous for athletes, many of whom played offense, defense and special teams. It was not unusual for a player to lose 20 pounds over the course of a hot game, and some had a parched, bug-eyed look as they trudged to the Memorial Stadium locker rooms after the final whistle.

Bible and Ed Olle, athletic business manager (and Bible's successor as AD), were prudent men, very careful with money. This fact, more than anything, delayed the stadium lighting project. While the Athletics Council still owed over $300,000 for the 1948 stadium expansion, some people believed that night football would spur game attendance, more quickly reducing the debt.

Players, coaches and fans at the 1953 UT-LSU game in Baton Rouge saw how pleasant nocturnal football could be. The Longhorns' first nationally televised regular-season game, against Oklahoma that season, hinted of the growing importance of television. If a game were to be televised, even a day game in bad weather, lights were all but mandatory. By then Bible seemed to have changed his tune, calling lighted stadiums the key to better attendance and media coverage of SWC football. "Suppose, for example, we have games being played in Dallas and Waco on the same day," he told the *Daily Texan*. "The day game could be televised and not hurt the night game's crowd."

Yet there was no hurry, as polls were taken among the student body (81 percent approved of lighting the stadium) and the Ex-Students' Association (76 percent favored it). Bible weighed concerns about travel and hotel accommodations, the safety of coeds, bringing children to night games and the effect on band days. In the fall semester of 1954, UT architecture students designed models for the lighting project, including one with lamps cantilevered out over the field.

Finally in February 1955, the Athletics Council recommended that the stadium be lighted, with Carl J. Eckhardt, superintendent of buildings and grounds, doing the design. The Board of Regents concurred and invited bids. Brown & Root, the Houston company that had built Rice Stadium in 1950, quoted $123,290 for electrical and wiring construction. Wilder & Company of Fort Worth quoted $37,974 to build the supporting structures, and another $38,000 was earmarked for auxiliary lighting under and around the stadium.

One reason the Athletics Council could afford this project was its planned divestiture of Hill Hall, campus home to UT athletes since 1938. An unsavory "Animal House" stigma had developed at Hill Hall, described sarcastically by the *Daily Texan* as "a den of highwaymen, marijuana addicts, scholastic reprobates and academic unmanageables." The athletes would be somewhat dispersed among other students, and a financial benefit would occur when the university took over the cost of operating the dormitory. This plan was only achieved in part, because the Athletics Council continued funding Hill Hall (now Moore-Hill), where most scholarship athletes lived until the completion of Jester Center in 1969.

The lighting work began in May 1955, continued through the summer and almost up to the opening game. Eight sets of 100-foot towers were erected, four on the east side and four on the west. Each set had 72 lamps and provided 110 candlepower on the field; only a couple of pro stadiums had stronger lights. Suddenly Memorial Stadium had a new look.

On September 17, 1955, 47,000 people saw the first night game ever in Memorial Stadium as Texas Tech beat the Longhorns, 20-14. Never before had UT lost a home opener. The next week, when the team beat Tulane, 35-21, fans were finally able to walk out of the stadium, look up and see an orange Tower illuminating the night.

Installation of lights was a major step in the development of Memorial Stadium, then in its 32nd year. Objections to the change were soon assuaged, and few people longed for those early-season day games played in stifling heat. This left Arkansas as the only Southwest Conference school with an unlighted home stadium.

ANOTHER FOOTBALL VALLEY

Lighting the stadium may have helped divert attention from the Longhorn football program. Ed Price's teams had done well early on, winning one SWC title, but they soon slipped into mediocrity and worse. As the 1955 team compiled a 5-5 record, two now-cherished items became a part of Texas football.

First, a wealthy Dallas booster, D. Harold Byrd, bought an eight-foot drum (built in 1922) from the University of Chicago, where it had sat unused for years. Byrd had the drum renovated, painted, set on a four-wheel cart and shipped to Austin. The Longhorn Band gratefully accepted the drum, nicknamed "Big Bertha," and has continued to use it during halftime performances at nearly every home football game since.

The 1955 season also saw the introduction of the "Hook 'em, Horns" hand sign although, as mentioned earlier, that phrase had gotten some use since at least 1925. Head cheerleader Harley Clark unveiled the sign at a Gregory Gym pep rally the night before the TCU game. It was instantly popular and seemed to give Longhorn fans a certain identity, especially when done in unison. But the "Hook 'em, Horns" sign did not help the next day against the Frogs, who won by a score of 47-20.

One of the primary responsibilities of a sports information director is to keep media people happy on game days, which Wilbur Evans did in the Memorial Stadium press box. He provided food, statistics and relevant information to writers, photographers, cameramen and radio and television announcers. Evans kept them in as much comfort as possible, considering that the press box was not heated until 1963.

Soon after the 1948 stadium expansion, denizens of the press box had begun complaining about having to walk, and often carry equipment, up so many rows. As a result, the Athletics Council had a 131-foot elevator installed in 1956. Set to the south side, it stopped at both floors and the roof of the press box.

Things went poorly for the Longhorns in 1956, as they finished with a 1-9 record, including the first loss ever to Texas A&M at Memorial Stadium, the long-time "Aggie Graveyard." Several times the Aggies had come to Austin heavily favored, but a tie in 1948 was the best they could do. Bear Bryant's team (on NCAA probation for recruiting violations) won despite a big Texas pep rally underneath the stadium stands, despite a Wednesday night bonfire rally with 7,000 people, despite a two-page *Daily Texan* ad headed "Aggie Submission . . . Texas Tradition."

In an interesting sidenote, UT students at that game collected $6,920.63 for Hungarians fleeing the Soviet invasion of their country.

One member of the 1956 Longhorn team was sophomore fullback and kicker Fred Bednarski. A Polish refugee during World War II, Bednarski had grown up playing soccer. He transferred his talents to football, becoming the first soccer-style kicker. At the time, it seemed a peculiar way to kick, and few fans knew they were witnessing the beginning of a revolution in football kicking. By 1990, less than 1 percent of college kickers used the traditional straight-ahead style.

Bednarski's kicking was not enough to help the undermanned 1956 Texas team. The wolves, who had made Blair Cherry's life miserable a few years earlier, began howling for Price's resignation, and they finally got it. "There might be differences of opinion as to the cause or causes, but we can all agree on one thing: We are not having a happy season," he told the Athletics Council.

DARRELL ROYAL HIRED

In 1957, UT would need both a head football coach and an athletic director, since Bible was going into semiretirement. Replacing him was Ed Olle, a multi-sport star in the 1920s who had served for many years as athletic business manager. The new coach was Darrell Royal, then better known for his work as a quarterback, defensive back and kicker at Oklahoma in the late 1940s than for his college coaching. A three-year record of 17-13 at Mississippi State and Washington did not seem all that impressive.

But Royal needs no introduction to anyone with the faintest knowledge of Longhorn sports history. He coached UT for 20 years, from 1957-1976, winning 167 games, losing 47 and tying 5. His teams won or shared 11 SWC championships, made 16 bowl appearances and were voted undisputed national champions in 1963 and 1969. "DKR" was twice national coach of the year, and he did it all with a flair that enamored players, fans and media.

It has been said that Dana X. Bible saved Texas football twice: when he came to Austin in 1937 and two decades later when he hired Royal. The

1

3

2

1. The original Clark Field (located at the southeast corner of Speedway and 24th Street) was the precursor to Memorial Stadium. **2.** William L. McGill, one of the key figures in the 1924 stadium fundraising drive. **3.** Louis Jordan, the Longhorn football and track star who was killed in combat during World War I. A flagpole dedicated to him stood in the south end of Memorial Stadium until 1967.

Texas Memorial Stadium - University of Texas.
Showing construction as of early in 1925.

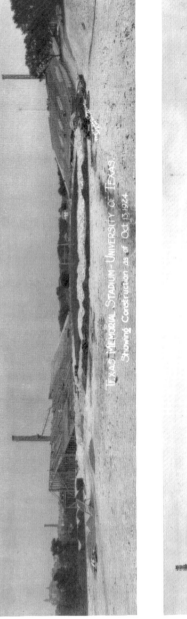

Texas Memorial Stadium - University of Texas.
Showing Construction as of Oct 13, 1924.

Dedication of Memorial Stadium   University of Texas - Thanksgiving, 1924.
Attendance- 33,000.
Texas- 7 - A·M·O.

4

5

6

(Opposite page) **4.** Stadium construction was rushed during the summer and fall of 1924. (This page) **5.** Ride 'em, cowboy! Track coach Clyde Littlefield (right) and five of his sprinters pose in western garb at the stadium in 1936. **6.** Surrounded by his teammates, Jack Crain pulls on Bevo's horns.

7. Not an empty seat in Memorial Stadium during this 1940s Texas game.

8

9

10

8 & **9.** Longhorn teammates Bobby Layne and Tom Landry. **10.** Dana X. Bible brought the UT football program out of a deep valley in the 1930s and served as athletic director for 20 years.

UNIVERSITY OF **TEXAS**

★

LOUISIANA STATE UNIVERSITY

MEMORIAL STADIUM   SEPTEMBER 18, 1948

11

11. Cover of game program, Texas vs. LSU, on September 18, 1948. The expanded Memorial Stadium (seating capacity of 60,130) was rededicated that day to honor Texans who died in World War II.

12. 1953: A jubilant Longhorn squad celebrates in the home locker room after upsetting No. 3-ranked Baylor. **13.** Another packed house in the early 1950s.

14

15

16

Mr. Track . . .

By Bill McClanahan

(Opposite page) **14.** Eddie Southern dominated the 1955 UIL meet and later became one of the university's greatest track stars. **15.** The Longhorn Band, with Big Bertha, parading on the Memorial Stadium turf. **16.** L. Theo Bellmont (left) congratulates H. J. Lutcher Stark for his induction to the Longhorn Hall of Honor in 1958, 34 years after they led the drive to build Memorial Stadium. (This page) **17.** A *Dallas Morning News* cartoon notes the retirement of Clyde Littlefield, whose UT coaching career spanned the presidencies of Warren G. Harding and John F. Kennedy. **18.** Workers apply artificial turf to the stadium floor, summer of 1969.

17

19. Darrell Royal and fullback Steve Worster, whose jersey number matched the team's winning streak from 1968-1970. **20.** UT students protest the removal of trees during the "Battle of Waller Creek," October 1969. (Opposite page) **21.** 1970: In one of Memorial Stadium's most dramatic plays ever, Cotton Speyrer takes Eddie Phillips' pass and heads for the end zone against UCLA in the waning seconds. Bruin linebacker Bob Pifferini gives futile chase. **22.** The upper deck and Bellmont Hall going up in February 1971.

19

20

21

22

23. Regent Frank Erwin spearheaded the Memorial Stadium expansion from 1969-1972. **24.** Freddie Steinmark, the UT defensive back who died of cancer in 1971. The stadium's south-end scoreboard is dedicated to him. **25.** Looking north, we see Memorial Stadium and Clark Field, which was razed following the 1974 baseball season.

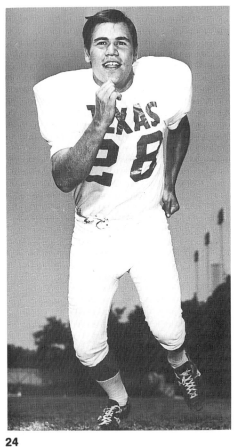

23

24

25

26. A crowd of 80,000 fills the stadium in 1974 to hear ZZ Top and other bands.
27. Memorial Stadium in the mid-1970s.

28

29

30

31

(Opposite page) **28.** UT coach Fred Akers and Earl Campbell exchange a soul shake at the 1977 Heisman Trophy dinner in New York. Campbell's mother, Ann, shares the proud moment. **29.** Campbell in action. **30.** Cheerleader Pam McGee jumps for joy during the 1978 Texas-Arkansas game. (This page) **31.** Longhorn football and track star Johnny "Lam" Jones. **32** & **33.** Two views of Eric Metcalf: Long jumping for Stan Huntsman's UT track team and putting the moves on an Oregon State defender.

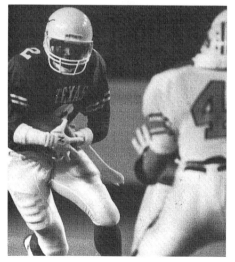

33

32

34

35

34. The Neuhaus-Royal Athletic Center, south of the stadium, under construction in 1986. **35.** Carlette Guidry, probably the finest female track and field athlete in university history. **36.** John Mackovic is introduced as the new Longhorn football coach, December 1991.

36

depths to which the program had fallen in the mid-1930s and again in the mid-1950s are comparable.

One of the first things Royal did upon arriving in Austin was to inspect Memorial Stadium, which he found in need of attention. He was offended by grass growing high up the seven-foot fence surrounding the stadium. In fact, Royal did not like the fence at all and urged its removal. And he certainly did not like to see peeling paint in the locker rooms or some of the ragged furniture in the coaches' office. Although his primary task was to rebuild Longhorn football, Royal soon had these and other cosmetic changes done to the stadium and its grounds.

Besides a spiffier stadium and an improved record, a lot of things happened when Royal got to UT. The Longhorn Hall of Honor was begun in 1957, and the names of the first inductees have all appeared in these pages: L. Theo Bellmont, Billy Disch, Louis Jordan and Daniel Penick. The person most responsible for starting the Hall of Honor was Olle, aided by Gus "Pig" Dittmar, Tiny Gooch and F. T. "Star" Baldwin.

In August 1957, Memorial Stadium hosted its first professional football game. An exhibition contest between the Chicago Cardinals and the Green Bay Packers, sponsored for charity by the Kiwanis Club, drew 19,000 spectators. Two more NFL preseason games were held at the stadium: the Cardinals vs. the Baltimore Colts in 1958 and the Cardinals vs. the Pittsburgh Steelers (with UT-ex Bobby Layne) in 1959. These games came to a halt when Royal decided that the university ought not help its "competition." And there has not been another one since, although in 1990, the Dallas Cowboys and Houston Oilers discussed playing a preseason game in Austin.

The 1948 stadium expansion had taken place amid controversy, because returning veterans had trouble finding housing on or near the crowded Texas campus. Some students and faculty had protested the use of money and scarce material to enlarge the stadium, so a compromise was reached. "Dormitory" areas were built on the second floor at both ends of the west stands, providing lavatories and toilets, but no showers. It was barracks-style living with cots and mattresses on the floor, and few UT students ever chose to reside there. The rooms got heaviest use during youth camps and when UIL track meets were held in the stadium. They soon fell into disuse and became little more than dusty storage areas.

T ROOM

But not completely. During the early and mid-1950s, some Longhorn football players discovered these two 45' × 100' rooms overlooking San Jacinto Boulevard, and began using them for romantic interludes and as hangout spots in the hours before a game. Royal put an end to that and anyway, the athletic department had plans for both rooms. The southern one was turned into a weightlifting area, while the other became a social club of sorts.

Wally Scott, co-captain of the 1942 team, had not lost his enthusiasm for Texas football. By then a successful Austin attorney, he was active in the Longhorn Club, the primary booster organization for UT athletics. Scott led an effort to have the northern of the two dormitory areas converted into a new T Room (succeeding the one at Gregory Gym), honoring lettermen from all sports. Beginning in 1958, Scott and five other people raised two-thirds of the $85,000 this room would cost.

Completed and ready for use in the 1960 season, the T Room's northern wall featured a 31' × 5 1/2' montage of UT football, basketball, baseball, track, tennis and swimming history. At Royal's suggestion, Austin photographer Dewey Mears put it together.

This room, with individual and team photos covering most of the walls, accommodates up to 400 people at a time. It has been used to host press conferences, woo high school athletes and for other social events. The main draw is the glass-encased Heisman Trophy that Earl Campbell won in 1977. But its main purpose has always been to provide current and former athletes a place to meet. Modernized a couple of times since 1960, the T Room has helped strengthen the traditions of Longhorn sports.

Memorial Stadium got a significant personnel change after the 1957 football season. Shorty Alderson had handled public address duties since 1941, but he was having health problems and furthermore, his work as stadium announcer had come under increasing criticism. While Alderson was a respected, well-loved man who knew football inside and out, he was no pro with the stadium microphone. He often got flustered, he meandered a good bit, and some people thought he was too much of a cheerleader.

The way Alderson mangled, indeed mutilated, Longhorn running back Rene Ramirez' name during the 1957 season brought matters to a head. Alderson had to be replaced, and he was, by Wally Pryor, a 1950 Texas grad who had majored in radio and television. A former swimming star, Pryor had announced at Gregory Gym swim meets since 1953 and basketball games since 1956. He stepped into the stadium's public address booth in 1958 and has called football games ever since.

But the main person in Texas athletics was Royal, who, with excellent assistants like Mike Campbell, Jim Pittman, Bill Ellington, T Jones and Charley Shira (not to mention trainer Frank Medina) put his teams in superb physical condition, taught them the fundamentals of the game and motivated them. Although not the classic rah-rah sort, Royal could have his players walk onto a football field feeling 10 feet tall.

"We talked about our record at Memorial Stadium, and I tried to let them know that they were a link in a great chain of tradition and history," Royal recalled. "I tied the old in with the present, the happenings with Mr. Bible and his great teams, and Clyde Littlefield."

While it took Royal a couple of years, he finally got the stadium turf replaced. The sod and grass first planted in 1924 was wearing out. Over the years, the grass had been fertilized, watered, lined with chalk, mowed and occasionally sprinkled with seed by Jake Bleymaier and his successor, Clarence Franklin. After the 1958 season, Royal suggested that the entire field be dug up and replanted with new soil and grass. The project, directed by agricultural experts from Texas A&M, gave Memorial Stadium a plush new playing field. This second-generation grass field lasted only 10 years, however, before giving way to artificial turf.

During the Longhorns' 13-12 win over Baylor in 1959, a fan, Arthur Shipley, suffered a heart attack and died. Such tragedies were all too common at Memorial Stadium, happening nearly every season. They made necessary unsettling calls for a doctor over the public address system. So Olle instituted a new policy of stationing a physician in the press box to facilitate treatment of medical emergencies.

(This has developed into what is now, in the 1990s, a fully equipped game-day force of three doctors, 40 paramedics, three nurses and two dispatchers at the stadium, watching the fans rather than the players. Headed by Dr. Demetri Vacalis, they handle 85 patients during a typical three-hour football game.)

By this time, some of the key people in the 1924 stadium campaign had passed away, including Max Fichtenbaum in 1956 and William McGill in 1959. Lutcher Stark, long since retired in Orange, would die in 1965 and Bellmont two years later. It is telling that in the obituaries of these four men, all of whom had long and eventful lives, their work in erecting Memorial Stadium received prominent mention.

On October 29, 1960, the Horns beat SMU in Austin by a score of 17-7. But Texas had been favored to win by 20 points. Gamblers were suspected of having removed portions of the tarp over the stadium turf the night before, allowing a heavy rain to soak the field and thereby keep the score down. No one was ever arrested for this act, which made UT officials more conscious of stadium security.

TICKETS, ANYONE?

Since the early 1950s, *Alcalde*, the Texas alumni magazine, had printed letters, articles and editorials about seating problems for Longhorn games. The titles alone tell the story: "Read Why Most Texas Fans See Football Games from the End Zone," "Crying Towel Time," "The End-Zone Lament," "Ticket Priorities," "The Free and the Unequal" and "A Way Out of the End Zone."

Many people—alumni, students or the general public—could be quite vociferous about having consistently poor seats. Olle, along with Al Lundstedt and Bob Rochs (both of whom would spend over four decades working in the UT athletic department) were accustomed to getting an earful on this matter from anyone who did not sit on the 50-yard line. Memorial Stadium was sold out just once between the 1954 and 1960 seasons. But as Royal's teams kept winning, and as student enrollment grew, so did the demand for good seats.

The list of complimentary tickets, always for prime seating, reached 2,000. These went to various state officials, current and past members of the Board of Regents, administrators, lettermen, current team members, coaches and other well-connected people. This system provoked considerable griping, but it was necessary. For example, if the university pulled the free tickets from the governor and legislators, it might find itself losing appropriations long taken for granted.

Jack Maguire, then the executive director of the Ex-Students' Association, wrote in *Alcalde* "A tax-supported institution has to be mindful of its public relations and politics, and nothing wins friends faster than a 50-yard line seat when the Longhorns play. Such seats aren't usually drawn out of a hat."

And there were the so-called "priority groups." After the plums were handed out to those on the complimentary list, the faculty, Longhorn Club and dues-paying members of the Texas Exes scrambled to buy the best remaining seats on the west side. Students who had purchased a "blanket tax" were guaranteed a seat in the east stands or the end zone, determined by lottery.

Additional work was done to Memorial Stadium in the early 1960s. The old analog clock on the scoreboard was corroded and had caused problems in recent seasons, so the Athletics Council replaced it with a digital clock. Below the scoreboard, the Longhorns' football schedule was painted, orange on a white background. A new wooden fence, 420' × 10', spanned the south end behind the scoreboard, proving somewhat more successful in keeping local kids from sneaking into the stadium on game days.

Parking inside the stadium grounds had long been haphazard, with people leaving their cars on the grass and at odd angles. So $16,000 was expended on parking areas and sidewalks, and another $8,000 for irrigation of the rutted, parched grass surrounding the stadium.

At the Cotton Bowl game on January 1, 1962, the University of Mississippi made a surprising gesture of sportsmanship, unfurling a huge Texas flag, 111' × 63'. Ross Barnett, governor of Mississippi, presented the muslin banner to Texas Governor Price Daniel, who later gave it to the Longhorn Band. Service fraternity Alpha Phi Omega has since cared for the flag, and its appearance on the field at halftime of most UT games has been known to cause even non-orangebloods to sit up and take notice. Replaced three times, a nylon flag of slightly larger dimensions is used today.

The red, white and blue of the Texas flag did not change in 1962, but the UT athletic colors did. You will recall that a dark "burnt orange" was used for a while in the late 1920s and early 1930s. For this and other reasons, Royal (by then athletic director as well as head football coach) decided to ditch the familiar bright orange and go with a darker and, some thought, duller shade. He discussed the matter with team members, who went along with the new colors, but by no means was there unanimous support on the campus and beyond.

Nevertheless, burnt orange jerseys made their debut in the 1962 Texas-Oregon game at Memorial Stadium and remain in use today. School colors were specifically defined in 1970 as part of the Regents' Rules and Regulations.

SUCCESS ON THE FIELD

From 1961 through 1964, the Longhorns had a breathtaking run of success, winning 40 games, losing three and tying one. They were voted national champions in 1963, and Royal was named national coach of the year. Home attendance was strong, as nearly every game sold out, but it was hard not to notice that the stadium needed work in a variety of areas.

Sportswriters' complaints about the now-aging press box drew action in 1963 when it was remodeled, heated and a photography darkroom was added. The visitors' locker room (which also served UT track) was redone and a laundry facility was installed in the home locker room. New runways and pits for the high jump, broad jump and pole vault were built, along with additional store rooms.

Yet that barely began to address Memorial Stadium's manifold needs, which included piping and drainage to better clean the stadium; additional paving and lighting; replacing the old splintery wooden seats; renovation of the weight room; construction of a business office; a new layer of cinders on the track; and the most urgent need—an expansion of restroom facilities, especially on the east side.

Most of these things were taken care of one at a time, as Royal and the Athletics Council strove to prevent Memorial Stadium from becoming obsolete. In 1963, engineers did a study on the feasibility of adding a second deck to the east stands. This would have enabled more students to attend Longhorn games, but it never got beyond the conceptual stage.

No description of the stadium's atmosphere in those days would be complete without mentioning the bats and other varmints that lived or scavenged there. It was not unusual to see a stray dog roaming the field during a game, and sometimes play stopped so that the offending canine could be caught and removed. Raccoons, possums, skunks and even an occasional red fox would come over from the wooded, residential area east of the stadium and dine on peanut hulls, discarded hot dogs and other assorted trash. Due to improved sanitation and the virtual elimination of their former habitat, such animals are seldom seen today in Memorial Stadium.

Of course, the same cannot be said for the thousands of Mexican freetail bats that call it home for several months a year. The stadium suits them perfectly because of its countless crevices (where they pack in colonies), plus it is dark, cool and relatively free from predators. You can hear them, you can see them flying in and out, and you can surely smell their prodigious droppings, especially after a rain. While bats fill a crucial ecological niche, most Texas sports fans would prefer that they live elsewhere.

"The stadium is one big bat roost," said former athletic business manager Al Lundstedt. "And we haven't found a way to eliminate them yet. We tried nets, ultrasonic sound and cyanide gas before the environmental laws were changed. Now, we just try to clean up after them and hope it doesn't rain the day before a ball game."

Spring football training usually took place in the stadium, rather than Clark Field or Freshman Field. Until not long ago, extended full-contact scrimmages were the norm during spring training. This was when a player could prove himself, move up the depth charts and show the coaches that he could help the Longhorns win in the fall. "The strong get stronger, and the weak get weaker," players would remind each other during these hard-nosed workouts, which culminated with the annual Orange-White scrimmage.

Before the advent of artificial turf, Freshman Field, on the west side of Waller Creek, was the site of most in-season practices. For more than four decades, players would dress in the stadium and, instead of using the less-direct 21st Street bridge, cross the creek via a series of large stones a few inches above the water. Whether from camaraderie, machismo or a combination of the two, many a team member, and even an occasional coach, got tossed into the creek on the way back to the locker room after practice.

The freshmen—known as both the Shorthorns and the Yearlings—always worked out in this tree-lined area, where the wind never seemed to blow. Sometimes the varsity subs would scrimmage the freshmen in what was called the "Toilet Bowl."

UT freshman football, which would continue for a few seasons after first-year players were made eligible for the varsity in 1972, was nothing if not obscure. Playing an abbreviated schedule against such teams as the TCU Wogs, the Arkansas Shoats, the SMU Colts, the Texas A&M Fish, the Baylor Cubs and the Rice Owlets, these young men wore hand-me-down uniforms and shoes, and had very few spectators. But at least they got to play in Memorial Stadium, a tantalizing taste of the big time.

By the mid-1960s, the Villa Capri Motel two blocks east of the stadium had become a favorite gathering spot for football fans. But not just for fans, since suite 2001 of the sprawling complex hosted Royal's post-game meetings with sportswriters. There, in a relaxed setting, Royal would review the game with such writers as Jack Gallagher, Dave Campbell, Mickey Herskowitz, Dan Jenkins, Blackie Sherrod and Lou Maysel. The Wishbone offense received its name during one of these sessions.

THE GATHERING STORM

After years of bouncing from one temporary home to another (such as the Waggener House, the Texas Union and the Home Economics Building), in February 1965, the Ex-Students' Association moved into the new $410,000 Lila B. Etter Alumni Center. What is remarkable is that it stood directly across San Jacinto Boulevard from Memorial Stadium. The Texas Exes, who were so deeply involved in financing the stadium in 1924, had been offered this spot by the Board of Regents. The alumni were delighted with the location as well as the building erected there.

So you can imagine their dismay when regents chairman W. W. Heath announced on March 12, 1965 that the land under Memorial Stadium might be better utilized. He recited a litany of problems on UT's congested campus, especially the need for additional parking, classroom, office and dormitory space. And while Heath stopped short of declaring that the stadium would soon meet the wrecking ball, he left no doubt that might be its fate.

While some students and alumni were stunned to consider the demolition of Memorial Stadium, the idea had been around for a while. The *Daily Texan* editorialized this view in 1947, and the Athletics Council, fully aware of the stadium's deficiencies, had quietly discussed it in the mid-1950s. The appearance of the stadium from some angles was, admittedly, less than inspiring, and yet many people were quick to defend it, not the least of them L. Theo Bellmont. The white-haired, 84-year old gentleman told *Daily Texan* reporter Sam Keach, Jr. that he opposed razing Memorial Stadium. "They'll have a tough time tearing it down," he said. "It has a lot of steel in it and was built to last."

Darrell Royal, whose opinion carried considerable weight, realized that the call was not entirely his. At first, he was reluctant but accepting of what appeared to be the stadium's fate. He told a student group on March 23 that Memorial Stadium, as it was then situated, did not satisfy all of UT's needs. Royal expressed no preference for an alternate site, only that he wanted to maintain an on-campus practice field.

Soon the regents' Buildings and Grounds Committee, the Faculty Building Committee and a special committee headed by Dr. Laurence Haskew, vice chancellor for developmental affairs, began looking at every aspect of the matter. The possibility of "removal of intercollegiate athletics from the main university to some other location," in Heath's words, upset quite a few people, especially alumni.

"I remember writing *Alcalde* editorials on it," said Maguire. "I was absolutely opposed and I don't recall any member who wanted to move it. We were pretty solidly against that. In any big university, the alumni organization wields a lot of power, political and otherwise, and we used all the clout we had. We spoke to the governor, and we spoke to legislators, of whom 60 to 65 percent were our alumni."

The governor in 1965 was John B. Connally, one-time president of the UT Student Assembly and a dues-paying member of the Texas Exes. And one legislator, Jack Crain of Nocona, a former Longhorn football star, raised hell in the Capitol a mile south of the campus. Maguire, Royal and Texas Exes president Frank Denius met with every regent individually at the Alumni Center. They emphasized the importance of keeping the stadium right there on San Jacinto Boulevard.

Despite the instant and heartfelt protests, Heath issued another lengthy statement on July 16 that made clear the regents' inclinations. The perimeter of the campus was expanding (mostly to the east), and the 32 acres occupied by the stadium, Clark Field and Freshman Field might have a higher priority than sports.

"When these intercollegiate athletic facilities were located, the university was a much smaller institution and it was not felt that such land would be needed for academic purposes," said Heath. "It is therefore apparent that the use of this land for academic purposes is highly desirable, and the board would be derelict in its duty if it did not investigate the economic feasibility of relocating these facilities on either the Brackenridge or the Balcones tracts."

BALCONES STADIUM?

Heath's first-mentioned alternative, the Brackenridge Tract, was the 500 acres along the Colorado River to which the university had almost moved in 1921. But it was isolated, and a stadium there would surely generate major traffic problems. The Balcones Tract in north Austin, site of UT's Balcones Research Center, was a more likely candidate. Located at the intersection of Burnet Road and Highway 183, its main drawback was the distance—eight miles—from the campus.

The Balcones Research Center in 1965 was nothing like the busy area it is today, home to a wide array of scientific ventures ranging from the Nuclear Engineering Teaching Laboratory to the Bureau of Economic Geology to the Center for Research in Water Resources. In addition, the person most responsible for the development of BRC from a World War II magnesium plant in the middle of a goat patch to its current state was Dr. J. Neils Thompson, a 1930s-era Texas football player and head of the Athletics Council from 1962-1979.

"There's no way I wanted the stadium out there," recalled Thompson, a civil engineer. "That would have destroyed what we were working for at Balcones, which is now coming to fruition. I never considered it a feasible, serious matter."

Still, the Athletics Council conducted a thorough analysis of Memorial Stadium and other options. If a new stadium were to be built, Balcones seemed to be the spot. During the summer of 1965, Thompson and other engineers formulated a conceptual plan for a huge athletic complex with a central dressing area and separate facilities for football, basketball, baseball, track, swimming and tennis. It would have provided abundant parking, in contrast to that around Memorial Stadium on game day. But with cost estimates ranging from $15-$27 million, how could UT afford it?

"Most of the problems were involved in transport of athletes from campus to practice sites every day and students to events," said Lundstedt. "We considered trains, buses and everything. We were open to it because we didn't have the ability to say 'no.' If the university had wanted to do this, it would have. But I'll tell you, the opposition came from the folks across the street, the alumni association. Just imagine people coming to Austin for athletic events and possibly never seeing the campus."

For those not overly bound by sentiment, it was nevertheless tempting. The Houston Astrodome had just opened, and its architecture and very name were bright, bold and forward-looking. By comparison, UT's stadium seemed almost dowdy with its gray walls and a name that focused on the past. If a new arena were not in the offing, then the old one had to be considerably brought up to date and enlarged.

David McWilliams, a senior on the 1963 national championship football team who was then finishing up his degree, also opposed moving. "I was just graduating and I started to see it as a fan," said McWilliams, the Longhorn head coach from 1987-1991. "I wanted to be able to come back to Memorial Stadium. That's when I realized what the stadium meant to me and the university."

On August 13, 1965, the Athletics Council announced 17 "opinions" and four "recommendations" regarding the long-range development of facilities. While clearly opposing removal of the stadium, the council believed that if this were necessary, the new one should be located at Balcones. Furthermore, it had to be first-class to gain acceptance by the campus and general public. Some of the opinions succinctly told why leaving Memorial Stadium was a bad idea:

• "By moving off-campus, the university would lose some of the long-recognized benefits of an intercollegiate athletic program such as the unifying influence, the close association with examples of personal sacrifice and heroism and the balance that comes from the inclusion of athletics as well as academic and cultural activities."

• "By moving off-campus, the student-athlete would have his participation in the academic community reduced, and it would be difficult to avoid fostering a professional rather than a collegiate atmosphere for him."

• "The present athletic site serves a real function on the campus by relieving the trend toward a dense collection of buildings with teeming occupancy throughout the school day."

• "The athletic facilities on the campus are well worth the value of the land on which they are located."

THE VIEW FROM UT'S FOURTH ESTATE

Within a week though, *Daily Texan* sports editor Paul Burka weighed in with the opinion that both the stadium and the Southwest Conference had outlived their usefulness. The *Daily Texan* followed that with an editorial entitled "Time to Move," which stated "Students at this university are not likely to lose interest in their football team if the stadium is removed from the campus. The *Texan* hopes that the Board of Regents seriously will consider relocation of Memorial Stadium."

It did not take Royal long to conclude that this would be a most unfortunate action. Never a supporter of the proposed move, the Longhorn coach had become a fierce advocate of keeping Memorial Stadium. "I'm not sure how close it came to happening. But I know that I was unquestionably opposed," he later said. "For the football program, it would have been a big, big blow, no matter what kind of stadium they built at Balcones. When asked, I expressed my opinion so there would be no mistake on how I felt about it. I can't imagine them moving the stadium. It just means too much to the students and the guys playing. It belongs right there."

At the beginning of the 1965 football season (with the team ranked No. 2 in the nation), Bellmont, in one of his last public statements, told a reporter "I agree with Royal that athletics will always have to remain on campus. The regents allotted that ground for the purpose of building a stadium, and the alumni have spent a fortune building their club."

Aside from Heath, *Daily Texan* writers and a few iconoclastic professors, no one really seemed in favor of moving. "I made sure we inspected the stadium, and it turns out it was structurally sound," remembered Dr. Norman Hackerman, then acting president of the university. "If not, knocking it down would have been a lot easier, and that was the critical point. And it was in a pretty good spot. Most of the faculty doesn't care one way or another, but some of them don't think college football is a legitimate part of the university. And the farther away from campus, the better they like it."

If there was any doubt about where the Ex-Students' Association stood on this subject, its Executive Council passed a unanimous resolution on September 29, 1965 that Memorial Stadium and Clark Field should remain. The council members also resolved that if new facilities must be built, the campus was the place to put them.

In an *Alcalde* editorial entitled "Is it Worth $16,000,000 for Texas to Have a Misplaced Stadium?" Maguire acknowledged that given the alumni's new home, they selfishly wanted to keep the football and baseball stadiums nearby. Adhering to what he called the quaint notion that college sports were carried on primarily for the benefit of students, faculty and alumni, Maguire presented many reasons, including one that had almost been forgotten: "It is a Memorial Stadium, built in memory of University of Texas students and alumni who gave their lives in World War I. The thousands of students and alumni who gave money to build Memorial Stadium more than 40 years ago aren't anxious to see it torn down."

Maguire suggested instead a program to "refurbish and landscape both Clark Field and Memorial Stadium so that they would offer an attractive campus view instead of eyesores of peeling paint and sagging fences."

Another person with strong feelings on the matter was Austin architect Howard Simmons, who said "Tearing down Memorial Stadium will be the death of Texas football." So he proposed decking both sides of the stadium with a total seating capacity of 100,000, though that would have ignored and even compounded other problems. Simmons later offered plans for a "Texas Super Bowl" in south Austin, but UT officials paid him little attention.

In an October 1965 *Alcalde* article, "Where Are We Going Next?" Anita Brewer assayed the likely growth of the UT campus for the next 10 years. Naturally, she discussed the future of the stadium and the approach taken by the Board of Regents. The article contained an aerial photograph of a packed Memorial Stadium with the Longhorn Band spelling out "Texas" on the field. An ominous question mark was superimposed over the captionless picture.

The role of President Lyndon B. Johnson in all of this was never entirely clear. UT had already forged an agreement with the federal government to build what would become the LBJ Library/Museum and the LBJ School of Public Affairs. Expected to take up at least 14 acres, this complex for tourists, graduate students and other scholars was to be set on a bluff on Red River Street, overlooking both Memorial Stadium and Clark Field. There was muffled suspicion about Johnson: Did he want the stadium gone? Would it be turned into a parking lot for the shrine to his presidency?

Johnson, not a Texas alumnus, had attended a few games over the years, but he could hardly be described as a football fan. Had he wanted the stadium removed, it probably would have been, but Johnson surely knew of the protests going on. If he were responsible for such a major change on the UT campus, resentment against LBJ and his library might last a generation or more. What likely happened is that the president chose not to antagonize his future neighbors. Having 60,000 people in Memorial Stadium across the street five days every fall might not be a bad thing, and the juxtaposition of a college football stadium and a presidential library could be an interesting one. Johnson almost certainly gave his OK to keep the stadium there.

STAYING—FOR NOW

Finally, after eight months of suspense, on November 23, 1965, the Board of Regents announced its decision. Clark Field and Penick Courts had to go, while Memorial Stadium and Freshman Field would remain for the time being. The tentative nature of this plan was apparent, since the land on which the stadium sat was still seen as prime real estate. "We believe that statement at this or any other time of intention to demolish Memorial Stadium should be dependent upon demonstrable immediate need for concrete and fiscally possible usage of the groundsite for academic purposes," said Heath, with some verbosity. ". . . the west portion of the Balcones Tract [is to] be held open to take care of any such future contingency as long as same is not required for other purposes."

Heath closed by recommending (as the Athletics Council and Ex-Students had already done) that the stadium's needs be identified and that its function and appearance be enhanced.

Memorial Stadium had gotten a reprieve, shaky though it was, since the issue had been postponed more than decided. Longhorn football and track would continue in their familiar home, but baseball and tennis faced uncertain futures. Some people thought it was the beginning of a de-emphasis of the two sports. Tennis coach Wilmer Allison was most displeased with the plan, saying "One of the best setups for tennis in the U.S. is being destroyed. Our courts are unequalled except for those at Forest Hills or Wimbledon." Allison expressed hope that the courts might be transferred to a spot just south of the stadium, which is exactly what happened two years later.

Baseball coach Bibb Falk responded more calmly than Allison. He figured that the new baseball park, wherever it was located, would be an improvement over Clark Field. Falk did not expect to be moving soon, and he was right; Longhorn baseball remained at Clark Field for nine more seasons before jumping over the highway to Disch-Falk Field in 1975. Even when it was torn down, the memory-laden area served as a parking lot for another four years until construction of the Performing Arts Center.

It is interesting that no mention was made about providing a new arena for UT basketball. Gregory Gym, which had gotten a $1.75 million southern annex in 1963, remained an excellent recreational facility. But it was thoroughly outdated for intercollegiate competition, with the worst seating in the Southwest Conference, according to basketball coach Harold Bradley.

We have already noted the views and actions of most of the principals: Heath, Johnson, Thompson, Hackerman, Maguire and Royal. One more person must be accounted for, though, and that is Frank C. Erwin, Jr. A regent since 1963 and soon to be chairman, Erwin has been called, whether with respect or derision, the H. J. Lutcher Stark of his day. While lacking Stark's immense wealth, Erwin was similarly blunt and dynamic, and took great interest in UT athletics. When the issue of moving the stadium arose, he gave it a hard look. Like other regents and state officials, Erwin was bombarded with passionate pleas to leave Memorial Stadium alone, and soon he began speaking publicly and privately for just that.

Minor changes had already begun to be made. Assistant track coach Cleburne Price was appointed superintendent of stadium grounds in 1965, and while he was given limited manpower and funds, Price labored to improve the appearance of Memorial Stadium. He soon had orange and white paint covering the aisle steps and portals throughout the stadium, as well as in locker rooms, concession areas and the press box. Price was responsible for flying the pennants of SWC institutions on flagpoles at the stadium's north end.

Memorial Stadium turned into something of a fortress on August 1, 1966, when Charles Whitman went on a noontime shooting spree from atop the Tower, killing a total of 16 people and wounding 31. Law enforcement officers took aim at Whitman from a variety of campus buildings, including the stadium's west side. Its walls provided shelter for several people. The carnage did not stop until UT policemen Ramiro Martinez and Houston McCoy killed Whitman in a dramatic encounter behind the Tower parapet.

FACELIFT

Frank Erwin knew that the stadium needed all kinds of work, and this opinion was bolstered when he attended an Arkansas-Texas football game in Little Rock. He saw that War Memorial Stadium was cramped and badly worn at the edges. On the airplane ride back to Austin, he spoke pointedly about such conditions and saw that they only resembled those at UT's Memorial Stadium. While Royal and the Athletics Council were aware that the regents' 1965 decision to keep the stadium was far from binding, they went ahead with a number of projects costing around $200,000. Some were cosmetic and others were functional, but put together, they helped bring the old building somewhat up to speed. Most of the work was completed before the Longhorns' 1967 home opener against Texas Tech.

Penick Courts had served UT tennis well for four decades, but they stood in the way of the East Mall Project which straightened 23rd Street and turned it into a boulevard. As Allison had suggested, the courts were taken down and moved to a spot just south of the stadium scoreboard and the Louis Jordan flagpole. The new Penick Courts (renamed Penick-Allison in 1977) had a south grandstand making use of some materials from the old facility, and were lined on the west and north by a row of tall juniper trees.

The old 1 1/2-story groundskeeper's house northeast of the stadium was razed that summer, and a new tractor and tool shed were built under the north stands. Progress came at the cost of this house on the stadium grounds where, since 1924, first the Bleymaier family and then the Franklin family had lived.

Royal was not the only person who disliked the seven-foot barbed-wire fence that had long surrounded the stadium. With gray walls and light poles as a backdrop, the fence suggested a prison more than a collegiate athletic arena, and no one complained about its removal. Tips Iron and Steel Company won the contract to build iron gates at the 13 arches in the north end and at other entry points. Seven squatty concrete ticket booths were built adjacent to the stadium, so fans no longer had to practically stand in the street to buy game tickets. A nine-foot orange and white facsimile of the UT seal, designed by architect Charles Harris, was erected in the central north arch under the steer head and bronze letters spelling out "Texas Memorial Stadium."

Architect Roland G. Roessner, a member of the Athletics Council, worked on many aspects of the 1967 stadium facelift. After some discussion about the exact shade of orange to use, the 20 oblong niches on the horseshoe columns were painted. This, combined with the seal, the gates and the open areas left by the departed tennis courts and house, gave the north end of Memorial Stadium a much nicer appearance.

One project that would have really changed the stadium's look on the inside was shelved due to unexpected costs. The weatherbeaten, splintery wooden benches had torn many a woman's hose over the years, and some had come loose and even broken. The Athletics Council debated encasing the wooden seats with nylon or installing precast concrete seats, but both methods proved too expensive. So for the time being, they continued replacing the worst of the wooden benches on a piecemeal basis.

Since Royal realized the importance of nice locker rooms to a prospective athlete, and since those in Memorial Stadium did not measure up, more work was done there. The home locker room under the west stands was enlarged, with 60 new lockers and benches, and assorted rooms for trainers, managers and the like. Appended to the visitors' locker room was a new shower and lounge for game officials. They had previously put up with cramped quarters on the east side of the stadium, which were then turned over to the UT tennis team. A new hot water system was installed, serving home, visitors' and officials' showers, as well as a small laundry room.

This facelift had no effect on the Longhorns' performance in 1967, as they struggled to their third straight 6-4 regular season record. It was an increasingly politicized time, as seen in a series of game-day protests outside the stadium by the Negro Association for Progress. One leader, O. B. Harris, told reporters "We're protesting Negro history, football and everything else racist around here."

The Board of Regents did not seem to consider Memorial Stadium's new look a sign of permanence, issuing another statement about the stadium remaining intact, but with the familiar "unless and until" caveat. The 1967 Athletics Council proceedings offer a glimpse of the stadium's future and that of the entire athletic program, which had always been driven by football revenue. Noting that students (who paid just $12 of their blanket tax to attend five home games) were taking up more and more seats, Thompson said ". . . a large number of long-time friends of the university have given up coming to football games. . . . The enrollment trend augurs for an extreme shortage of seats in Memorial Stadium at an earlier date than anticipated."

GROWING PAINS

The 1967 refurbishing of Memorial Stadium (which, unfortunately, did not address the matter of restrooms) had barely been completed before the Athletics Council began looking at expansion. Thompson recommended a feasibility study by two companies, Osborn Engineering of Cleveland and Lockwood, Andrews & Newnam (LAN) of Houston. Both had experience in the field of stadium design and enlargement. Osborn had worked on D.C. Stadium—since renamed Robert F. Kennedy Stadium—in the nation's capital, Cleveland Municipal Stadium, Yankee Stadium and those on the campuses of Michigan, Minnesota, Purdue and Notre Dame, among others. LAN, meanwhile, had worked on the Astrodome, Memorial Stadium (Owen Field) at Oklahoma, Kyle Field at Texas A&M and the much-admired Rice Stadium.

For a fee of $28,000, Osborn and LAN were appointed to do a two-part study of UT's options, but only after lengthy meetings with Thompson, who, it will be recalled, was a civil engineer, and had already concluded that the stadium had to stay. And if it were to be enlarged, he had come to the following conclusions:

• Removing the track and lowering the playing field to gain additional seating would cost around $500,000;

• Any expansion would be in the range of 12,000-15,000 seats;

• Double-decking the east side would cost around $1.5 million, not including relocation of lights; and

• Selling seat options, an idea not relished in the past, would be the likely way to pay for the work.

The UT Athletics Council took a pragmatic, flexible approach to augmenting the stadium. Yet the notion of moving the track elsewhere came as a surprise to track coach Jack Patterson, his team and its fans. They understandably had a hard time envisioning the Texas Relays and other home meets held anywhere outside of Memorial Stadium. As it turned out, moving the track and lowering the field substantially proved unfeasible for a number of reasons and never came close to happening.

A moderate-sized upper deck on the east side seemed imminent. The UT regents and administration reviewed a model of the expanded stadium and were happy with the design. But, according to Athletics Council minutes, "it wasn't until someone commented about the height of the east-side second deck in relation to the . . . Johnson Library that there began to be concern and the decision to take a second look. After the meeting, Mr. Erwin and others went to the vicinity of the Johnson Library and examined the relative heights of these two structures. It became apparent that the top of the proposed deck would be several feet higher than the top of the Johnson Library. The structure is in direct line of sight from the Johnson Library to the Capitol."

Even if Lady Bird Johnson (who would become a regent in 1971) were not the first person to raise this issue, she and presumably her husband expressed displeasure over the possible addition of an east-side upper deck. One other factor that militated against building on the east side was that fans there would face the sun during day games. While it would have been easier and cheaper to build on the eastern slope (as in 1924 and in 1948), this option was closed.

MORE OFF-CAMPUS POSSIBILITIES

The stadium was to be expanded, right? Well, perhaps. The Board of Regents remained unconvinced that staying on campus was the thing to do. So Osborn and LAN proceeded to review the Athletics Council's studies and came up with one of their own. In July 1968, these associated engineering firms completed a report entitled "Site Comparison Study/Off-Campus Athletic Complex."

The criteria included a total of 300 acres to accommodate spectator parking and these facilities: an 80,000-seat football stadium in bowl configuration, decked on both sides, with provisions for future expansion to 100,000; a dual-purpose fieldhouse for basketball (20,000 seats) and swimming (1,000 seats); a 20,000-seat outdoor track stadium; a 3,000-seat baseball park; and a 1,000-seat tennis facility with eight courts.

The report examined six places in Austin where UT teams might compete in the future. Dismissed almost out of hand were sites at the university's Brackenridge Tract and at the intersection of Highway 290 and Interstate 35. Of the four remaining sites, Balcones was regarded as the *least* desirable, in part because of its remoteness from campus and the fact that the proposed

MoPac Expressway would eventually bisect the whole complex. Plus, a set of often-used railroad tracks sat on its eastern border.

Next up the ladder was a site at the intersection of highways 290 and 183. It offered several advantages, including plenty of undeveloped land and access to freeways, but rugged topography would raise clearing and grading costs.

The intersection of Ben White Boulevard and Montopolis Drive in southeast Austin got slightly higher marks from Osborn and LAN due to land availability, access and topography, but considerable utility extensions would be needed.

Of the four main options, the best was adjacent to Austin State Hospital, two miles north of the university, near the conjunction of Lamar Boulevard and Guadalupe Street. This land, owned by the Texas Department of Mental Health and Mental Retardation, was well suited to development because of utilities and drainage, but even it had inherent limitations. First of all, only 154 acres were available, barely half of what was needed, and it was bound by residential areas, a cemetery, Austin State Hospital, Texas School for the Blind and the State Health Department. In addition, UT's Whitaker Intramural Fields had been moved from campus to the northeast corner of this area in February 1967. According to the report, "From the standpoint of overall urban planning in Austin, development of this site as an athletic complex may not necessarily represent the best use of the site."

To say the least. Just a glance at the schematic map drawn by Osborn and LAN shows the five athletic facilities jammed together on this site with minimal parking or greenery. And building there would have had a severe impact on long-settled surrounding neighborhoods.

Besides its relative proximity to the UT campus, this site may have been ranked first mostly because it would cost least, an estimated $24.4 million ($3 million less than the others), plus land costs. Osborn and LAN concluded that from an engineering standpoint, an athletic complex could be constructed at any of the locations examined, but it was a lukewarm recommendation. The report had hardly been turned over to the Athletics Council before it was rejected.

If any of the choices had been truly attractive, then moving off campus might yet have happened, but the dollar figures alone scared people off. Athletics Council surplus and money raised through seat options could not conceivably pay for the multi-sport complex desired. The issue was dead in the water. The UT athletic department still had to make some hard decisions about its facilities, but one thing was certain: Memorial Stadium would stay where it was.

Six

The Stadium in Maturity: 1968-Present

After it became apparent that moving Texas athletic facilities off campus would not happen, Osborn and Lockwood, Andrews & Newnam quickly started work on their second report, entitled "Feasibility Study/Memorial Stadium Expansion." They delivered it in September 1968. While the engineers prefaced their report by affirming Memorial Stadium's structural soundness, they noted that fewer than half of its 60,130 permanent seats provided optimum viewing.

"Good seats are generally considered to be those located along the sidelines and between the goal lines at a height of five feet or more above the playing field," the report stated. By this definition, there should have been no thought of putting a matching horseshoe in the south end, thus raising the number of "bad" seats. But it was discussed since construction costs would be low and no alteration to the existing structure would be necessary.

Still, this option never had a chance. The Penick Courts sat in the south end, close to where 5,430 end-zone bleacher seats could be erected for sellout football games. An elevated southern horseshoe would have overhung both the track on one side and the tennis courts on the other. In addition, J. Neils Thompson believed that an enclosed bowl might have been suffocatingly hot for afternoon games. (But that had not prevented Osborn and LAN from planning a bowl stadium for their off-campus feasibility study.)

For a variety of reasons then, expansion of Memorial Stadium to the east or to the south was unlikely, which left only the west, not without its own problems. The most obvious included unfavorable topography, construction of a new press box and moving a portion of San Jacinto Boulevard to the west. And while it would cost much more than the Athletics Council could possibly pay, Thompson, Erwin, President Hackerman, Osborn and LAN, and the capable people at the UT System Office of Facilities Planning and Construction found a way to do it.

Put a building, an ostensibly academic building, underneath the proposed west-side upper deck, and let the university foot much of the bill. This would make use of otherwise dead space, would help deflect anticipated criticism and would probably look better, too. Some Athletics Council members initially urged that the building hold dormitory rooms, like LSU's Tiger Stadium or Tennessee's Neyland Stadium, but that never got far.

The idea of combining academics and athletics in one building made sense to the university, which had been considering erection of an annex on the north side of Gregory Gym. Multiple use of buildings, land and parking space was an appealing concept for the crowded campus. And since constructing a new facility or expanding Memorial Stadium to the east or south had been ruled out, UT's decision-makers saw this as the way to go.

While the Athletics Council claimed that such a structure "would not create an overpowering appearance" to the west, it would absolutely dwarf the Lila B. Etter Alumni Center across San Jacinto Boulevard. But by this time, the Texas Exes were just relieved that the stadium would remain. As the Longhorn football team began a 30-game winning streak capped by an undisputed national title in 1969, the Athletics Council got the regents' approval of the west-side upper deck and accompanying building. Estimated cost: $5.5-$6 million. UT applied for federal money to help finance the academic portion of the project, but the government declined.

Parts of UT's diverse community grumbled that the plans and negotiations were too secretive. Soon though, contracts were signed with Osborn (for architectural and mechanical engineering) and LAN (structural and electrical engineering), and with the joint construction companies of H. A. Lott of Houston and Lyda Inc. of San Antonio. Those with a sense of history noted that in the 1948 Memorial Stadium expansion, the construction superintendent was none other than Lott, and one of his key men was Gerald Lyda. UT architect Charles Harris would serve as project manager.

In January 1969, Thompson publicly announced that Memorial Stadium would be double-decked on the west side and supported by what was at first called the "San Jacinto Classroom and Office Building," later the "Building to House Physical Education Facilities and Offices," and finally "L. Theo

Bellmont Hall." He predicted that the job would be completed in time for the 1970 football season.

Some people—including the very architects and engineers who were to design it—expressed incredulity at that schedule. The rush to design and build the project would lead to trouble down the road. But Lou Maysel of the *Austin American-Statesman* reminded his readers that in the 1920s, Texas had put on a whirlwind fundraising drive and constructed a 27,000-seat stadium in just over a year.

The primary architect of Memorial Stadium's west-side expansion was Al Papesh of Osborn. He first designed a straight 10,000-seat deck with a press box on top. The UT people wanted something else, so Papesh came up with a curved, longer deck (with nearly 15,000 seats), supported by an 11-story building. Papesh and his associates worked with guidance from Thompson and Erwin, who had traveled around the country looking at college football stadiums; they regarded Camp Randall Stadium at the University of Wisconsin as the prototype for what would be done at Texas. In 1966, the Madison facility—which predated Memorial Stadium by seven years—got a single 13,000-seat curved second deck.

Construction on Memorial Stadium would extend far beyond the 1970 football season, would cost much more than $6 million, would add several major aspects to the job, and would cause a storm of debate about its propriety. While the engineers and architects worked furiously, there was little visible change to the stadium in the spring of 1969.

SO LONG, BERMUDA GRASS

To make way for the massive Jester Center dormitory, in 1967 the Intramural Fields were moved off campus and named after former football coach and intramural director Berry Whitaker. Ever since, the stadium had received heavier use by students, leading to a noticeable deterioration of the track and turf, which cost $150,000 per year to maintain. Athletics Council members expected that artificial turf would eventually come to UT, but only in the early or mid-1970s, when stadium expansion work was complete.

Synthetic playing surfaces were something of a novelty then, having begun at the Houston Astrodome in 1966. They quickly became recruiting boons, and when Royal learned that Razorback Stadium at Arkansas was getting artificial turf, Texas had to have it as well. Laying artificial turf on the Memorial Stadium floor would also benefit the Longhorn Band, ROTC, physical education classes, intramurals and the student population in general. For these reasons, the UT athletic department believed it should not bear sole financial responsibility for the new turf and track. The regents agreed to pay a quarter of its estimated $565,000 cost.

The *Daily Texan* soon questioned the expenditure of so much money on artificial turf instead of on scholarships or programs for underprivileged students. In the newspaper's "Firing Line" section, classics professor Dr. Karl Galinsky pointed out that UT was spending $11 million—his figure—to expand the stadium, but only a small fraction of that for graduate fellowships and for books. While conveniently overlooking the genuine need for a modernized stadium and the fact that athletic funds were not transferable, Galinsky and other critics had some powerful logic on their side.

Nevertheless, Memorial Stadium was getting a rug. Royal recalled "I thought artificial turf was the thing to do, and I still do. It's so much neater, there's no trimming, and it's for all kinds of weather. I like it, and it's great for the game. We can have joggers and kids playing all the time, and the band can come and work out when they want. It's good PR to open the stadium up."

Work began in the summer of 1969, shortly before Apollo 11 astronauts Neil Armstrong and Edwin Aldrin put the first human footprints on the moon. UT athletic officials expected the installation of artificial turf both inside the stadium and at Freshman Field to take no more than 30 days. But the task proved rather difficult, entailing the removal of three feet of dirt and rock, building a drainage system and surveying the field.

Vastly oversimplifying what was done, the next steps included applying (1) six inches of a compacted limestone base, (2) a 1 1/2-inch layer of rough asphalt, (3) a 1 1/2-inch layer of smooth asphalt, (4) a 1/2-inch rubber pad, and (5) the carpet itself, Astroturf, made by Monsanto. Thirty-five rolls, each 15 feet long, were glued to the rubber pad, then given the markings of a football field.

Goalpost foundations were set in the north and south end zones, but even this was different. Gone were the old H-shaped goalposts, replaced by a modern "slingshot" type, and the field was moved 10 yards south to better suit option seat buyers in the coming years. Of course, this meant that seats in the north end got correspondingly worse. The high jump pit was moved to the north end of the field, which now had more room.

And let's not forget the cinder track, to be replaced by 3M's Tartan Track. After removal of the old track, thick liquid was poured over an asphalt base, hardening into granulated rubber known as polypropylene. It looked pink to some people, although 3M preferred to call it "rust-colored." This 440-yard all-weather track would spare fallen runners from painful cinder burns and help them achieve faster times, whether in sprints or distance events. As of 1969, no longer would UT cheerleaders have their shoes covered by black cinders during the course of a game.

Excavation, a drainage system, artificial turf and a rubber track came to just over $1 million, providing more ammunition for the critics, who only got louder. But time would prove that the decision to convert to synthetic surfaces was a wise one. First of all, the stadium was thrown open to students and others. Second, football on artificial turf was a much faster game than on grass, and mudbaths became a thing of the past. (However, the effect of artificial turf on football injuries remains a matter of debate.) Finally, rubber tracks have every advantage over cinders.

Other things changed, too. Royal told his assistant coaches that he would not allow them to spit tobacco juice on the new turf. Bevo, the steer mascot, had no grass to chew on at the south end of the field, and stadium workers no longer watered, mowed, raked and fertilized, learning to use such new machinery as a scrubber, a brush and a vacuum for water removal.

The bright new turf and track were given their baptism on September 27, 1969 when UT played Texas Tech before 65,200 fans. The Red Raiders had beaten Texas two straight years, but not this time, getting bombed, 49-7. Three days later, the *Daily Texan* ran a rather uncharacteristic editorial, "Football's Contribution," saying that the sport still had a unifying effect on students and alumni, and that rightly or wrongly, it drew recognition to the university. That was nice, because Longhorn football, the expansion of Memorial Stadium and the actions of regent Frank Erwin were about to become the focus of intense interest ranging beyond the state's borders.

TROUBLE ON THE BANKS OF WALLER CREEK

In the late 1960s, the University of Texas, like many other schools across the country, was in upheaval. Protests against the war in Vietnam, countercultural lifestyles and rebellion toward authority were the order of the day. While tame compared to Berkeley or Ann Arbor, Austin was probably the most freewheeling college town in the South during those times.

For several months, it had been known that the expansion of Memorial Stadium would require moving a portion of San Jacinto Boulevard 56 feet to the west, closer to Waller Creek. The loss of about 15 cypress and oak trees, some of them with trunks four feet thick, was inevitable, and as the day for their removal neared, protests grew more vocal. The university was accused of secret planning, environmental boorishness and a stubborn refusal to compromise.

On Monday, October 20, workers equipped with chainsaws and bull-dozers met a small group of students chanting slogans and carrying such signs as "Trees Give More Shade Than Alumni Seats," "Don't Rape Mother Nature" and "No Bulldozing Here." Some joined hands and encircled trees to prevent their felling. Ralph Butler, the construction superintendent, was almost apologetic in urging the students to cease and desist, but they refused, also defying Dean of Students Stephen McClellan.

The protesters were back on Tuesday, their numbers swelled to 50, which included a few UT professors. With the help of a temporary restraining order, they again succeeded in keeping the trees from being cut down. Many vigorous discussions in the free speech area of the Texas Union patio focused on the issue, as well as letters and articles in the *Daily Texan* and *Austin American-Statesman.* The administration brushed aside an alternate plan put forward by UT architecture students.

Taking no chances, some protesters slept at the site to guard against any overnight tree-cutting. Wednesday was the climactic day, though. Some university administrators asked Erwin to hold off, but he had seen enough. He jumped into his orange Cadillac and stormed down to the creek to take charge.

The number of protesters and observers had grown to 400, and some of them put it all on the line by climbing high into the disputed trees or lying down in front of bulldozers. Campus, city and state police were on hand, taking orders from Erwin, who made an oft-repeated statement: "Arrest all the people you have to. Once these trees are down, there won't be anything left to protest." The police complied, arresting 27 people for disturbing the peace. Pictures of officers on ladders, pulling students out of trees, appeared in newspapers and on television screens from coast to coast.

It was a nasty scene, with the chairman of the University of Texas' Board of Regents applauding and cheering and trading insults with anyone he perceived to be in opposition. When the protesters were finally removed, the bulldozers and chainsaws roared into action, and the trees came down. With all the confusion and noise, 27 trees were cut down, rather than the 15 called for. Waller Creek was scarred, and so, some claimed, was the university's spirit. Students dragged tree limbs up to the steps of the Tower and engaged in a spontaneous, angry protest.

"Axe Erwin" bumper stickers became fashionable, as construction work resumed. Royal's football team did not seem distracted in the least, beating Rice, 31-0, the following Saturday. But spectators entering and leaving Memorial Stadium's west side that day could not help seeing the now-ravaged Waller Creek.

UT English professor Dr. Joseph Jones had stopped attending football games twenty years earlier, and occasionally offered half-serious motions in the Faculty Senate that the sport be abolished. In his 1986 book, *Life on Waller Creek*, Jones wrote "Why, indeed, was the stadium being so lavishly enlarged and embellished? . . . the old incentives had died along with 'school spirit'—a casualty of commercialization over several decades. Too many students were cynical about 'their' football team to generate enthusiasm for such development, long since having written off high-pressure intercollegiate sports as a money-bags enterprise being steadily professionalized and corrupted in Austin as elsewhere."

And yet things were not quite so cut and dried as that. While the football team remained undefeated, student enthusiasm grew. On December 3, 1969, with the Longhorns ranked No. 1 in the nation, an estimated 26,000-30,000 people attended a Memorial Stadium pep rally before the "Big Shootout" against Arkansas. James Street, Ted Koy, Steve Worster and the rest of the players entered the stadium in convertibles before a cheering throng. They even got some high culture, as jazz musician Herbie Mann (who was in town for a concert) did an upbeat version of "The Eyes of Texas." When UT won that memorable game the following Saturday in Fayetteville, there were nine hours of havoc on the Drag. The team went on to beat Notre Dame in the Cotton Bowl, and the sunset was burnt orange. Winning does something to you.

CONSTRUCTION COMMENCES, SLOWLY

Work on enlarging Memorial Stadium was expected to begin in earnest just after the last home game of the 1969 season, but a series of problems prevented that. Builders Lott and Lyda were understaffed early on, and UT officials blamed the students' protest at Waller Creek for a three-week delay. The new part of San Jacinto Boulevard had to be ready before work could start on the stadium. On April 10, Lundstedt admitted that completion by the 1970 football season was unrealistic, and that 1971 was a better target date.

While Longhorn players were being fitted for national championship rings, Lott and Lyda built a short railroad track between the stadium and the street, and mounted two cranes on it that could move north and south as required. The west-side lights were taken down, and the old press box and elevator were demolished. The area west of the stadium took on the look of a construction site, with scattered refuse and heavy equipment, often noisy and somewhat dangerous.

The first substantial change was the erection of an 11-story tower that would hold four elevators. Deep piers were drilled into the limestone bed, and slowly, very slowly, the steel and concrete infrastructure began to take shape. The ivy-covered walls on the stadium's west side were gradually obscured. Amid all the construction work, the 43rd running of the Texas Relays took place on the new rubber track, which got good reviews.

Meanwhile, things were happening to further alter the interior of Memorial Stadium. The Athletics Council printed and distributed 50,000 color brochures detailing the plan to sell west-side seat options, which would raise $1.5 million to help pay for the construction work. Before being made available to the general public, $400 (between the 40-yard lines), $300 (from the 30- to the 40-yard lines) and $200 (from the 20- to the 30-yard lines) options were offered to former lettermen, faculty, members of the Longhorn Club and the Ex-Students' Association. Never included in the option plan, however, were the top four rows of the lower stadium between the west-side 20-yard lines. This area formed the core of the complimentary seating list.

"People jumped on the seat options like a blue jay on a june bug," said Lundstedt. "It gave them the right to buy a ticket for a designated seat, and it was a tremendous deal, because it lasted for 10 years."

Options were sold for the first 17 rows of the entire upper deck, again with the more expensive ones in the center. But these sold more slowly, since people were not sure just how good the viewing would be from up there.

In an effort to entice upper-deck buyers, a full-page ad was placed in *Alcalde* with the headline "UT Football: Option 1970" stating "They will be comfortable seats, as the design will provide ample room. . . . In the lower stands we will have to fit these seats into the existing space, and knee room may be at a minimum in some instances." This seemingly minor problem would lead to major headaches in the next three years.

Option buyers were promised contoured, chair-back seats, but of what kind? The Athletics Council looked for a new type of seating throughout the entire stadium. It would not do to have donors in fancy new chairs while other people sat on the old wooden benches. For reasons of aesthetics, comfort and fairness, all of the seats would have to be replaced.

ALUMINUM SEATS INSTALLED

The Athletics Council vetoed precast concrete seats (too heavy) and fiberglass (questions of durability), settling on aluminum. In the summer of 1970, Southern Extrusions Company of Magnolia, Arkansas was engaged to build and install aluminum benches and chairs in Memorial Stadium. The work crew, employing several UT athletes, removed the wooden planks, tightened the existing vertical standards to the concrete and then attached the seats, which were light and durable.

The wood-to-aluminum seating change, headed by stadium superintendent Glen Swenson, led to a brief labor strike. Union steelworkers walked off the job to protest the use of non-union labor by Southern Extrusions, but the conflict was soon resolved. Another strike by carpenters and plasterers further delayed work in July.

The number of seating sections was reduced from 48 to 32 by the elimination of intermediate vertical aisles in the stadium's east and west stands. Done primarily because these aisles did not connect directly to portals and generated too much up-and-down traffic, it also had the effect of adding two seats per row from each of these former aisles, for a total of 2,250 new seats. Unfortunately, on game day, fans in the middle of a row now had to squeeze past twice as many people to reach an aisle on their way to restrooms or concessions.

Finished in time for the 1970 Texas football season, the aluminum seats, along with the artificial turf and rubber track, gave the stadium's interior a whole new look. It helped compensate for the mess and noise of the construction work, which would last for another two years.

By no means was the expansion of Memorial Stadium the only construction project on the UT campus at the time. A total of 16 works, costing an estimated $71 million, were then ongoing, including the Humanities Research Center, the Communications Building, Sid Richardson Hall and the Physics-Math-Astronomy Building (now Robert Lee Moore Hall). And others would begin soon. The *Cactus* yearbook asked rhetorically if all the "progress" was worth it: "down with trees . . . parking lots closed and new ones constructed . . . swinging cranes . . . noisy bulldozers . . . blasting . . . drilling . . . hammering . . . sawing . . . grinding engines . . . piles of dirt . . . dust-filled air . . . streets closed for construction . . . fenced-off areas . . . the urban atmosphere . . . fewer trees . . . less space between buildings . . . expansion . . . is it progress?"

The university had long coveted the land east of Memorial Stadium, and by 1970 most of it had been annexed by means of eminent domain and urban renewal. Dozens of old houses and apartment buildings were torn down, eliminating a sizable chunk of low-income housing for students and others. This might have become another bitter controversy a year earlier, but by the fall semester of 1970, the inflammatory campus mood had begun to wane.

Although the Longhorns were the defending national champions and had plenty of big guns returning, they were not the No. 1 team in the country as the season began. That honor went to Ohio State, but by early November, with its winning streak approaching 30, Texas got the top spot and kept it the rest of the regular season. United Press International, which held its final vote before bowl games, overwhelmingly picked UT as the 1970 national champion. But after a 24-11 Cotton Bowl loss to Notre Dame, the Associated Press and most others chose Nebraska, dropping Texas to third in the rankings.

Apart from that final game, Royal's fourteenth Longhorn team was just as strong as the one before. It outscored opponents 412-125 in the regular season, including a 42-7 home victory over Arkansas, known as the "Big Shootout II." That game, attended by former President Johnson, was briefly interrupted when two antiwar protesters ran onto the field with a banner. They were escorted out of the stadium, but not arrested. Athletic department officials have since pointed to this incident in support of the strictly enforced no-banners policy at Memorial Stadium.

During the 1970 and 1971 seasons, Texas hosted no night football games since the stadium lacked west-side lights. A temporary, plywood-covered press box costing $40,000 was built and lifted by crane to the top of the east-side stands. Called jokingly the "Jones Ramsey Memorial Press Box" for UT's crusty sports information director, it was regarded as a major inconvenience by most of the people who used it. Facing the sun, the flimsy press box got rather hot during these afternoon games. Some sportswriters and coaches used it with trepidation, afraid it might topple backward out of the stadium.

Osborn and LAN's original design had the stadium press box at the top of the upper deck (according to the prototype, Wisconsin's stadium). But Ramsey, Lou Maysel of the *Austin American-Statesman*, Jimmy Banks of the *Dallas Morning News* and others questioned that. "They wanted to put the press box on the very top of the damn thing, up in the nosebleed section," said Maysel. "We told the architects why that wouldn't work. It was partly for selfish reasons. You'd need binoculars to see, and it would work to the disadvantage of game photography, too."

Osborn architects went back to the drawing board and designed a press box that would fit underneath the deck. Constrained by time and by specifications already in use, they produced plans for the new one but again, problems appeared.

"DESIGN BUSTS"

For reasons of spectator safety, during the 1970 football season, none of the cantilevered supporting beams for the upper deck were installed. But by January 1971, these 18 huge beams were in place, and construction progressed with the help of night-shift crews working under the east-side lights. While a photo deck was planned for the second level of the press box, problems arose with sight lines to the field. The beams, which doubled as storm drains, seriously obscured any view from this area. Long before the first game of the 1971 season, it was obvious that a kicked ball or even an arched pass would disappear from sight. In fact, you could hardly see the east sideline in the erstwhile photo deck. The beams hung down about 15 feet too far and created an oppressive atmosphere.

Frank Erwin, by training a construction claims attorney, was livid when he found out about this. He disparaged the architects and engineers and threatened to sue, but if the university—principally Erwin—had not forced them to hurry so much, it might have avoided this "design bust." At a February 16 meeting with athletic and administration officials, Ramsey commented "We're the University of Texas. We don't want some Mickey Mouse solution."

UT System Deputy Chancellor E. Don Walker suggested building a "porch" in front of and below the press box to accommodate photographers and television camera operators. Although not ideal, this compromise solution was adopted, and Osborn and LAN gave $25,000 to help cover the cost ($60,000), although the companies insisted they were not at fault.

"There was a misunderstanding by us as to the university's intended use of the upper deck of the press box," said Harry Badger of LAN. "When this was discovered, it was too late in the construction process to redesign these beams. Frank Erwin was fine when things went well, but when they didn't, he became quite upset."

Perhaps we can trace some of the design and engineering problems that developed during this period to mere geography. Osborn in Cleveland and LAN in Houston were just too far apart for an ideal working arrangement.

The pouring of concrete into the upper deck and building below accelerated in the spring and summer of 1971, as 54 rows and an 11-story ramp at each end were constructed. Another problem had to be addressed, though. Upper-deck spectators could not see the northwest and southwest corners of the football field, so the field was shifted a few feet to the east.

The stadium's new addition was far from complete when Texas Tech came to Austin for the home opener on September 25. Fences with dire warning signs were erected at both ends of the deck, and people sat on rough concrete (except in the option areas, where folding chairs were provided), since aluminum seats did not go in until the next season. At 76,639, it was the biggest crowd to ever see a college football game in the state.

Speaking over a new PA system, stadium announcer Wally Pryor added a note of levity that day when, on behalf of the university, the architects, engineers and contractors, he thanked the people in the upper deck for testing its structural strength. The building held though, and while some people did not like sitting up so high—the top row is actually higher than the east-side lights—others found it a nice place to watch a football game. When the upper deck of Interstate 35 was completed a couple of years later, it provided motorists with an impressive view of the stadium's west side, whether empty or full.

A $57,000 auxiliary scoreboard was built atop the stadium's horseshoe because people in the south part of the upper deck could hardly see the one at their end of the field. The old southern scoreboard was due for replacement the next year, anyway, since a large, swept-wing scoreboard was already under construction. Reaching 56 feet high and 44 feet across, it would be dedicated to Freddie Steinmark, the UT defensive back who had died of cancer in June 1971. Few people seemed to notice when the Louis Jordan flagpole was taken down. The plaque at its base, commemorating the revered Longhorn lineman killed in World War I, sits today in a storeroom in the southeast corner of Memorial Stadium.

After the 1971 season, the north and south ends of the upper deck were completed, and aluminum benches and chairs matching those in the lower stadium were installed. An orange interlocking "UT" was painted in the center of the upper deck, and a steel mesh "cow catcher" was appended to the ledge to prevent binoculars, soft drinks, handbags and other items from falling on fans below.

SPECTACULAR ACCIDENT

Electrical wiring was in place when workers began the process of lifting lights to the top of the upper deck. This did not come off without a hitch, either. On February 8, 1972, one of the Lott/Lyda cranes attempted to raise a 53,000-pound concrete lighting fixture to the top of the stadium. It was just 15 feet off the ground when the boom cables snapped. The fixture fell onto a truck and blew out its tires, and at the same time, cables and assorted pieces of steel headed earthward from 140 feet. Gerald Lyda, who happened to be directly underneath, somehow escaped injury. "Later, I noticed that my new suit had big holes in it. I'm not sure what from, but it must have been the fear coming out," he joked.

The crane's disabled boom briefly swayed over the Lila B. Etter Alumni Center, which was evacuated, but the crane operator managed to lower it to the ground. This man then climbed down from his perch, very pale, walked to his car, and drove away without saying a word. He never returned to the job.

Despite this accident, work went forth. When installed, the new mercury-vapor lights (as opposed to incandescent lights on the east) and their fixtures rose 216 feet above the playing field.

Yet another design bust appeared, one that could not be blamed on hired engineers and architects. As described earlier, people in the lower stadium's west-side option seats had limited leg room. And since they had paid between $200 and $400 for those chair-back seats, they issued numerous complaints during the 1970 and 1971 seasons. The UT Athletics Council responded by taking out the seats and laboriously overpouring concrete to eliminate every fifth row.

This resulted in the displacement of nearly 2,000 prime seats, so the decision was made to extend the option area from the 20-yard lines another 10 yards in each direction. To support the weight of the extra concrete, several steel braces were installed underneath the west-side stands. The difficulty and expense of this operation thwarted the Athletics Council's plans to eventually convert the whole stadium to chair-back seats. While the workers were at it, they also reinforced the north-end horseshoe, now supporting the auxiliary scoreboard.

Thompson had an idea for using the eight 100-foot lightpoles removed from the stadium's west side after the 1969 season. He suggested putting six of them just behind the south scoreboard and converting them into flagpoles for the six flags of Texas. It was a notion that would warm the hearts of patriotic Texans and those conscious of recycling. So ever since, for all major athletic events in Memorial Stadium, the flags of France, Spain, Mexico, Texas, the Confederacy and the United States have flown from there. The remaining two poles were placed at Disch-Falk Field (for the Texas and American flags) when it opened in 1975.

"Finally, A Flashy New Home for the 'Horns" was the title of a 1972 Vaughn Aldredge article in *Texas Football Newsmagazine*. He wrote "Completion of the remodeling culminates a frustrating period for Texas officials and fans, who have waited almost five years to see rumors turn to plans and plans finally become concrete."

The stadium's upper deck was ready in time for the 1972 football season, although the building underneath it still had a way to go. By February 1973, most of the finishing touches had been applied, including the planting of 14 live oak trees in the walkway between the stadium and San Jacinto Boulevard.

The stadium's academic building finally got a name—L. Theo Bellmont Hall. How fitting that the university would recognize the man who not only shared with H. J. Lutcher Stark the primary responsibility for erecting Memorial Stadium in 1924, but who did so much for physical education, and intramural and intercollegiate sports. Frank Erwin suggested the name; he was a close friend of former Longhorn athlete and basketball coach Jack Gray, who had married Bellmont's daughter, Margaret.

And what was Bellmont Hall? It was 200,000 square feet spread out over 11 floors, holding three multi-purpose gymnasiums, eight handball/racquetball courts, 12 squash courts, a 250-seat lecture hall, dozens of offices and classrooms, and abundant space for what would become a cutting-edge Department of Kinesiology and Health Education. It housed most of the athletic department, plus the campus police. Ticket offices and trophy cases adorned the ground floor, where UT registration took place until 1977.

The final design bust involved poor ventilation of gyms and lockers at Bellmont Hall. To address the problem, larger exhaust fans were installed throughout the building, which compounded the total cost of the project. The original estimate of $5.5-$6 million had gone up to $9.7 million, then $12.8 million, then $15.5 million, then $18 million and probably more. No final dollar figure was ever released or, for that matter, a breakdown of who—the athletic department or the university—paid for what.

While some people thought that the stadium's king-sized look was appropriate for the football program, the university and the state, others were disturbed both at its cost and appearance. When viewed from the west, the stadium, now the third tallest building on campus, conjured up such terms as "gigantic," "enormous" and "overwhelming."

UT regent Ed Clark called it a "monstrosity," and a project that had just gotten out of hand. "Every time I look up those straight walls, and every time I think about it, it almost puts a crick in my neck," he told the *Austin American-Statesman.* "Then I see those seats way up in the sky, and I'm mildly shocked."

Joseph Jones, who never masked his dislike for big-time college sports, wrote "Surely the architect must have been aware, somewhere along the line, that an upper deck of that configuration, and most of all in that incredible suspension, resembled nothing in art or nature so much as the blade of a titanic bulldozer. . . . Who could ever have achieved anything so grotesquely symbolic by sheer accident?"

While James Cole did not design the upper deck himself, he was manager of structural engineering for Lockwood, Andrews & Newnam during that time, and he does not entirely disagree with such critiques. "I think the upper deck is disproportionately large. It should have been looked at more closely during design. It's too big," he said.

In 1974, the stadium's 50th year, *Cactus* writers Richard Justice and Randy Edwards bemoaned what they regarded as an outdated emphasis on sports. Acknowledging that Memorial Stadium was "a venerated athletic facility fairly dripping with tradition," they questioned its expansion and appropriation of $37 million for new baseball (Disch-Falk Field), basketball (the Special Events Center, later named for Frank Erwin) and swimming (Texas Swimming Center) facilities. As Justice and Edwards saw it, student interest in intercollegiate athletics was low: "Sportswriters, athletes and coaches were excited, but it was a troubled excitement comparable to a child eating candy, knowing his teeth will decay."

Furthermore, the Athletics Council received a report from the Student Advisory Committee stating "There is a great deal of discontent among students with regard to seating at football games. They feel that football at the university caters to 'alumni and VIPs' and disregards the desires of the students."

EXPENSIVE, BUT WORTH IT

The upper deck and Bellmont Hall, garish though they appeared to some, quickly proved their value. The recreational and intramural load on Gregory Gym was eased, the athletic department had a more spacious home, and research in the various fields of physical education got a boost. Although sellouts became less frequent, more people could now attend Longhorn football games in the stadium, with a permanent seating capacity of 75,504. That was and still is the number of tickets printed per game. But athletic officials claimed that the stadium actually held 77,809, when everyone—including football players, photographers and popcorn vendors—was counted.

Game-day traffic problems were relieved somewhat in the early 1970s with greater cooperation among Austin's Urban Transportation Department, the Austin Police Department and campus police. One-way traffic on streets around the stadium helped, as did a shuttle bus system with off-campus parking.

Several things happened at or around the stadium in 1974. The 165-foot moonlight tower at the corner of 23rd and Red River streets had been there since the 1920s. It came down as the result of an industrial accident; a backhoe doing excavation hit one of the supports, causing the tower to collapse. Some people rejoiced at this development, since the tower lent little aesthetically to either the stadium or the LBJ Library it had stood between.

Also that year, Memorial Stadium was a suicide scene, as a despondent young man jumped from the open-air 11th floor of Bellmont Hall, landing just 20 yards away from a pair of pedestrians. After this incident, campus police closed off access to ramps leading to the top floor.

An unforgettable event in stadium history occurred on September 1, 1974: the "ZZ Top and Friends First Annual Texas Size Rompin' Stompin' Barn Dance and Barbecue." Sponsored by UT Student Government, this day-long concert also featured music by Joe Cocker, Santana and Bad Company. Instead of the expected crowd of 50,000, a whopping 80,000 showed and filled every inch of the field, track and seats in the lower stadium. No one—the promoters, police, concessionaires or drug crisis workers—was prepared for so many people. The 90° temperature led to 30 cases of heat prostration.

As fate would have it, much of the craziness took place on the stadium's second-generation Astroturf, which had been installed just that summer. Vandalism was widespread, including several stains, burns and a Texas-shaped hole cut in the new turf. When Darrell Royal and other UT officials saw the results the next morning (as the last stoned concert-goers were led away), they were incensed. There have not been any more such concerts at Memorial Stadium; even Willie Nelson's 1986 request to hold a show benefiting financially strapped farmers was denied.

Ever since the 1969 national championship year, Royal had been asked questions about retirement, although the Longhorns won SWC titles in 1970, 1971, 1972 and 1973, and tied for it in 1975. But Royal's 20th season as Texas head coach would be his last, and not a very happy one, with a 5-5-1 record punctuated by a 30-0 loss to Houston before a sellout crowd at the stadium. A remarkable 42-game home winning streak ended, one that stretched back to the 1968 season. Royal's coaching career came to an end against Arkansas on the night of December 4, 1976 in Austin. Coincidentally, Razorback coach Frank Broyles was retiring too, after 19 years. It was a couple of weary warriors who met at midfield after the 29-12 UT win.

Royal's choice as his replacement, Mike Campbell, was passed over for the job, which went to Fred Akers, a longtime Texas assistant who had been head coach at Wyoming the previous two seasons. During his 10-year reign in Austin, Akers would coach a couple of near-national champions in 1977 and 1983. Royal continued as athletic director until January 1980, and has since worked as special assistant to the UT president.

In 1977, at Akers' request, the stadium's home locker room got a makeover, with most of the attention going to the lecture room—new seats, indirect lighting, wood paneling and carpet. The track was resurfaced and converted from 440 yards to 400 meters, although its 190-foot diameter from side to side did not meet NCAA guidelines, which suggest 207 feet.

Due to leaking roofs in the stadium's locker rooms, a waterproofing compound was applied to the stands over these areas at a cost of $50,000. When the stadium is empty, this work can be seen by a discerning eye.

Soon there was a more visible change to the Longhorns' football uniforms, with TEXAS emblazoned on the front of the jersey and two orange stripes running from hip to knee. Players' names on the backs of the jerseys had first appeared in 1975.

Heisman Trophy-bound Earl Campbell ran for 153 yards and two touchdowns in a late-season win over TCU in 1977. On that day, the stadium was dedicated for the third time. Just as it was built to honor Texas' World War I soldiers in 1924, and as a 1948 ceremony encompassed those who served in World War II, the university chose to include Korea and Vietnam war veterans. A sloping granite marker was erected near the top of the stadium's horseshoe, reading "Texas Memorial Stadium/Rededicated November 12, 1977/in Memory of All American Veterans of All Wars." Note that the words go beyond the state of Texas, and by inference, into the future.

In the spring of 1982, some College Station students attempted to steal the marker. They pried it off its foundation and were halfway out the stadium when apprehended by campus police. They paid for construction and placement of a new marker, while the old, battered one found its way to the Waxahachie home of UT alumnus Perry Giles.

Complaints had long been voiced about low sanitation standards in the concessions facilities. Gene Seaton, who had turned concessions from a poorly managed money-loser into the opposite, stated that the prevailing conditions would not have been tolerated anywhere else on campus. Soon concessions areas were expanded and modernized under the east and west stands, and a larger concessions office was erected under the north stands in 1979.

The visitors' locker room was enlarged and remodeled, and accommodations for game officials were turned over to visiting coaches. The officials moved from there to the small locker room in the southeast corner of the stadium, sharing it with the Texas men's tennis team.

J. Neils Thompson, closing out his active service on the Athletics Council, was behind the erection of the first—and still the only—"Monuments of Honor" on the stadium's west side. Three bronze plaques, 48" × 27", designed by Dr. David Deming of the UT Art Department, were built featuring Clyde Littlefield, Dana X. Bible and Ed Olle. They were unveiled during a halftime ceremony at the 1979 Texas-Baylor game. For whatever reasons, no other monuments have been set alongside these, which need updating, since they give the impression that Littlefield and Bible are still alive.

One summer afternoon around this time, a topless female jogger caused a slight stir. Only a few people were present that day, most of whom stared in disbelief, but stadium superintendent Glen Swenson hopped into his pickup truck and drove onto the track alongside the woman. He implored her to put on a shirt, but she ignored him, and completed her workout *au naturel.*

ARSON

A different sort of excitement arose on the night of September 17, 1981, when flames engulfed the sixth-floor Bellmont Hall office of women's athletic director Dr. Donna Lopiano. There were no injuries or important records lost, but it was an intense fire, causing $150,000 in damage. A former UT employee, Verna Hodges, was later indicted on charges of arson. That was the worst, but not the only case of crime (mostly petty vandalism) then taking place at Memorial Stadium. Campus police chief Don Cannon came under some criticism for not preventing it, especially since he and his staff had headquarters there.

Some clannish UT boosters viewed 44-year old DeLoss Dodds as an outsider when he became athletic director in September 1981. But he arrived in Austin with an impressive resume: a track star at Kansas State in the 1950s (he competed in the Texas Relays), then the Wildcats' track coach and athletic director, and assistant commissioner of the Big Eight Conference. Dodds had experience with the NCAA and a reputation for running things in a strong but even-handed way.

He was well prepared to "deal with the changing face of college athletics" in the words of UT sports information director Bill Little. Dodds would guide Texas into the economically murky 1980s and 1990s by converting the athletic department offices to computers and by use of broad-based fundraising. While about 70 percent of college athletic departments lose money, Dodds and his staff have balanced the $16 million budget, avoided major scandals and had success in a variety of sports.

At the urging of UT President Lorene Rogers, the Athletics Council debated the installation of private suites or some sort of VIP area at the stadium. Such facilities were then associated mostly with pro stadiums, but some colleges found them conducive to fundraising. That is where the Texas Longhorn Education Foundation (TLEF) comes in. This group, begun in 1978 by Frank Erwin, former Texas player Howard Terry and others, soon supplanted the Longhorn Club and raised money for athletic scholarships.

By October 1981, it was decided to build the $1 million Centennial Room above the stadium's press box. This, of course, was to have been the site of the photo deck 10 years earlier, until design problems became apparent. Since the 1972 season, handicapped fans had sat in this open space, and most liked it despite the ever-present bats and the upper-deck beams that curtailed viewing. It was better than the former custom of having their wheelchairs lined up along the stadium's retaining walls. But in 1981, to make way for the Centennial Room, these people were shifted to two lower, but less-central areas of the stadium.

The Centennial Room, built by B & B Developers, is a temperature-controlled, glass-enclosed area 90 yards long and 25 feet wide, with 10 closed-circuit television monitors and two bars. Yes, alcohol is served. TLEF and administration officials had to repeatedly tell the *Daily Texan* why only a select group of people were allowed to drink during games. Ronald Brown, vice president for student affairs, stated that since it was a controlled area, liquor could be served by the Texas Union, which had a mixed beverage license. But there was no intention of making alcohol available to other fans. "It's been a longstanding university policy not to serve liquor in the stadium," said Brown. "We've never felt it was a good thing to do."

First used on September 18, 1982 when Texas hosted Utah, the Centennial Room has proven a popular place to watch a game—if you can get in. Only TLEF members who pay $4,000 in annual dues (known as the 200 Longhorns Club), high-level UT administrators and their guests are allowed entrance. There, they can eat, drink and socialize, see instant replays on TV monitors and do it all in utter comfort. The Centennial Room has probably stolen a bit of the T Room's cachet, although some people sample both during the course of a game. It is also the site of numerous social events throughout the year having nothing to do with athletics. But even when empty, Memorial Stadium makes for a pleasing backdrop.

A couple of school traditions had come to an end by the early 1980s. The annual bonfire before the UT-Texas A&M game was terminated because of the trouble and danger involved. (Of course, that has not yet prevented the Aggies from ending theirs.) And it was curtains for Band Day, an annual event at Memorial Stadium since before the time of Dana X. Bible. Started as a way to help fill the huge stadium, it was a chance for high school musicians to play before a larger crowd than most of them had ever seen. Band Day was a colorful, if cacophonous, spectacle destined to end because the university gave away as many as 7,000 tickets. In effect, it has been replaced by the UIL marching band competition, held at the stadium every November since 1978 and attracting up to 30,000 spectators.

It was again time for the Athletics Council to draw from the reserve fund for synthetic surfaces. An estimated 2,000 people used the stadium's track and football field daily—not including scholarship athletes. Since both track and turf were getting ragged, bids were taken to replace them. The number of companies making synthetic surfaces had grown since the 1960s, along with their claims for excellence, so the Athletics Council looked for more than just the lowest bidders.

Finally, the German-made Rekortan track was chosen, at $262,450, and Superturf, a more natural shade of green, at $499,378. Installation on the floor of Memorial Stadium took place in the summer of 1982. Unlike the first two generations of artificial turf (1969 and 1974), this one gave a hint of whose stadium it was, as two white steer heads were painted in each end zone.

NEUHAUS-ROYAL

Although the home locker room had been updated in 1977, it was a source of increasing dissatisfaction. Some blue-chip recruits, unimpressed with tradition, took one look at it and crossed the University of Texas off their lists. Naturally, this irked Fred Akers, and he was pleased when the Athletics Council began discussing a big, modern facility just south of the stadium.

UT President Peter Flawn was convinced of the need to move out of the old locker room. On October 26, 1982, he wrote to Executive Vice Chancellor Bryce Jordan: "The current football facilities under Memorial Stadium on the west side are very old, very crowded, un-air conditioned and difficult to maintain. They are inferior to facilities at other Southwest Conference schools. They do not support our recruiting efforts. Our football program now operates without a practice field. All practices must be scheduled at Memorial Stadium."

Even before a new facility was designed and before the Board of Regents approved preliminary plans, the Longhorn Foundation (despite the similarity in names, a different entity from the TLEF) had raised $2.7 million. In January 1984, the regents gave the expected OK, fundraising continued, and it was decided to name the building in honor of Vernon F. "Doc" Neuhaus, a longtime benefactor of UT sports. Soon the Athletics Council chose to split the honor between Neuhaus and Darrell Royal. (Following Royal's retirement from coaching in 1976, some of his admirers wanted to rename the stadium after him.)

The Neuhaus-Royal Athletic Center was designed by the architectural firm of O'Connell, Robertson & Grobe and built by Badgett Construction

Company for a total project cost of $7 million. Half of the money came from private donations and half from UT athletic department surplus.

So what about the tennis courts, supplanted by Neuhaus-Royal? As with baseball and basketball, Longhorn tennis moved off campus, though only two blocks south, on Trinity Street. When completed in 1986, the new Penick-Allison (it had been renamed in 1977) Tennis Center far surpassed its two predecessors. Costing $3 million, it had 12 courts, lights, locker rooms, scoreboards and a 2,000-seat grandstand. Men's tennis coach Dave Snyder and women's coach Jeff Moore were quite happy with the new complex, although their teams must share it with physical education classes and the UT Division of Recreational Sports.

"The consensus is that this is the best all-purpose college tennis facility in the United States," said Moore.

A new option seating plan was instituted for the 1982-1985 football seasons, with people paying $800, $400, $200 or $100 for Memorial Stadium's 10,934 contoured, chair-back seats. Since 1986 though, location and priority of option seats have been determined by contributions to the TLEF's "Annual Giving Scholarship Program."

While Neuhaus-Royal was being planned, designed and built, other things were happening at the stadium:

• $36,000 was spent on remodeling the second floor of Bellmont Hall, nerve center of UT men's athletics;

• $15,000 went toward repairing ramps under the stadium's east-side stands;

• $95,000 was spent to build Longhorns LTD, a street-level store selling Texas paraphernalia;

• $146,000 was invested in the athletic department ticket and business offices on the first floor of Bellmont Hall;

• $30,000 was used for new electrical wiring;

• $24,000 went toward converting the former home locker room into the men's track locker room (to be shared with visiting football teams); and

• $27,000 was spent on turning the former visitors' locker room into the UT women's track locker room.

In addition, the university built a $4.7-million parking garage two blocks north of the stadium. With room for 1,000 vehicles, it would relieve parking on the east side of campus every day of the year, not just for home football games.

The Athletics Council debated, but took no action on renovating the northern exterior of the stadium, which was characterized by fungus, stains and peeling paint. A more urgent problem was the restrooms. Inadequate to game-day demands even 30 years earlier, they now begged for attention. In an interoffice memo, assistant athletic director T Jones stated that the east-side restrooms were particularly bad, with only 20 commodes serving female spectators there. A row of unisex porta-potties helped somewhat, although everyone agreed that these were unbecoming to the state's flagship university, which had a $1.3 billion endowment. The matter was studied and delayed a couple of times before anything changed, but in the summer of 1986, restrooms under the east-side stands were renovated for about $100,000.

At a meet-the-players social function on the stadium's upper deck two weeks prior to the 1986 season, Akers admitted a certain fondness for the old locker room and the history it had witnessed. He then pointed south toward the recently completed Neuhaus-Royal Athletic Center and predicted that it would come to have traditions of its own.

The 38,225-square-foot facility is much more than a locker room. The most visible thing from outside is a 70-yard rooftop football practice field. In a minor glitch, one of the plaques on the building's north end incorrectly states that the Longhorns won a national championship in 1967. Inside, you will find paintings of Doc Neuhaus and Darrell Royal, an entire wall of team MVPs dating back to 1956, and a large mural that features Earl Campbell running behind a UT offensive lineman, both preceded by a herd of charging steers. There are a series of lecture rooms and coaches' offices, a world-class weight-training room, a large rehabilitation pool and a laundry area.

Texas now had one of the best collegiate training centers in the country. Neuhaus-Royal was expected to boost recruiting efforts, enhance athletic performance and speed rehabilitation. The facility had been in use for nearly two months before its dedication on October 18, 1986, when the Longhorns played Arkansas in front of 67,344 spectators. The Hogs won the game, 21-14.

DEATH MARCH

The 1986 football season was rife with dissension among students, players, alumni and the UT athletic department. At the center of it all was Fred Akers, who would be fired by Dodds on November 29. *Austin American-Statesman* sports columnist John Maher likened that season to the Bataan Death March. In producing the first losing record in 30 years, Akers was under immense pressure and criticism about everything from his play-calling to off-field discipline to the three-piece suits he favored.

Akers had a lot to show for his 10 years as Longhorn head coach: a record of 86-31-2, with nine bowl appearances and four teams that finished in the Associated Press top ten. He coached 60 all-Southwest Conference players, 21 all-Americans, two Lombardi Award winners, an Outland Trophy winner and a Heisman Trophy winner.

And yet problems had been mounting for two seasons. In 1985 and especially in 1986, many fans at Memorial Stadium grew disenchanted. Dodds saw that the most powerful and wealthy alumni (some of whom had helped finance the Neuhaus-Royal Athletic Center) tilted irreversibly against Akers, and the deed was done two days after a season-ending 16-3 loss to Texas A&M. *Sports Illustrated* magazine devoted seven pages to the story.

The media throughout Texas believed that the new Longhorn coach would be David McWilliams, who had worked as an assistant to Royal and Akers, but was then running the show at Texas Tech. Considered UT's favorite son, he tried to dodge all questions on the topic and insisted that he was happy in Lubbock.

Dodds conducted a six-day "nationwide search" for a new coach and to no one's surprise, the choice was McWilliams. Red Raider partisans screamed and called him harsh names, but McWilliams, one of the captains of the 1963 Longhorn national championship team, was coming home. He would instigate only minor changes to the football uniform, removing the dual pant stripes and putting a small steer head on the left hip. Akers rebounded quickly, taking the head coaching job at Purdue, although he lasted just four seasons before getting fired there, too.

For several years, at UT and elsewhere, the need to bring in ever more revenue had made some people uncomfortable. Fundraising, marketing, promotions, advertising and lucrative television contracts seemed to have become the name of the game in the increasingly risky world of big-time college athletics. Just to stay solvent, such means were necessary.

In response to the "Long Range Planning Study" done in 1987 by a marketing consultant, Athletics Council member John Stuart protested. As paraphrased in the council's minutes, "He felt that too much commercialism did not fit the image of the University of Texas. He further stated that this is an academic institution, and we need to maintain and improve that image. There should be a vision of how athletics fits into the overall institutional image."

Stuart reminded his colleagues that both men's and women's athletics were auxiliary enterprises of the university, under the direction of the vice president for student affairs. Perhaps in response to these and other criticisms, the Athletics Council debated adding an academic component to Neuhaus-Royal. When that proved unfeasible, attention shifted to a large area at the northwest corner of the stadium, adjacent to the T Room. Costing $840,000 to build and equip, this series of rooms, computers and support personnel would help Longhorn athletes stay eligible and look toward graduation and post-sports careers.

RENAME THE STADIUM?

Before this project was finished, a handful of men long involved with Texas athletics formed a plan to rename Memorial Stadium for Dana X. Bible, who had inspired deep loyalty among his players and co-workers. The chief proponent was former sports information director Bill Sansing, who had the active support of Bible-era players like Rooster Andrews, Noble Doss, Malcolm Kutner and Wally Scott.

"I worked and begged the university to name the stadium for Mr. Bible. He's the one man who really built athletics at the University of Texas," said Sansing. "We thought he had been shortchanged in recognition and should have a major facility named after him." With the athletic department's tacit permission, Sansing met with UT President William Cunningham and stated his case, but the odds were never good. Cunningham turned down the proposal because the very name "Memorial Stadium" had come to mean so much to several generations of people who passed through the university.

Sansing offered a compromise, "Dana X. Bible Memorial Stadium," or simply naming the football field after him, but those did not fly, either. Bible's advocates were then presented with the option of naming the study area, then nearing completion, in honor of the illustrious Longhorn coach and AD. While this obviously lacked the marquee value of the whole stadium, they accepted, and since opening in November 1988, the Dana X. Bible Academic Center has, to a large extent, achieved its goals.

Soon more construction started south of Neuhaus-Royal. The $12.5-million Recreational Sports Center would ease some of the ever-growing demand on Gregory Gym and Bellmont Hall. Ready for use in October 1990, it serves today as home to Mick Haley's powerful UT women's volleyball team.

While all of this was going on, Memorial Stadium got a long-overdue cosmetic change, brought on by a single letter. The writer deplored the condition of the bronze plaques on the portal walls. Dulled by exposure to weather for more than 60 years, these monuments to Texans killed in World War I looked their age. So all 197 (26 had been lost or stolen over the years) were taken down, given a chemical treatment to produce a shinier patina and replaced in alphabetical order, but not in their original positions. The southernmost portals, east and west, had been part of the 1948 stadium expansion, and therefore never held any of the plaques until 1988. Following this fairly inexpensive but tedious process, all 22 of the lower stadium's portals would hold between eight and 11 plaques. Still, nothing was done to the six Southwest Conference plaques on the stadium's outer north wall or the big tablet at the top of the horseshoe.

The University of Texas, which takes its athletic traditions seriously, has retired the jersey of only one football player—Earl Campbell. Few would argue that Campbell's number, 20, should not be given that status. After all, he gained 4,443 yards rushing, won the Heisman Trophy and led the Longhorns to the brink of a national championship in 1977. Campbell was in the second year of a Hall-of-Fame career with the Houston Oilers—and later the New Orleans Saints—when the Athletics Council recommended, and the Board of Regents agreed, to honor him in this way.

In August 1988, the Athletics Council considered extending the honor to a couple of other players who had performed with distinction: quarterback Bobby Layne (who had actually worn three different numbers) from the 1940s and linebacker/guard Tommy Nobis from the 1960s. While both were quite deserving, the idea fell through.

Civil engineering professor Dr. David Fowler, who was an Athletics Council member, and J. Neils Thompson, then sitting as an *ex officio* member, inspected the stadium's concrete in 1988. Their conclusions were a mixture of good news and bad news. "We studied all the concrete in this whole stadium," Thompson said. "Some of it's not in very good shape, especially the slab in the north end, but it's not a structural problem because the columns are sound. That's the important part. This building is open to the elements just like a bridge, yet you have to avoid getting water on the reinforcing steel. . . . The stadium is still in good shape. You just have to keep maintaining it."

NEW SCOREBOARD

Creeping commercialism was a concern to everyone from Athletics Council members to fans sitting in the stadium's knothole section. Some schools never had a problem with advertising at football games and saw it as a handy way to balance the budget. UT professed to disdain such means, and there was even a regents' rule to that effect. Yet it was not adhered to completely: Walsh & Burney erected a large billboard at each end of the stadium before the 1924 dedication game, and the University Co-op had a plug on the old scoreboards at the stadium and Gregory Gym. When the Erwin Center opened in 1977, its scoreboard carried a series of revolving ads.

The issue would not go away, as the Athletics Council discussed it with regularity beginning in the mid-1970s. A small step was taken in that direction in 1984, when fans began noticing a fast-food ad on the backs of their game tickets. It was a compromise, with more to follow. In October 1988, Dodds suggested the installation of new scoreboards for both Memorial Stadium and Disch-Falk Field. Sponsors would be required, and so would a waiver of the rule against such advertising.

Within two months, an agreement had been reached that would put a big, modern scoreboard at the north end of the stadium and one in center field at Disch-Falk. Coca-Cola would pay the entire cost, $700,000, and in return, the Coke logo appears at the bottom and middle of the scoreboards, flanked by smaller logos of the *Austin American-Statesman* and North Carolina National Bank. The latter two companies pay for their spots. As part of the agreement, during a game the scoreboard flashes 10 Coca-Cola messages, all 15 seconds long, and five each of the *Austin American-Statesman* and NCNB.

The four-color animated scoreboard, built by American Sign Company of Spokane, Washington, is designed to give additional information about players and the progress of a game. With dimensions of 38' × 42', it is supported by a pair of steel columns set 30 feet deep just outside the horseshoe. Traditionalists grumbled a bit about the aesthetic impact on the stadium, from inside and out. But this much-needed and rather tastefully designed scoreboard made its debut on September 30, 1989 when Texas played Penn State before 75,232 fans.

That night, stadium announcer Wally Pryor was instructed to read a statement that caught some fans by surprise. Shortly before kickoff, he said "The university would request that, out of courtesy to the people around you, you not smoke inside Memorial Stadium. Those of you who want to smoke, please do so in areas under the spectator seating area. Thank you for your cooperation."

Put politely as possible, this was not a rule or command, but a request, one that continues to be made before all UT home football games. It became policy in 1991, although enforcement is lax. Considering that cigars were a part of stadium concessions in the 1920s, a startling societal change had taken place.

The Longhorns and Nittany Lions played that night on a new layer of artificial turf, installed in the summer of 1989, along with a new rubber track. This one had a bold look. In 20-foot letters (white with orange trim), the words TEXAS appeared in the north end zone and LONGHORNS in the south, with a steer head facing west on the 50-yard line.

The first three generations of artificial turf at the stadium—1969, 1974 and 1982—had been glued to a rubber mat atop an asphalt base, but this time, it was sewn together. "There were problems with gluing the turf down," said

Lex Acker, an architect at the UT System Office of Facilities Planning and Construction. "You had to patch it and reglue, and water drained slowly. Now, the rolls are sewn together, and it's somewhat loose, so water goes through the carpet and disperses underneath. This way, the turf flexes and has a self-healing tendency. It's cooler and more tactile, which some consider better for the players. The fibers hold their shape much better than on the older versions."

The placement of a new track and turf at Memorial Stadium in 1989 caused a public relations mess. The Texas Special Olympics, a track meet designed for the mentally disabled, had been held at the stadium since 1974. But the meet's timing conflicted with the need to install the synthetic surfaces. President Cunningham repeatedly explained why the construction schedule could not be altered, and compromises were offered and rejected on both ends. Finally, the Texas Special Olympics made arrangements to hold the meet at Bobcat Stadium in San Marcos. It was not an amicable parting, and the media, oversimplifying a complex issue, portrayed UT as a cold-hearted giant.

In 1981, the Division of Recreational Sports had built a jogging trail and outdoor basketball and racquetball courts at the former Freshman Field, renamed Clark Field. Eight years later, the UT athletic department installed a full-sized grass practice field there. Longhorn players once again "crossed the creek" for some practice sessions, a tradition almost as old as the stadium itself.

However, it has not been an ideal practice field for a number of reasons. When John Mackovic replaced David McWilliams as Texas head coach in December 1991, he indicated the need for a better and more secure practice field. The land just east of Neuhaus-Royal will probably become the scene of Longhorn football workouts.

HAIL TO THE CHIEF

On May 19, 1990, Memorial Stadium hosted an event that recalled "Pappy" Lee O'Daniel's gubernatorial inauguration there 51 years earlier. On a stage built at the 50-yard line, President George Bush would give the commencement address to 4,700 graduates among a crowd of 40,000. Students, their families and others who wanted to witness a presidential speech (Bush also received an honorary law degree) sat in the west stands and upper deck.

The event was not without controversy. While conservative students were pleased and honored to have the president at their graduation ceremony, those to the left side of the political spectrum protested mildly. At Bush's introduction, one group of students bellowed "Give 'em hell, George!" to which another group retorted "Go away, George!"

"While an estimated 100 protesters shouted and blew horns and whistles outside the stadium, the ceremony itself was not disrupted," according to the 1990 *Cactus*. "One protester was arrested and nine others on the top level of the stadium were quickly escorted out by UTPD and Secret Service, but the rest of the president's address was not interrupted. Nevertheless, the constant sound of whistles and horns floating into the stadium was an audible reminder that not everyone was happy with the chosen commencement speaker."

Ever since Thanksgiving Day in 1988, the nearby Lila B. Etter Alumni Center had been the scene of construction. Roy Vaughan, executive director of the Texas Exes, led a long fundraising drive that eventually came to more than $7 million. The building grew from 14,000 square feet to 45,000 square feet, with an underground parking garage, many new offices and social areas, and a spacious outdoor plaza with a Longhorn motif. More than 8,000 ex-students gave from $100-$1 million to pay for the construction, and got their names set on terra cotta tiles, bronze plaques or entire rooms and hallways. The enlarged alumni center, designed by architecture professor Dr. Charles Moore, was equal to any in the country. It opened for public inspection on September 22, 1990, when UT played Colorado in the stadium across the street.

After two straight losing seasons, there was some pressure on the team to perform, and the Horns came through in magnificent fashion. They won the SWC title for the first time in seven years with a 10-2 record. Attendance at home games jumped from 54,768 in 1989 to 76,007 in 1990, ninth best in the nation.

"There is everything right and nothing wrong with the happiness the University of Texas football team has brought this community," wrote *Austin American-Statesman* sports columnist Kevin Lyttle before the regular season finale against Texas A&M. ". . . when you walk inside Memorial Stadium on Saturday morning, take a moment to reflect on the present. Look around at the 83,000 fans and think about all the improbable events this year that have led up to this, that have hooked all these people."

It belied the notion that college football had become primarily a television game and that ticket-buying fans were little more than a studio audience. Even though the game was broadcast nationally, only those present in the stadium that day caught all the sound and fury. David McWilliams' team broke a six-year losing streak to Texas A&M by a score of 28-27. The rivalry between the Longhorns and Aggies had hardly changed since Thanksgiving Day in 1924, when the two schools dedicated Memorial Stadium.

25 Great Football Games
at Memorial Stadium

More than 350 University of Texas varsity football games have taken place at Memorial Stadium since its erection in 1924. In many of those games, the Longhorns or their opponents—sometimes both—have boasted powerful teams and fought to exciting finishes. And yet there have been occasional mismatches and times when two poor teams played ho-hum games before paltry audiences. Texas weather, famed for its variability, has made for games played under sparkling skies, ice storms, fierce heat, driving rain and most other meteorological conditions.

Any attempt, no matter how objective, to rate the top games in the stadium's history just begs for debate. Because far more than 25 great football games have occurred there, some real worthies are bound to be excluded. Besides certain games that would make almost anyone's list, this is a sample of who played and what happened at Memorial Stadium between the mid-1920s and the early 1990s. A few of the games are seen as "great" because of an individual performance or some other unique factor.

Not all of these are Texas victories—two are high school championship games—since the Horns have suffered some close and some devastating defeats in Austin. A slight bias toward offense (touchdown runs and passes) over defense (tackles and interceptions) is freely admitted. While some UT football fans can brag of not missing a home game since the Depression,

World War II or some other major event, no one around today has seen them all.

Without further ado then, let's take a look, in chronological order, at 25 of the best football games ever held in Memorial Stadium.

SMU 21, TEXAS 17 (OCTOBER 30, 1926)

Some people were becoming disenchanted with Doc Stewart by 1926, but if the Longhorns beat SMU in the sixth game of the season, he might still have retained his head coaching job. And with eight minutes left in the game, a UT victory seemed assured until some Frank Merriwell heroics by Mustang quarterback Gerald Mann, a future attorney general of Texas.

Around 15,000 people gathered at Memorial Stadium, its north-end horseshoe nearing completion, to learn of Chris Cortemeglia's post-game travel plans. The brash SMU player had promised to walk back to Dallas if Texas won, and it had not gone unnoticed by the Austin newspapers, UT fans and players. Since this was a strong and talented SMU squad, heavily favored to win, most people expected Cortemeglia to be on the north-bound train with his teammates Saturday night.

On the game's first play from scrimmage, Texas running back Rufus King lateraled the ball to Rosy Stallter (one of the heroes of the 1924 stadium dedication game against Texas A&M), who passed to Bill Ford for a 70-yard touchdown. Mann tied the game at 7-7 with a 25-yard scoring run, but a touchdown and a field goal had the Longhorns ahead, 17-7, in the fourth quarter.

SMU coach Ray Morrison put in fresh reserves, which took a toll on the smaller, tiring UT players. Mann, nicknamed "the Little Red Arrow," threw a 42-yard TD pass to Ross Love, and two minutes later, won the game on a defensive play. At the Texas 22-yard line, King was hit by either Cortemeglia or Stanley Dawson—accounts differ—and fumbled the ball into the eager hands of Mann, who sped across the goal line for a 21-17 win. While the Mustang Band gleefully played "Peruna," UT fans wondered how the game had been lost.

Dick Vaughn of the *Daily Texan* called it "the most sensational game ever played in the [two-year old] Memorial Stadium," and Frank White of the *Austin American-Statesman* wrote "The Mustang-Longhorn clash Saturday was one of those kinds of football battles that has earned the title of 'The King of Sports' for the grid game. No horse race, track meet, baseball game, basketball contest or other sport could ever give the assembled fans the thrills of elation and despair that ran through first one side and then the other of the stands at Memorial Stadium."

TEXAS 19, TEXAS A&M 0 (NOVEMBER 29, 1928)

Even prior to the formation of the Southwest Conference, the Thanksgiving Day classic between the Longhorns and Aggies had aroused more interest than any other game in the state. Big crowds for the Texas A&M series had proven the insufficiency of old Clark Field. After the stadium was built, the numbers just kept growing, with record crowds in 1924 (33,000), 1926 (35,000) and again in 1928 (42,571). It would be another 12 years before so many people packed Memorial Stadium.

Texas A&M came to Austin for the 1928 season finale near the bottom of the conference standings, while if the Longhorns won, the SWC title was theirs for the first time since 1920. Because the stadium still lacked locker rooms, players from both teams dressed elsewhere. The Aggies entered the field from the north end, the Horns from the south. Both coaches, Dana X. Bible and Clyde Littlefield, had expressed confidence in their teams, but UT would hand Bible a 19-0 defeat, the worst he ever suffered at Texas A&M.

Sophomore running back Dexter Shelley, who played without a helmet, had been a star all season long, and he did well against the Aggies with a one-yard touchdown run, as well as his passing and punting. Ed Beular threw scoring passes of 20 and five yards to Bill Ford, and the offensive line, with players like Jack Cowley, Ike Sewell and Alfred "Big Un" Rose, dominated by using off-tackle plays and end runs.

The victory and conference championship proved a fitting climax for L. Theo Bellmont, since his deposition as Texas athletic director was about to become final. It also quieted some of Littlefield's critics, who thought a more demonstrative man should lead the team. Bible had coached his last game at Texas A&M. He would go to Nebraska for a successful eight-year stretch and in 1937, became UT's football coach and AD.

It had been a good game, especially from a Longhorn viewpoint, but it was the crowd, that huge crowd gathered to watch and cheer, that was most remarkable. "The vast crowd represented a colorful cross section of Texas, mightiest of states," wrote Lloyd Gregory in the *Houston Post*. "Beautiful girls, young men, businessmen, statesmen, women, young children, all had assembled to see the flower of the state's young manhood do battle. . . . The varsity memorial stadium, set on the side of an oak-fringed hill, presented an inspiring sight."

TCU 28, TEXAS 0 (NOVEMBER 16, 1935)

UT's decline in the mid-1930s might have been avoided if a fellow from Sweetwater had been allowed to play both football and baseball. But when Sammy Baugh got no such assurance, he chose TCU instead, where he became a good baseball player and one of the greatest football players in Southwest Conference history.

Baugh was a junior in 1935 when the Horned Frogs visited Austin with an 8-0 record, and they had little trouble winning their ninth, 28-0, before 12,000 fans. Texas actually had a promising start, driving 68 yards to the TCU three, before being halted. But it was soon apparent that coach Dutch Meyer's team far outclassed the Longhorns. Whenever Baugh went back to pass, he had plenty of time, throwing for three touchdowns.

"The staid memorial horseshoe has entertained some fine aerial circuses in its day, but never one more effective than Saturday's," wrote an *Austin American-Statesman* reporter. But Baugh did more than just pass. He returned punts (one for 32 yards), ran from scrimmage and exhibited his renowned punting a few times.

The final TCU score came near the end of the third quarter when Tracy Kellow blocked a Texas punt, and his teammate, Walter Roach, took it in 20 yards for a touchdown. It was a day of futility for the Longhorns, who completed none—zero—of 15 passes and gave up four interceptions. The only real bright spot was the play of running back Jud Atchison, who coach Jack Chevigny had drafted from the UT track team.

The *Daily Texan* characterized the game this way: "Sporting receivers with uncanny accuracy, Sammy Baugh's unerring right arm literally hurled the purple horde to their ninth straight victory. It was the worst defeat the Longhorns have received in history with the exception of the 30-0 rout dealt by the Frogs in 1933" [sic.—In 1904, UT lost to the University of Chicago by a score of 68-0].

TCU finished the regular season 11-1 and beat LSU in the Sugar Bowl, while the Longhorns lost to Arkansas and Texas A&M to go 4-6, a record which at that time really *was* the worst in school history.

TEXAS 7, TEXAS A&M 6 (NOVEMBER 24, 1938)

Of all the traditions that have grown up around Memorial Stadium, none rivals the way the Longhorns dominated Texas A&M in the early years. Prior to 1938, the Aggies had lost all seven games in the stadium, managing to score (a field goal and a safety) only in 1926. But the jinx seemed in danger since UT had lost 10 straight games, going back to 1937. Texas A&M entered the contest with a pair of superb running backs, senior Dick Todd and sophomore John Kimbrough.

Just the most blindly loyal orangebloods picked Texas to win, especially after the varsity lost a scrimmage game to the freshmen earlier in the week. But Dana X. Bible (then in his second year as UT coach) insisted that the players' spirits were good, and he would not abandon hope for victory on Thanksgiving Day. Although the squad lacked size and speed, Bible offered no alibis, only the promise that better times were ahead.

It was a cold day, cold enough to make most of the 35,000 fans present wish they had brought an extra blanket. While Todd made some big gains, Kimbrough was held in check, and Texas intercepted six passes. Twice in the first period and twice in the third, UT got inside the Texas A&M 10-yard line, only to be stymied.

Early in the fourth quarter, following a Gilly Davis punt return to the Aggie 45-yard line, the Horns had the wind at their backs, and began to drive toward the south goal. Wally Lawson gained 15 yards up the middle, Beefus Bryan went around right end to the Aggie 17, and Lawson got another four. Nelson Puett, Jr. then broke through left tackle for nine yards, setting up his scoring run on the next play. Puett headed right, behind blocks from Bernie Esunas and John Peterson, and leaped across the goal line.

While the crowd erupted in cheers, the fiesty Puett got into a shoving match with some Texas A&M players, and Bible pulled him from the game. Lawson kicked the extra point (the only successful one all season) for a 7-0 lead, which held until the final minute, when an Aggie punt pinned UT on its own goal line. Instead of taking an intentional safety, Bible called for a double reverse, with nearly disastrous results.

Bobby Moers, better known for his basketball skills than for football, was hit by Marshall Robnett and fumbled the ball, which Alvin Olbrich recovered for the first Aggie touchdown ever in Memorial Stadium. Only 20 seconds remained on the clock when Todd lined up to kick the tying extra point. But with perfect timing, Roy Baines jumped on the shoulders of teammate Ted Dawson and then on those of the Texas A&M center to block the kick, preserving UT's 7-6 win.

The Longhorn Band performed a triumphal march around the cinder track, some students attempted to tear down the north goal post, and victory-starved alumni celebrated with coaches and players inside the locker room. A teary-eyed Bible called it "the happiest day in all my years of coaching."

TEXAS 14, ARKANSAS 13 (OCTOBER 21, 1939)

Nocona's Jack Crain, one of the brightest names in Texas football history, at first merited just a one-year "make-good" scholarship. But he quickly proved himself the star of the freshman team and gave Bible hope for the future. In the first two games of the 1939 season, Crain scored touchdowns in victories over Florida and Wisconsin, and his two 71-yard touchdown runs against Oklahoma won even more attention.

Crain was a 5' 7", 165-pound runner with speed, power, change of pace and a fierce stiff-arm. There were other talented sophomores on that 1939 Longhorn team, such as Pete Layden, Malcolm Kutner, Noble Doss and Chal Daniel, but Crain was first among equals.

The Arkansas Razorbacks had beaten Texas four straight years, most recently a 42-6 win in Little Rock in 1938. Crain did not seem overly impressed, however, because at a pep rally the night before the game, he announced "We're going to bring in some Hog meat."

Crain's 13 yards on eight carries did little damage to Arkansas, but he had a splendid 83-yard punt return in the first quarter which set up a TD by Layden. With half a minute left to play and the Longhorns behind by a score of 13-7, Crain struck his memorable thunderbolt.

The ball sat on the UT 33-yard line. Knowing that the Razorback defense was intent on stopping Crain, quarterback John Gill suggested that the two of them switch positions. Fullback R. B. Patrick threw a bullet pass to Crain in the right flat, where he got a block from Gill. By the time Crain reached midfield, it was obvious that he would score, and he did, setting off a wild celebration by the 17,000 fans—or at least those still there, because many had already given up and departed.

Stunned Arkansas players flung themselves face-down on the stadium turf, while fans rushed out onto the field, shoving game officials aside. With the score tied, 13-13, and eight seconds left, the field had to be cleared by the use of some strong-arm tactics on the part of players from both teams. Crain—of course—kicked the extra point, at which time the fans again took over the field.

Enraged officials assessed a 15-yard penalty on the ensuing kickoff, which the Hogs' Guy Gray took all the way to the UT 17-yard line before Kutner stopped him. As the clock expired, the crowd again rushed the field, carrying Crain and several other players to the locker room.

Bible would later call the 1939 Arkansas game, and Jack Crain's scamper to glory, the turning point in his tenure as UT head coach. Crain, called by the *Austin American-Statesman* "a stubby-legged, wild-running chunk of a boy from the plains country," would have other big moments in a Texas uniform, but none bigger than this.

TEXAS 7, TEXAS A&M 0 (NOVEMBER 28, 1940)

After the 1938 loss to UT, Texas A&M had won 19 consecutive games. The Aggies were voted national champions in 1939 and were heavy favorites to end their string of failures at Memorial Stadium. Homer Norton's team had all the incentive in the world to win on Thanksgiving Day, 1940: a second undefeated season, a trip to the Rose Bowl and recognition as a football powerhouse unlike any the SWC had ever seen.

Yet they were facing a Longhorn team much better than the one they had beaten, 20-0, in College Station the previous season. Crain, Layden, Doss, Daniel and Kutner were true veterans now and were joined by other skillful players. They carried a 6-2 record into the game, along with a passionate belief that Texas A&M must not win at Memorial Stadium.

Bible, who had worked his players hard in the days before the game, ignored all the talk about the Aggies' invincibility, and distributed copies of the inspirational poem "It Can Be Done." In the locker room, minutes before kickoff, master-motivator Bible called Memorial Stadium hallowed ground, not only because of the athletic rituals enacted on its turf, but because it was dedicated to Texans who had died in World War I.

Of the SWC-record 45,000 fans, those who arrived late missed all the scoring. The Longhorns won the coin toss and chose to receive. After a kickoff return brought the ball to the 30-yard line, Layden took the snap and headed right before turning and throwing a 33-yard strike to Crain. After an incompletion, Layden lofted another pass to Doss, who got behind John Kimbrough. In what would later be called "the Impossible Catch," Doss watched the ball come over his shoulder, cradled it and went out of bounds at the one-yard line.

On the fourth play from scrimmage, Layden broke a tackle by Texas A&M's Jim Thomason and scored standing up. Crain kicked the extra point, and with just 58 seconds elapsed, the Longhorns were where no other team had been all season—ahead of the Aggies. The ferocious Kimbrough (described by Harold Ratliff of the Associated Press as "a 210-pound cyclone of a man") brought his team right back, but they could not break the goal line.

The weather, cool and cloudy, enabled Bible to rely on his top few players, 13 to be exact. When the game ended with the Horns still ahead by a 7-0 score, those young men were elevated to the pantheon of football greatness as "the Immortal 13." While 6,000 Aggie cadets sat gloomily in the stands, the UT faithful celebrated. Thirty minutes after the game's conclusion, many were still there, doing snake dances and carrying on.

The Aggie locker room was a scene of dejection and tears, compounded by a lack of hot water in the showers. The Longhorn players, meanwhile, were serenaded by students, alumni and other fans singing "The Eyes of Texas." As each player departed the locker room, he got cheers from the adoring mob, including H. J. Lutcher Stark, who was keeping a lower profile by 1940.

The famed Aggie jinx was never more palpable than during this titanic game, and although it was bound to end eventually, it went on a few more years. Texas A&M would manage a 14-14 tie in 1948, but not until 1956, in their 17th attempt, did the Aggies win in Memorial Stadium.

RANDOLPH FIELD 42, TEXAS 6 (OCTOBER 7, 1944)

The quality of college football declined noticeably during World War II, as many athletes and coaches volunteered or were drafted into the armed services. While Baylor dropped the sport in 1943 and 1944, Texas and other SWC schools did the best they could with the talent remaining on their campuses.

An interesting phenomenon of the war years was the emergence of football teams at various army, navy and air bases around the country, masquerading as college teams. The skills of such squads varied wildly; some were woefully bad, and others were veritable all-star teams. For example, in 1942, UT defeated Corpus Christi Naval Air Station, 40-0, and in 1943, Blackland Army Air Field took it on the chin, 65-6. But Randolph Field tied the Longhorns, 7-7, in that year's Cotton Bowl.

The Randolph Field Ramblers were back in 1944 and had amassed some tremendous athletic talent (witness their 59-0 win over Rice), including former Longhorn stars Pete Layden and Jack Freeman, plus Jack Russell of Baylor, Martin Ruby of Texas A&M, Don Looney of TCU, Jake Leicht of Oregon and Bill Dudley of Virginia and the NFL's Pittsburgh Steelers. Texas assistant coach Blair Cherry scouted the opponent and came back with a grim report: "What team wouldn't be tough and experienced with a total of 135 years of collegiate, professional and service ball behind them?"

The Ramblers were favored to win by 33 points, but Bible would not wave the white flag just yet, even though freshman star Bobby Layne had injured an ankle in the season opener and was unable to play. Around 18,000 people attended the game under sunny skies, and they saw Randolph Field score two touchdowns in the first 3 1/2 minutes, then sit back and capitalize on UT's mistakes. Zeke Martin threw a 20-yard TD pass to Roger "Pud" Evans late in the first quarter for the only Longhorn score, while Rooster Andrews' dropkick extra-point attempt was blocked.

Randolph Field scored in every quarter, ending with Layden's 97-yard interception return, which made it 42-6. After the game, Rambler coach Frank Tritico lightly praised Texas, while Bible said "There's no substitute for experience, as the great Randolph Field club proved today. . . . I think my boys should be commended for the fine stand they made against superior numbers."

Tritico's team had been criticized for its merciless pounding of Rice the week before, and some people thought the Ramblers were loafing against UT in an attempt to hold the score down. Some dared ask why the team personnel, mostly officers, were playing football in the states and not involved in combat overseas. At the very least, Texas had company, because UCLA, Auburn and Northwestern, among others, lost to service teams on the same day.

ODESSA 21, SAN ANTONIO JEFFERSON 14 (DECEMBER 28, 1946)

"Kyle Rote is sheer perfection in every way," wrote Johnny James of the *San Antonio Light,* proving that overstated, flowery sportswriting was still in use in 1946. Wilbur Evans called Rote "the best all-around backfielder to roam over Texas gridirons since the days of Booty Johnson" (the legendary Waco High School star of the 1920s). Rote had done a lot for the San Antonio Jefferson Mustangs in the past three years to merit such praise. As a senior, he carried them to the state title game against Odessa High School.

The Bronchos had some studs of their own, including Byron "Santone" Townsend, Pug Gabriel and flashy quarterback Hayden Fry. Undefeated and untied in 13 games, Odessa was a 10-point favorite to win the crown. Memorial Stadium was familiar territory to both head coaches, as Bones Irvin of Jefferson played there for Texas A&M in the 1920s and Joe Coleman of Odessa for TCU in the 1930s.

This would be the third state championship game held at the stadium; Austin High School beat Dallas Sunset in 1942, and Port Arthur Jefferson beat Highland Park in 1944. UT did more than just turn the stadium over to the UIL, because Bible, Olle, ticket manager Alice Archer and others gave up much of their Christmas holidays to prepare for the game.

A round-trip ticket from San Antonio on the Missouri-Pacific train cost $3.68, and an estimated 15,000 people came via rail or automobile to cheer for Rote and the Mustangs. Between 8,000 and 10,000 fans traveled 400 miles from Odessa, as Memorial Stadium approached a sellout with a paid attendance of 38,000. The UIL issued a record number of press passes.

On a windy, unseasonably warm winter day, the teams lined up for the 2:30 P.M. kickoff. The heaviest starting player was 187-pound Steve Dowden of Odessa. The stars lived up to their advance billing, as both Townsend and Rote scored on the ground, and both threw for a TD. A 68-33 offensive-play differential and a couple of third-quarter breaks helped Odessa win, 21-14.

Townsend played another year for Odessa, became a Longhorn and earned all-SWC honors as a junior in 1950. Fry quarterbacked at Baylor, and went on to become head coach at SMU, North Texas and Iowa, while Kyle Rote had a fabled career at SMU and then with the New York Giants.

TEXAS 34, NORTH CAROLINA 0 (OCTOBER 4, 1947)

After impressive victories over Texas Tech (33-0) and Oregon (38-13), people were beginning to ask: How good were the 1947 Longhorns? Blair Cherry had taken over the head coaching duties from Bible, and with much help from the capable and charismatic Bobby Layne, the team streaked to a 10-1 record and No. 5 in the final Associated Press poll. Their most dominant performance came against North Carolina in Memorial Stadium.

UT was an underdog, albeit a slight one, entering the game. The Tarheels had beaten a good Georgia team the week before and boasted the fast and shifty Charlie "Choo-Choo" Justice in the backfield.

Of course, Cherry had some potent weapons as well, starting with Layne, and including receivers Max Bumgardner, Dale Schwartzkopf and Peppy Blount, linemen Joe Magliolo, Dick Harris and Danny Wolfe, and runners Randall Clay, Byron Gillory and future Dallas Cowboys head coach Tom Landry.

Some 47,000 fans gathered at the stadium on a hot day to watch that week's premier intersectional game. On the Longhorns' sixth play from scrimmage, Layne threw a 44-yard touchdown pass to Gillory, and the "upset" had begun. It was 20-0 at the half and 34-0 at game's end, with two short TD runs by Clay, one by Landry, and a 28-yard scoring pass from Raymond Jones to Blount, who had recently been elected to the Texas Legislature.

Justice gained only 18 yards on six carries, which led some wags to remark that "Justice was done" and "Choo-Choo didn't run." UT assistant coach Bully Gilstrap attributed the many Tarheel injuries to "putting the leather to them." Despite complaining about the heat from the moment they arrived in Austin, the North Carolina players were gracious in defeat. Justice compared Gillory to Illinois star Buddy Young, and fullback Walt Pupa said "They're a great team. They sure beat the hell out of us today, didn't they?"

UNC coach Carl Snavely said "They had too much speed and got faster as we got slower," and called Layne "a wonderful player. I haven't seen anyone better." Layne, known for his strong metabolism (he often caroused until just before gametime and then put on a dazzling show), finished his college career with 3,145 yards passing, and he gained plenty of ground as a runner, too. Four times all-conference and a consensus all-American as a senior, Bobby Layne went on to a 15-year pro career that included three championships with the Detroit Lions. It was the play of Layne, as much as anything, that brought enough people into Memorial Stadium that it had to be expanded in 1948.

SMU 21, TEXAS 6 (OCTOBER 30, 1948)

The last time Doak Walker had played in Memorial Stadium was during the 1944 high school state championship game. It is well known that he nearly followed teammate Bobby Layne to Austin, but ended up at SMU. After an all-Southwest Conference freshman season in 1945, Walker served in the merchant marine for a year and returned to school no worse for wear, earning consensus all-American honors in 1947, 1948 (when he won the Heisman Trophy) and 1949. The 5' 11", 165-pound Walker excelled as a runner, passer, receiver, kicker, kick returner and defender. He was probably the best pre-integration football player in SWC history.

Walker's No. 8-ranked Mustangs had beaten Layne's No. 3 Longhorns, 14-13, in Dallas the year before, and while Layne had begun his pro career by 1948, the teams would meet for another memorable battle in Austin. Neither team was undefeated this time, but partisan enthusiasm was even higher. UT students held three large rallies, a torchlight parade down the heavily decorated Drag and an auto caravan through the campus. Thirty minutes before kickoff on Saturday, the recently expanded Memorial Stadium was packed with 66,000 vocal fans, 18,000 more than it had ever held before.

They saw an exciting game that was dominated, naturally, by the golden boy, Doak Walker. On the game's third snap, he faded back to pass, and finding no receivers open, escaped Longhorn defenders and blew down the east sideline for a 67-yard touchdown. UT came back in the second quarter on a 13-play drive, as QB Paul Campbell mixed passes with runs by Ray Borneman and Randall Clay. Borneman plunged over for the score, but the extra point attempt failed, leaving it 7-6.

Walker scored again just before the half, and in the third quarter, he threw a short pass to Raleigh Blakeley, who lateraled to sophomore star Kyle Rote for an easy 18-yard touchdown that left the Longhorns dispirited. Texas outgained SMU on the ground by a margin of 231-136, and had 23 first downs to the Ponies' 13, but the score read 21-6 in favor of SMU, breaking a 16-game home winning streak.

Walker had been involved in every Mustang score, including kicking three extra points, and proved—in a time before the game became so specialized—that he could do everything with a football but peel it and eat it. As Wilbur Evans wrote in the *Austin American-Statesman*, "The ace in the hole in Matty Bell's stacked hand once again was Dynamic Doak Walker, surely the greatest football player ever to roam the wide-open spaces of Southwest gridirons."

TEXAS 21, BAYLOR 20 (NOVEMBER 7, 1953)

The week before the 1953 Baylor game, spirits were riding high on the Forty Acres, although the Longhorns had just a 4-3 record. Pep rallies took place almost daily, some of them unplanned. One was at the Governor's Mansion, another was at the intersection of Congress Avenue and Seventh Street, and still another began at Martin's Kum-Bak hamburger stand. On Thursday night, police had to disperse 500 frenzied students racing between dormitories.

Assistant football coach Ox Emerson (who had played at UT in 1929 and 1930) said it was "the greatest manifestation of school spirit I've ever seen." Dean of Men Jack Holland volunteered to take a dip in the Littlefield Fountain if Texas beat the Bears.

That prospect seemed unlikely since BU had rolled up a 6-0 record and No. 3 national ranking, the best in school history. Some pundits called Baylor a "superteam" that should have been ahead of Notre Dame and Maryland, Nos. 1 and 2. Running, passing, kicking, blocking and tackling—the senior-dominated Bear squad did it all.

But Baylor coach George Sauer used the crying towel in the days before the game, as if UT were the 16-point favorite, not his team. Maybe he knew something, because Ed Price's Longhorns won, 21-20, on a cold, misty afternoon at Memorial Stadium.

On the fourth play from scrimmage, tackle Buck Lansford hit Bear quarterback Cotton Davidson, causing him to fumble. Texas promptly drove for a TD, courtesy of running back Dougal Cameron. Baylor's L. G. ("Long Gone") Dupre scored the first of his three touchdowns, but Carlton Massey blocked the extra point kick, leaving UT ahead, 7-6. Sophomore quarterback Charley Brewer's timely passing and the work of running backs Delano Womack, Ed Kelley and Cameron had the Longhorns up, 21-13, entering the final quarter. Dupre made a sensational scoring catch with 10:40 left, but the Bears were still a point short.

Their final drive ended when Johnny Tatum intercepted Davidson's pass at the UT 41. Brewer then led a drive that consumed the rest of the clock. "Smokey," the Texas Cowboys' cannon, got its first use that day, booming at the beginning and end of the game, and with every score.

Sauer was sour to the media, keeping them locked out for 10 minutes, then answering questions brusquely. But it was another story in the home locker room, packed with well-wishers, photographers and reporters; some players danced and cried with joy.

As a result of UT's win over Baylor, Holland did indeed get dunked in the fountain, Price was named UPI coach of the week, and the Horns jumped to No. 10 in the nation, while BU fell six places to No. 9. Victories over TCU and Texas A&M left Texas with a 7-3 record, while Massey won all-American recognition.

TCU 47, TEXAS 20 (NOVEMBER 12, 1955)

In the mid- to late 1950s, the TCU Horned Frogs were a power to contend with in the Southwest Conference. Their most memorable season may have been 1955, when they came to Austin and Jim Swink laid it on the Longhorns.

Swink, a quiet, burr-headed running back, had been recruited out of Rusk primarily to play basketball. Although he did take part in the hardcourt game while at TCU, Swink's football skills really blossomed during his junior year, when he was a consensus all-American. Entering the game against UT, Swink had gained 851 yards on 103 carries for an eye-catching 8.3-yard average. No wonder Longhorn coach Ed Price urged his players to "get number 23" during practice that week.

As things turned out, they did not get him very much at all. Texas had the worst defense in the conference, and it showed that afternoon as the Frogs romped to a 47-20 win before 55,000 fans. Swink gained 235 yards on just 15 carries, with touchdowns of 1, 62, 57, and 34 yards. He kicked two extra points, intercepted a pass, and returned one punt and two kickoffs. Before it was over, some observers were doing the unthinkable: comparing him to Doak Walker. Verne Boatner of the *Daily Texan* wrote that Swink had put on "the greatest one-man show ever seen in Memorial Stadium."

The Longhorns were actually in the game through the third quarter, when UT defensive back Curtis Reeves intercepted a pass and sprinted 83 yards to the goal line. But Swink quickly ended any hope of a comeback with his third and fourth touchdowns. Throughout the game, he got strong blocking from all-conference linemen Hugh Pitts and Norman Hamilton, and met only feeble resistance from the Texas defense. At the time, the 27-point defeat was UT's worst ever at Memorial Stadium.

Swink was lionized after the game by players and coaches from both teams, as well as the media. Flem Hall of the *Fort Worth Star-Telegram* wrote "Swink ran with an artistry that wrung shouting applause from even the most loyal Texas fans." The Frogs won the 1955 SWC title with the help of a 21-6 UT upset of Texas A&M in College Station.

TEXAS 19, RICE 14 (OCTOBER 26, 1957)

Darrell Royal's first Texas team was not his most talented, but it hustled and played aggressively. The Longhorns carried a 3-2 record into the Rice game and sought to prove that they were no longer pushovers, despite the presence of six sophomores in the starting lineup.

One of them, running back Rene Ramirez, had emerged from obscurity earlier in the season, but it was against the high-flying Owls, who were headed for the Cotton Bowl, that he really made a name for himself. Around 50,000 people gathered in 40° weather for the 8 P.M. kickoff, and they saw little of note until Ramirez (nicknamed the "Galloping Gaucho") stole a King Hill pass at the Rice 40-yard line late in the first half. Bobby Lackey, who had taken over quarterbacking duties from Walt Fondren, drove the team to a score with just two seconds left on the clock.

For most of the third quarter, the two teams exchanged punts, penalties and fumbles, but the game got hot during a five-minute span. Ramirez' one-yard TD run put Texas up 12-0, then Rice, aided by two major penalties, drove 70 yards in 90 seconds for a score. In the twinkling of an eye, the Owls had the ball back, and Howard Hoelscher went around right end for a 33-yard touchdown to take the lead, 14-12.

The ensuing kickoff went under Monte Lee's legs and was grabbed by Ramirez at the 20-yard line. He set sail up the east sideline, was in the clear at midfield, shook off a tackle attempt by Hill at the 40 and got a final block from teammate George Blanch at the 30 before crossing the goal line. It was the first time a Longhorn player had returned a kickoff all the way since Hugh Wolfe did it against Minnesota 21 years earlier.

Rice had a couple of fourth-quarter drives, both of which ended in fumbles, as UT took a surprise 19-14 win that merited a No. 13 national ranking. Ramirez' totals looked this way: 76 yards rushing and one touchdown on eight carries, a 22-yard punt return, one pass completion, two pass receptions, an interception and his brilliant 80-yard kickoff return that won the game.

In the locker room, Ramirez exclaimed "This is my greatest thrill ever. I saw this big hole, and there I go. Oh, San Antone, I did it!"

TEXAS 7, ARKANSAS 3 (OCTOBER 20, 1962)

"Two dynasties are gonna bump," wrote Lou Maysel of the *Austin American-Statesman* about the 1962 Texas-Arkansas football game. These teams had risen to the top of the Southwest Conference and were getting national attention. Both were undefeated (4-0), and the Longhorns were ranked No. 1, the Hogs No. 7, entering their night-time matchup in Memorial

Stadium. Frank Broyles' players had extra incentive, remembering UT's 33-7 win in Fayetteville the year before.

Tom McKnelly's 41-yard field goal gave the Razorbacks a 3-0 lead, which they held at halftime. They seemed to have the game in hand in the third period when quarterback Billy Moore led a drive to the UT three-yard line. Johnny Treadwell and Pat Culpepper were about to prove why Royal had called them the best pair of linebackers in the country.

Danny Brabham, the 6' 4", 218-pound Arkansas fullback, took the handoff and tried to jump over the line. While Marvin Kubin and Clayton Lacy hit him low, Treadwell and Culpepper hit him high. The ball popped out of Brabham's arms, and defensive back Joe Dixon recovered in the end zone. The Razorbacks' chance to widen their lead had vanished, and the teams went into the fourth quarter battling not just each other, but fatigue and the muggy 75° weather.

With eight minutes left, the Longhorns took possession of the ball at their own 15-yard line. The Texas offense had been less than scintillating to that point, but it was time for what would later be called "the big drive." QB Duke Carlisle completed passes of 12 yards to Tommy Lucas, 11 yards to Sandy Sands and then to Sands again for 14.

Royal sent in Johnny Genung for the exhausted Carlisle, who had been playing both offense and defense. Genung did not miss a beat in making first downs and depleting the clock. A fourth-down pass up the middle to Charlie Talbert kept the drive going, along with the running of Ray Poage, Tommy "T-Bird" Ford and Jerry Cook.

The 64,350 fans' voices were augmented by the reverberation of jumping up and down on the stadium's wooden seats and the roar of "Smokey." During a game, the Texas Cowboys ordinarily fired the cannon only after a score. But caught up in the moment, they began firing it after every first down and then after every play. With 36 seconds left on the clock, the Horns had worked the ball to the Arkansas three-yard line. The play Royal called, "18 sweep to the right," was run to perfection. Genung pitched to Ford, who followed the blocks of Poage, Sands and Ernie Koy, Jr., broke a tackle by Moore and fell into the end zone. Tony Crosby's kick made it 7-3, the final score.

It was a bitter loss for the Hogs, who had the upper hand most of the night. Broyles, boarding the team bus at the stadium's south end, recalled Brabham's fumble and said "We should have scored. That's our fault. Our kids are broken-hearted."

That defensive play by Treadwell and Culpepper would stick in people's minds, as would the magnificent 20-play drive that took up almost half of the final quarter. Although the teams scored just 10 points, it was one of the best games ever witnessed in Memorial Stadium. The Longhorns had an emotional letdown the next week, when they were tied by an inferior Rice team, 14-14, hurting their chances for a national championship.

TEXAS 7, BAYLOR 0 (NOVEMBER 9, 1963)

Having come so close the year before, Royal's team was reaching for the brass ring in 1963, but the pass-happy Baylor Bears would make a strong challenge in the season's eighth game. There was an unusual amount of psychological warfare in the preceding week. For instance, Royal was quoted as saying that no UT partisan would wear green socks with a blue suit. Inferring that he doubted their sophistication, BU people took offense. Many of them, including head coach John Bridgers, made a point of wearing loud green socks to the game in Austin.

The state's newspapers played up the contrasting football ideologies, since the Bears, with the Don Trull-to-Lawrence Elkins combination, led the country in passing, while the Horns led in rushing. In addition, on the morning of the game, the UT Board of Regents voted to open student activities, including athletics, to everyone, regardless of race. Integration of Longhorn football, if not imminent, was now just a matter of time.

After the opening kickoff, Baylor drove—mostly via the air—to the Texas 14 before stalling. UT answered with a second-quarter march that ended with a missed Tony Crosby field goal. The players went to their locker rooms at halftime in a scoreless tie. In the third quarter, Tom Stockton's one-yard TD put the Longhorns up, 7-0. That lead looked safe as quarterback Duke Carlisle marched the team to the Bears' 13-yard line with just over two minutes left in the game.

But Baylor's Ken Hodge recovered a fumble on the next play. With the right kind of offense to travel the length of the field in a hurry, Bridgers felt confident. Before Trull could begin throwing, however, UT assistant coach Mike Campbell, sitting in the Memorial Stadium press box, suggested leaving Carlisle in to play his safety position. Completions of 18, 11 and 9 yards to Elkins, a couple of running plays and a 27-yard pass interference penalty brought Baylor to the Texas 19 with 29 seconds to play.

Then the Bears went for it all. Elkins ran a post route and had beaten defensive back Joe Dixon in the end zone. Trull's throw spiraled toward the sure hands of Elkins, but Carlisle drifted across, leaped and intercepted the ball. As pandemonium reigned in the stands, the game was effectively over.

Dixon told reporters "I expected him [Elkins] to go outside, and he went in. I saw six points going until Duke came. I wanted to kiss him. . . . Duke made a tremendous play, absolutely tremendous. He saved my life."

The Longhorns finished the regular season with a 10-0 record and had no trouble beating Navy, led by Roger Staubach, in the Cotton Bowl. The 1963 national championship was made possible by the win over Baylor and Carlisle's big play, which Lou Maysel would later describe as "perhaps the greatest single defensive gem the stadium has seen."

ARKANSAS 14, TEXAS 13 (OCTOBER 17, 1964)

According to the *Daily Texan*, this was "college football at its finest . . . a capacity crowd standing through an unbelievable second half . . . no one leaving the field after it was over . . . an artistic football game played on one of the nation's finest fields . . . a big rivalry and a big game with a big meaning." For the first time since 1961, UT lost a regular-season game, and it was to the Arkansas Razorbacks by a score of 14-13.

The Longhorns went into the contest as the defending national champions, ranked No. 1, with a 15-game winning streak. They were favored by nearly two touchdowns over No. 8-ranked Arkansas. And while Royal's team prided itself on kick coverage, there would be one major slip that evening in Memorial Stadium. In the second quarter, Ernie Koy, Jr. punted 47 yards to Ken Hatfield, the nation's top kick returner (and a future Hog head coach). Fielding the ball at his 19-yard line, Hatfield slung off one tackler and fell in behind a wall of blockers to his left. He did not stop until he reached the end zone, putting Arkansas ahead.

Texas tied it up early in the fourth period with a gritty 14-play, 46-yard drive that culminated in Phil Harris' two-yard TD run. Arkansas came back with a 75-yard march kept alive by a penalty against UT for having 12 men on the field. Quarterback Fred Marshall connected with Bobby Crockett on a 34-yard touchdown strike to retake the lead, 14-7. Then, evoking the memory of "the big drive" two years earlier, the Horns began at their 30-yard line with 6:15 left in the game. Texas countered the blitzing, charging Razorback defense with some fierce running by Koy, and key passes from Marvin Kristynik to Barney Giles and Hix Green brought them to the Arkansas two, where Koy scored over right tackle with 1:27 remaining on the clock.

Royal called time out and conferred with his assistants on what to do. Disdaining a sure-thing extra point by kicker Tony Crosby that would tie the game, the coaches were virtually unanimous to go for the two-point conversion to win. Everyone in the stadium knew that a second national championship hung in the balance, and held their breath as Kristynik took the snap and wheeled right. Defensive end Jim Finch pressured Kristynik, who threw a feeble pass toward Green. It bounced short, and Razorback players began a wild celebration. Cries of "Whoo! Pig! Sooeey!" came from the 5,000 or so Arkansas fans present, some of whom took handfuls of the stadium's turf home to the Ozarks.

Although deeply disappointed, Royal went to the visitors' locker room after the game and congratulated them. Meanwhile, the eyes of Texas were crying in the home locker room. Linebacker/guard Tommy Nobis, who did not take losing lightly, stripped off his uniform, cut the tape from his ankles and walked to the shower, ignoring reporters' questions.

Royal refused to second-guess the two-point gamble that climaxed the game, saying "There was never any doubt about what we'd do. There was no hesitation, and there are no regrets. I felt that we were defending champions, and champions ought to go down swinging." A single point separated the Longhorns from another national title, as they won their last five regular-season games and beat Joe Namath and Alabama, 21-17, in the Orange Bowl.

TEXAS 20, HOUSTON 20 (SEPTEMBER 21, 1968)

Texas had played the University of Houston once before, in 1953, when Cougar football was in only its eighth year. UH had earned its identity by 1968 though, when it would lead the nation in total offense for the third straight season, with the help of some talented black athletes and the innovative Veer offense. Long an independent, Houston wanted admission to the Southwest Conference, and a win over UT would bolster its claim. Head coach Bill Yeoman said "Our game with the University of Texas this weekend has been a topic of conversation since last season ended."

Royal's program, meanwhile, was reeling, having struggled to 6-4 regular-season records in 1965, 1966 and 1967. But some promising sophomores, led by running back Steve Worster, and a new triple-option offense soon to be dubbed the "Wishbone" gave UT fans hope.

The Cougars' 54-7 nuking of Tulane the week before had them primed for Texas. The media fancied the game a showdown between Houston's Paul Gipson (1,100 yards rushing in 1967 and second-team all-American) and the Horns' Chris Gilbert (2,099 career yards rushing and poised to break Jim Swink's SWC record). Neither would disappoint that night. The game was a sellout, and no less an authority than Clyde Littlefield said that he had never seen so many people outside of Memorial Stadium, unable to get tickets.

For a while, it resembled a slugging contest between two heavyweights. Houston took a 7-0 lead on Gipson's one-yard run, but three plays later, Gilbert bolted 57 yards to tie it up. An eight-yard Gilbert TD putting the Longhorns ahead was followed by Gipson's 66-yard gallop, evening the score at 14-14.

UH capitalized on an interception, and again Gipson did the honors from five yards out. The extra point was missed, leaving the Cougars with a 20-14 lead. Bill Atessis of Texas pounced on a fumble at the Houston 20-yard line near the end of the third period, leading to Ted Koy's four-yard scoring run. That made it 20-20, but Rob Layne shanked the extra point.

Although the Houston offense would manage drives of 72 and 45 yards to the verge of the UT goal line, it failed to score. The weary Longhorns did not make a single first down after Koy's touchdown and were lucky to come away with a tie. The game ended with Texas sitting on the ball as the clock ran out, and for that perceived lack of gumption, Royal heard boos from fans of both schools.

The teams' running stars had been just as good as advertised. Gilbert had 159 yards on 21 carries and two touchdowns, while Gipson gained 173 yards on 28 carries and scored three times. Longhorn defender Loyd Wainscott went overboard in his praise of Gipson, saying "He's better than O. J. [Simpson], hands down."

Clark Nealon of the *Houston Post* wrote that UH "caught a blood and guts Southwest Conference team with deep tradition to goad it on, but the Cougars met it all head on and battled it out on the humid, 80° floor of Memorial Stadium. For tempo, hitting and thrills, this one goes down with the great ones in the history of Texas football."

The new Longhorn offense would require some fine tuning and a quarterback change (James Street taking over for Bill Bradley), but 1968 marked the beginning of another UT football dynasty with six straight Cotton Bowl appearances.

TEXAS 20, UCLA 17 (OCTOBER 3, 1970)

Darrell Royal's Longhorns, the defending national champions, easily dispatched California and Texas Tech in the first two games of the 1970 season. But the UCLA Bruins, despite their 22-point underdog status, would prove a much tougher foe.

The guys in the baby-blue jerseys were serious about ending UT's 22-game winning streak, as seen in just the second play from scrimmage. Linebacker Bob Pifferini read the triple option, busted Texas running back Billy Dale and recovered quarterback Eddie Phillips' errant pitchout. UCLA coach Tommy Prothro had designed his defense to stop the Wishbone by having an end, linebacker or defensive back charge through and disrupt things. For most of the game, this worked very well, and if it left them vulnerable to the pass, they did not seem too concerned about Phillips' arm.

While the Bruins managed a first-quarter field goal, they fell behind at the half, 13-3, due to a short Jim Bertelsen TD run and field goals of 55 and 47 yards by Happy Feller. The third quarter belonged to UCLA, with scoring drives of 89 and 95 yards led by quarterback Dennis Dummit, to go back up, 17-13. It did not look promising for Texas when a long drive was halted at the UCLA 12-yard line with 2:27 left in the game.

The Longhorns got the ball back near midfield with 58 seconds remaining. Trailing by four, they had to have a touchdown. The highly successful Wishbone was a methodical, grind-it-out offense, but UT needed a quick strike against a deep-prevent defense. At that point, Phillips had completed just five of 14 passes for a piddling 57 yards.

A 13-yard pass to tight end Tommy Woodard gave Texas a first down with 33 seconds left. Phillips threw an incompletion to stop the clock, since the Horns had used up all their timeouts. On second down, Phillips went back to pass, failed to find an open receiver, and fumbled the ball in front of the Bruin bench, but it went out of bounds. That nine-yard loss left UT with third down at its own 45, and 20 seconds to play. Who among the players, coaches, media people or 65,500 fans truly had a premonition that something big was about to happen?

Under a heavy rush, Phillips fired the ball 20 yards downfield toward Cotton Speyrer, angling in from his right split-end position. Three, possibly four, UCLA players were in the vicinity, and all of them misplayed the ball or Speyrer. Allan Ellis went for the interception over Speyrer's left shoulder and missed the ball, as did Doug Huff from the right. Speyrer caught it and instantly pivoted toward the goal line, away from Frank Jones. He and Pifferini could only give chase as the fleet Speyrer ran for the score.

People who were at Memorial Stadium that day in 1970 still remember the thunderous sound that erupted when the Longhorns completed this play. Feller's conversion made the score 20-17, which is how it ended. The winning streak remained intact, as did a run for another national title. Royal quieted the locker-room celebration somewhat when he reminded his team that it had not played very well. He complimented the defeated Bruins and stated "There is no question luck is involved, but as I've said before, you've got to be in a position to let luck happen."

Lou Maysel wrote in the next day's *Austin American-Statesman* "Forget about that miraculous comeback against Arkansas last year and also that great pressure drive against Notre Dame in the 1970 Cotton Bowl. Those were garden-variety thrillers. The University of Texas Longhorns pulled perhaps the most fabulous comeback of their entire football history with a 45-yard pass from Eddie Phillips to Cotton Speyrer when they seemed hopelessly beaten by UCLA Saturday at Memorial Stadium."

PLANO 21, GREGORY-PORTLAND 20 (DECEMBER 18, 1971)

It was the battle of the Wildcats, as both UIL Class 3A finalists Gregory-Portland and Plano had the same feline mascot.

Plano had not even been favored to win its district, but here it was with a 12-1 record, playing for the third state championship in school history. Running backs Pat Thomas (1,600 yards rushing) and Rucker Lewis were largely responsible. Undefeated Gregory-Portland had 1,000-yard rusher Alan Callicoat, receiver Mike Crosswhite and QB Marty Akins. Coached by his father, Ray, Akins was a three-year starter with a 32-2-1 record. During that time, he accounted for almost 6,000 total yards and was involved in 570 points.

Memorial Stadium's old south-end scoreboard was being dismantled, so for this one game, UT workers hauled a small one (designed for basketball) over from the Gregory Gym annex. On a cold, windy day, 11,500 people showed up for the title game of the state's second-highest classification; San Antonio Lee and Wichita Falls played for the Class 4A championship that weekend at Texas Stadium in Irving.

It turned out to be a fine game, as the teams traded touchdowns. Plano had most of its success on the ground, while Gregory-Portland went to the air. Akins' team led, 20-14, entering the final quarter. But with 10:55 left, Plano scored, and Thomas kicked the extra point for a 21-20 margin.

There matters stood until Akins engineered a 70-yard drive in the final two minutes. A penalty set the ball at the Plano 25-yard line, and with 14 seconds remaining, a hurried Akins field-goal attempt went wide and short. Plano would get the coveted UIL trophy.

Thomas had scored two touchdowns, gained 149 yards and kicked three extra points. Akins scored once, threw a 57-yard TD pass to Crosswhite and kicked two extra points. He audibled like a pro throughout the game and later revealed that he had played the last five weeks with a broken wrist.

Akins would spend the next four years as a Longhorn, making all-SWC his senior year and later becoming an attorney in Houston. Thomas, a two-time consensus all-American defensive back for Texas A&M, had a long career with the Los Angeles Rams.

TEXAS 38, ARKANSAS 7 (OCTOBER 19, 1974)

When Earl Campbell made his college debut in 1974, it was quickly apparent that this "can't-miss" prospect was the real thing. Halfway through the season, he had gained 386 yards and scored three touchdowns, despite sharing the fullback position with 1973 all-American Roosevelt Leaks, who was still suffering from a spring-training knee injury.

The No. 16-ranked Longhorns were 3-2 going into the nationally televised game against Arkansas, in which Campbell played a big part from both sides of the line of scrimmage. Texas intended to challenge the Razorbacks' SWC-leading defense against the run. Mike Dean put UT ahead with a 45-yard field goal, and Campbell added to that in the second quarter when he took a handoff from QB Marty Akins, stiff-armed an Arkansas player and motored 68 yards to a touchdown.

The "Tyler Rose" was not finished, however. With 30 seconds left in the half, the Hogs' Tommy Cheyne punted—or at least he tried to. Campbell charged through the line and arrived shortly after the snapped ball. Tackle Doug English grabbed the blocked punt on the bounce and strolled into the end zone with a lineman's dream, raising the score to 17-0.

"Earl did it all," said English after the game. "All I could see was the ball and the goal line. It's something I've always wanted to do."

The injury-riddled visitors would surrender another three touchdowns that day before Rolland Fuchs ran for a long score against the UT subs to make it 38-7. "No less than 10 injuries," reported Arkansas coach Frank Broyles. "Texas just whipped us in every phase of the game. We've never had so many injuries in a ball game, or been so physically beaten."

Austin American-Statesman sportswriter George Breazeale speculated that the worst injury of all was to the pride of the Razorbacks, SWC preseason favorites. Campbell, with 109 yards on eight carries, was named offensive player of the game, while defensive honors went to English.

The 1974 team, which would finish with an 8-4 record, was far from Royal's best, but it produced three all-time Longhorn greats, each of whom went on to distinguished pro careers: English with the Detroit Lions, Leaks with the Baltimore Colts and Buffalo Bills, and Campbell with the Houston Oilers and New Orleans Saints.

HOUSTON 10, TEXAS 7 (NOVEMBER 11, 1978)

Earl Campbell had taken his all-world act to the National Football League in 1978, and he was undoubtedly missed. But Fred Akers' second UT team adapted and carried a 6-1 record into its November showdown with Houston.

The Longhorns had a number of outstanding players, some of them destined to join Campbell in the pros: tackle Steve McMichael, linebackers Robin Sendlein and Bruce Scholtz, defensive backs Johnnie Johnson, Ricky Churchman and Glenn Blackwood, kicker Russell Erxleben, running back A. J. "Jam" Jones and receiver Johnny "Lam" Jones. Akers also had promising freshmen like quarterback Donnie Little, tight end Lawrence Sampleton, tackle Kenneth Sims and linebacker Doug Shankle.

Houston had some talent, too, as seen in the Cougars' 7-1 record. In the previous four weeks, they had beaten Texas A&M, SMU, Arkansas and TCU by a 158-43 margin. Texas was ranked No. 6 and UH No. 8 in the Southwest Conference game of the year, which pulled a record crowd of 83,053 to Memorial Stadium despite gray, overcast skies.

Akers and Houston coach Bill Yeoman denied any bad blood between the schools, although there were muffled accusations of cheating in the recruiting wars. And not everyone had been pleased to see the upstart Cougars winning the conference in their very first year, 1976.

The high-scoring game most people expected was instead a tense 10-7 UH victory. The first half was a scoreless tie, but Texas had several chances. Akers chose not to let Erxleben attempt a 42-yard field goal, Johnson's 54-yard punt return was nullified by a clipping penalty, and twice QB Randy McEachern had a receiver open for an apparent touchdown, but he threw poor passes.

Houston scored twice in the third quarter, as Emmett King took a pitchout from Danny Davis at the two-yard line, and Kenny Hatfield booted a 33-yard field goal. Little replaced McEachern and drove the Longhorns to an early fourth-quarter score, with "Jam" Jones going over from one yard out.

A 72-yard Houston drive, lasting six minutes, ended with an interception by Churchman, but UT could not make it back down the field and lost the game. The Cougars went on to lose a thriller to Notre Dame in the Cotton Bowl. Texas gave Maryland a 42-0 mauling in the Sun Bowl, as both conference teams finished with 9-3 records.

SMU 30, TEXAS 17 (OCTOBER 23, 1982)

"Ponies Ride Infractions to Big Time," read the headline of David McNabb's *Daily Texan* sports column the week before the 1982 Texas-SMU game in Memorial Stadium. NCAA probation for recruiting violations had kept the SWC-champion Mustangs out of the Cotton Bowl following the 1981 season, in which they went 10-1. And their lone defeat was administered by Fred Akers' Longhorns.

SMU brought a No. 4 national ranking, a 10-game winning streak and an attitude to Austin. When informed that the Longhorns were one-point favorites, SMU running back Eric Dickerson said "I'm not surprised they're favored. Texas. That's all you have to hear. Texas. It intimidates a lot of people, but it doesn't intimidate me or this team."

Dickerson, on his way to an all-American season, third place in Heisman Trophy voting, the conference's career rushing mark and over 12,000 yards in the NFL, provoked this response from UT linebacker Jeff Leiding: "I think they're scared. Deep down, they don't really think they can beat us. If we put a couple of sticks on Dickerson, he'll fold up and go tippy-toe."

With all the woofing back and forth, the stage was set for a big game, which drew an appropriately big crowd, 80,157, on a beautiful Indian-summer day. It was more than double the largest crowd SMU had drawn in six previous games that season. Early in the second quarter, Dickerson took a pitchout from quarterback Lance McIlhenny, cut between two blockers and sprinted 60 yards before being tackled by Fred Acorn and Jerry Gray. That set up Dickerson's two-yard score soon after.

Going into the fourth quarter, SMU led, 10-0, but a 51-yard touchdown pass from QB Robert Brewer to tight end Bobby Micho and a 41-yard Raul Allegre field goal tied it up. Texas seemed to have the momentum with 7:51 left and the Ponies on their own 21-yard line, facing third down and nine. Longhorn players on the west sideline were waving towels as McIlhenny faded back and threw a wobbly pass intended for Bobby Leach. But it went straight to defensive back Jitter Fields, bounced off his hands and into those of Leach, who completed a shocking 79-yard touchdown.

Another McIlhenny TD throw four minutes later had the Mustangs up, 23-10, but Brewer and Herkie Walls connected for a six-yard scoring pass with 1:50 left. Any hope of staging a comeback ended when McIlhenny did a play-action fake and threw a 46-yard touchdown pass to Craig James, leaving the score 30-17.

It was Mustang Mania at its best for the 9,000 SMU fans who had come to Austin. Dickerson, with 118 yards rushing, got to show his considerable stuff before a regional TV audience, against a top team. There was a profusion of microphones and minicams inside the winners' locker room, as the Dallas media generally treated it as the biggest Pony victory since Jerry LeVias in the 1960s, Don Meredith in the 1950s, or even Doak Walker in the 1940s.

McIlhenny said "I love the fans and the intensity of this place," while SMU head coach Bobby Collins remarked "Texas has an excellent football team, but we were able to come down here and win this big game in front of 80,000 people."

Only a 17-17 tie with Arkansas marred the 1982 season for the Mustangs, who beat Pittsburgh in the Cotton Bowl and finished No. 2 in the nation. Regardless of the NCAA sanctions, *Texas Football* magazine would later name this bunch the Southwest Conference team of the decade.

TEXAS 35, AUBURN 27 (SEPTEMBER 15, 1984)

Coming off an 11-1 season in which a fumbled punt kept them from a probable national championship, the Longhorns faced a real challenge in 1984. They would miss all-SWC players like Mike Ruether, Doug Dawson, Eric Holle, Mossy Cade and Fred Acorn. But the cupboard was not entirely bare, since Tony Degrate and Jerry Gray were back to anchor the defense.

Another team finishing 11-1 in 1983 was the Auburn Tigers, and who had been responsible for their only loss? Texas. Sophomore running back Bo Jackson—not yet a household name—said after the game "I feel like I've been run over by a herd of cows."

The teams met again in 1984, but this time in Austin. It was the season opener for No. 3-ranked UT, and the second game for Auburn, which had already lost once. The Tigers had fallen from a No. 1 ranking to No. 10, and after this game, they would drop even further.

"I hope they are aware of the tradition and atmosphere we're going to be playing in Saturday night," said Auburn coach Pat Dye. "Texas has one of the top traditions in the nation." The game was televised nationally on ESPN, and 78,348 fans saw it in person.

With a strong north wind at their backs, the Longhorns jumped to a 14-0 first-quarter lead when quarterback Todd Dodge bootlegged 10 yards for a score, and Terry Orr had a one-yard TD. Auburn responded with a touchdown and two field goals to trail at the half, 14-13.

A 32-yard scoring pass from Dodge to Brent Duhon was followed by an Auburn drive that ended with a six-yard TD run by Jackson. The Horns led, 21-19, late in the third quarter when Jackson took a handoff and found a hole in the UT defense. He turned on his speed (reputedly 4.15 seconds in the 40-yard dash) and headed for paydirt. Texas defensive back Jerry Gray had the angle on the 222-pound Jackson and finally corralled him after 53 yards. The Auburn star landed heavily on his right shoulder, but stayed in the game and carried two more times before coming out.

The Longhorns' defense held, and two Jerome Johnson touchdowns had them comfortably ahead midway through the final period. But the celebration began a little too soon, as Auburn rallied for a score, a two-point conversion and a successful onside kick with 2:33 left. An interception by Gray halted the comeback, however, for a 35-27 win.

Jackson's numbers came to 104 yards on 14 carries, a 21-yard reception and one score. He was diagnosed as having a separated shoulder, ending what the Auburn sports information department had hoped would be a Heisman Trophy season. Of course, Bo Jackson would be back. He won the 1985 Heisman, surprised everyone but himself by playing both pro football (Los Angeles Raiders) and baseball (Kansas City Royals and Chicago White Sox), and was the subject of so many innovative Nike commercials that he became a media icon of sorts.

TEXAS 24, TCU 21 (NOVEMBER 14, 1987)

Recruited out of a Virginia prep school in 1985, Eric Metcalf arrived in Austin loaded down with comparisons to his father, Terry, a star running back/receiver/kick returner for the St. Louis Cardinals and Washington Redskins in the 1970s. Somewhat underutilized during his first two years at UT, Metcalf burst into national prominence as a junior in 1987.

His greatest game that year—and there were several great ones—took place against TCU's Horned Frogs when both teams still entertained outside shots at the Southwest Conference title. TCU had a 5-4 record and a 20-year losing streak to Texas, but David McWilliams' first UT team was not exactly striking terror into anyone's heart. The Longhorns were coming off a disastrous 60-40 loss to Houston the week before, and a home game against one of the SWC's weak sisters was just what they needed.

The first score was a three-yard run by the 5' 9", 178-pound Metcalf. Linebacker Lee Brockman's 43-yard interception return of a David Rascoe pass made it 14-0, although the Frogs came right back with a scoring drive of their own. Texas quarterback Shannon Kelley, subbing for the injured Bret Stafford, threw just seven passes the entire game; what he mostly did was hand off to the cat-quick Metcalf.

Just under six minutes remained in the third period as the Horns faced second down and 14 from their 43-yard line. Then Metcalf escaped defensive end Tracy Simien and sprung loose. He got a block from teammate Gabriel Johnson at the 30-yard line and outran the other Frog defenders on a 57-yard touchdown equal to any his father ever scored in the National Football League.

A 17-point UT lead looked safe until Rascoe engineered a couple of fourth-quarter TDs, putting TCU within three, 24-21, but that is how it ended. Metcalf had the most productive day of his college career, with 280 total yards—206 yards rushing on 36 carries, 66 yards on kick returns, and an eight-yard reception.

Plenty of accolades followed. Kelley said "Eric is a superman. He's just a better athlete than anyone else out there."

When asked, McWilliams agreed that Metcalf's performance against TCU should draw some notice from all-America and Heisman Trophy voters. "We didn't intend to give Metcalf the ball 36 times," he said. "He's just a great football player. He's a multipurpose threat who can break any play."

Metcalf finished the season with 1,161 yards rushing (for a 5.2-yard average), 33 receptions (7.2-yard average), 24 punt returns (13.5-yard average), 11 kickoff returns (18.4-yard average), and scored 11 touchdowns. The SWC's offensive player of the year in 1987, before he was through, Metcalf would eclipse Earl Campbell as UT's total yardage leader. He went on to play for the Cleveland Browns.

TEXAS 45, HOUSTON 24 (NOVEMBER 10, 1990)

The proud Longhorn football heritage took quite a beating in 1988 (4-7) and 1989 (5-6), bottoming out with a 50-7 loss to Baylor in the final home game of the 1989 season. Allegations of players gambling and using steroids only made it worse. While some fans and sportswriters called for a complete overhaul of the program, McWilliams, with steady support from athletic director DeLoss Dodds, handled it all with aplomb.

Expectations were not too high as the 1990 season began, but the Longhorns benefited from a tough offseason conditioning program and the leadership of seniors like Kerry Cash, Chris Samuels, Brian Jones and Stan Thomas. After a 29-22 defeat by eventual national champion Colorado, they began inching up in the polls. Texas was 6-1 and ranked No. 14 when Houston came calling. The only major college team still unbeaten and untied, UH had an 8-0 record and a No. 6 ranking.

The Cougars also wore the NCAA's scarlet letter: P, for probation, so they were ineligible for postseason play. First-year Houston coach John Jenkins had no qualms about running up the score when he had the chance. He loudly campaigned for a higher team ranking and the Heisman Trophy for his quarterback, David Klingler. Earning the ire of some fellow Southwest Conference coaches, Jenkins bragged of his team's "unstoppable" Run-and-Shoot offense. UT's recent history against Houston was a string of nightmares, as the Horns lost 60-40 in 1987, 66-15 in 1988 and 47-9 in 1989. And although Texas had served notice that it was not the same team as before, some people in burnt orange feared another trip to the woodshed.

Averaging less than 30,000 in attendance for their home games in the Astrodome, the Cougars walked out on the floor of Memorial Stadium in front of 82,457 loud and involved people. It was a one-sided game, but this time UT gave, rather than getting, to the tune of 45-24. The Longhorn defense blitzed Klingler all night and held running back Chuck Weatherspoon—their chief nemesis the last two years—to just 50 yards rushing. UT freshman Butch Hadnot rumbled for 134 yards and three touchdowns, and quarterback Peter Gardere (20 out of 28 passing for 322 yards) looked more like a Heisman Trophy candidate than Klingler, who threw four interceptions.

Trailing 28-10 at the half, Houston still thought a win was possible, but Texas put up the next 17 points before easing the pressure in the fourth quarter. In the final minute, rowdy fans poured out of the stands and circled the field. Some attempted to tear down the north goalpost, drawing a rebuke from stadium announcer Wally Pryor.

After seeing the Run-and-Shoot offense unravel before his eyes, Jenkins struck an unaccustomed humble pose, saying "I felt like Jim Bowie and Davy Crockett at the Alamo. They just kept giving us the bayonet." The Longhorns' performance fed off the huge crowd and the ear-splitting noise it made all night long. John Maher of the *Austin American-Statesman* wrote that it was "the most electric game that's been staged here in half a dozen years." Maybe more.

McWilliams' Longhorns jumped to No. 7 in the nation following the rout of Houston, and then beat TCU, Baylor and Texas A&M to win the SWC title. Ranked third with a 10-1 record, they went into the Cotton Bowl game with a decent chance at the national championship, but got bombed by Miami, 46-3. Even this did not alter what UT had achieved during the 1990 season, proving once again that nothing can draw together a disparate college campus quite like a winning football team.

Track and Field at Memorial Stadium

I n terms of attendance, media coverage, generation of revenue and virtually all other criteria, track and field at the University of Texas has always lagged far behind football. It is safe to say that Memorial Stadium would not have been built solely on the popularity of track and field. Although architect Herbert M. Greene had instructions to design a dual-purpose facility, it was—and still is—primarily a football stadium.

Between 1924 and 1991, more than 80 Longhorn football games at Memorial Stadium have sold out, but it has never been anywhere near full for a track meet. Not for any of the five NCAA meets, 15 Southwest Conference meets, 65 runnings of the Texas Relays, 68 University Interscholastic League state meets or hundreds of other lesser meets held there. Of course, that is partly because Memorial Stadium has always been a large building, originally holding 27,000 spectators, and expanded to 40,500 in 1926, 60,130 in 1948, and 75,504 in 1971. Not even the most track-crazed region of the country could expect to fill such a stadium for anything less than the Olympics.

Still, UT has a long and rich tradition in the world's oldest sport, a tradition predating Memorial Stadium by 30 years. Back when they were toiling at the original Clark Field, Longhorn track teams dominated the SWC, winning five of the first nine titles. And the man most responsible for that was Clyde Littlefield.

Littlefield was a native of Pennsylvania whose family moved to Texas in 1904. He enjoyed a stellar schoolboy career in Beaumont and San Antonio in

157

the four major sports—football, baseball, basketball and track. In a time before athletic scholarships and recruiting, he arrived on the Forty Acres in 1912 with little fanfare. But it was the beginning of a distinguished 47-year association with the university.

"I was a poor boy," he said later. "I waited on tables and delivered papers early in the morning the first two years and was manager of the Kappa Alpha fraternity house the last two years to make my expenses."

Littlefield stood 6' 1 1/2", weighed 175 pounds and was fast, strong and competitive. He soon proved his value to the UT athletic program. Playing football in the fall, basketball in the winter and running track in the spring (he also played briefly for Billy Disch's baseball team), Littlefield found time to study, majoring in geology; he expected to follow his father into the oil business.

He kept up this schedule for his entire college career, earning 12 varsity letters, three more than anyone else in UT history. The Longhorn basketball team, on which he played center, went undefeated for three seasons. In football, he made the initial all-SWC team in 1915 and could throw 60-yard spirals with ease. And in track, Littlefield specialized as a hurdler. Over a four-year span, he lost just one low-hurdles race and was never beaten in the high hurdles. In 1914, he tied the world record in the 120-yard high hurdles with a time of 15.2 seconds, which lasted as an SWC record for 12 years. Strangely enough, Littlefield was not elected captain of the track team his senior season.

Having shown such excellence in three sports, for many years Littlefield was accorded unofficial recognition as the greatest athlete UT ever produced. When the university celebrated its centennial in 1983, an *Austin American-Statesman* reader poll sought to determine the top Longhorn of all time. Two years after his death and nearly seven decades after he stopped competing, Littlefield still had some supporters, coming in fourth behind Earl Campbell, Bobby Layne and James Street.

COACH LITTLEFIELD

Deciding against the life of an oilman, Littlefield knew he wanted to coach, and so he did, at Greenville High School, winning state titles in football and track. World War I had just concluded when Littlefield entered the Army. Serving as an infantry officer in Arkansas, he coached and played on the camp football team. It is the last recorded instance of him competing in any sport, unless we count the informal 1924 "Ragnots" football game at Clark Field.

Upon discharge from the Army in 1920, Littlefield found himself in demand as Texas, Texas A&M, Baylor and TCU all sought his coaching services. He returned to UT, although the pay was $600 a year lower than some of his other offers. And he would stay busy, coaching varsity track, freshman football and freshman basketball. Well-suited for the coaching profession, Littlefield was calm and patient by nature, yet he spoke with authority.

Littlefield's college coaching career did not get off to a rousing start, as the track team finished fifth in the SWC in 1921 and second in 1922. But he soon had Texas on top with five crowns in a row. Astute at recognizing and developing talent, Littlefield would watch the annual intramural track meet and ask a few young men to join his team. It was quite a thrill to get such an invitation from Clyde Littlefield, a chance to score some points in a meet and maybe even earn a letter.

Never an eager recruiter, Littlefield knew his own reputation and that of UT were usually enough to draw good athletes to Austin. These are just a few of the superlative track and field men who competed for him between 1921 and 1961: distance runner Jim Reese, high jumper Rufus Haggard, sprinter Harvey "Chink" Wallender, long jumper Jud Atchison, pole vaulter Beefus Bryan, distance runner Jerry Thompson, sprinter Charley Parker, sprinter Dean Smith, sprinter Charlie Thomas, javelin thrower Bruce Parker, sprinter Eddie Southern, distance runner Joe Villareal and sprinter Ralph Alspaugh.

The Longhorns won the SWC title 25 of Littlefield's 41 years at the helm, and his athletes set several national and world records over that time. Three of them, Thompson, Smith and Southern, reached the pinnacle of track and field, competing in the 1948, 1952 and 1956 Olympics, respectively. Although Littlefield's UT teams never won an NCAA championship, they had eight top-10 finishes.

Long before it was common, he emphasized proper running form, and even insisted that all team members—including weight men and distance runners—practice starts, since speed was the key ingredient in nearly every event. Although he took pride in fielding a complete team, Littlefield had an affinity for sprinters, hurdlers and relay men. "Racehorses," he called them.

"He never remembered your name unless you ran 9.5 or better," said one former Longhorn with slight exaggeration. "The first thing he'd ask when he got on the bus was 'Is the sprint relay team here?' If it was, he'd say 'Then let's go.'"

Littlefield, a non-political person, disliked confrontations and had few enemies. Although L. Theo Bellmont had brought him back to the university in 1920 and elevated him to the head football coaching post in 1927, Littlefield did nothing to support the athletic director when he was fired a year later. When told of the move divorcing Bellmont from the program he had lifted to success, Littlefield merely replied "You see I go ahead with my work regardless of the action and have nothing to remark on the proposition."

In the mid-1930s, after his seven-year stint as head football coach, Littlefield introduced the "blind" baton pass, which revolutionized relay events. Before, runners in the exchange zone had lost precious time passing the baton in a careful and slow manner. But with many repetitions on the Memorial Stadium oval, Texas relay men learned to pass in full stride, with the lead runner not even looking back. A strange sight at first, when the results became evident, it was universally adopted. The impact of the blind pass in relay races compares to that of the "Fosbury flop" in high jumping, soccer-style kicking in football or the jump shot in basketball.

Regarded as the dean of Southwest Conference track coaches even before he was halfway through his career, Littlefield contracted pneumonia in 1939. He lay in a coma for eight days until a doctor located sulfa drugs, saving his life. He directed that year's Texas Relays from a hospital bed.

Longhorn teams kept winning during World War II, despite the drain on manpower at UT and elsewhere. Some people thought Littlefield had slowed down a bit or even lost his touch from 1947-1953, winning just one SWC title. While the word "burnout" was not yet in vogue, it would be understandable if he had that experience. Of course, no one pressured him to quit, and besides, he had a rugged constitution and loved his job.

In 1954, Littlefield had the Longhorns back on top of the Southwest Conference, and they finished fourth in the NCAA meet at Ann Arbor. His skeptics were surprised when, as a virtual senior citizen, he caught a second wind and put together a string of winning teams based on fine sprinters like Dean Smith, Charlie Thomas, Bobby Whilden, Eddie Southern and Ralph Alspaugh. The mid- and late 1950s have come to be seen as something of a golden age in Texas track history.

Littlefield was nearly 70 years old when he coached his final season in 1961. In *Champions: University of Texas Track and Field*, Wilbur Evans and Carlton Stowers wrote "It was Clyde Littlefield who developed UT track into a nationally recognized power, who persuaded university officials that an event which would become known as the Texas Relays would provide a noteworthy athletic showcase for the campus, who lured and tutored a long succession of gifted athletes to Texas and escorted them across the United States to prove their abilities. . . . He left few coaching achievements undone."

END OF AN ERA

The honors given to Clyde Littlefield over the course of his 88-year life would fill an entire page, but here are just a few: *Cactus* dedication (1928), referee of the Drake Relays (1950), assistant Olympic coach (1952), *Coach and Athlete* magazine's coach of the year (1957), Texas Sports Hall of Fame (1958), Longhorn Hall of Honor (1961), Texas Relays dedication (1963) and National Track and Field Hall of Fame (1981). He left quite a legacy.

Who could possibly fill such big shoes? Littlefield recommended his longtime assistant, T. J. "Froggy" Lovvorn, who may have deserved more credit than he got for UT's recent success, but was not widely regarded as head coaching material. Littlefield's loyal act proved unwise, because Lovvorn lasted just two years. There was a stark contrast between Littlefield's dignified manner and the rough-hewn Lovvorn. Actually, Littlefield was still on the scene, serving as supervisor in 1962 and 1963. He must have been dismayed as he saw the program he had nurtured for 41 years enter a steep decline. Lovvorn's two teams finished second and fifth in the SWC and did not score a point at the NCAA meet either year. Athletic director Darrell Royal got Lovvorn's resignation after the 1963 season, replacing him with former Houston and Baylor track coach Jack Patterson.

He was no immediate sensation either, but at least Patterson restored the Longhorns' regional dominance with runners like Preston Davis, Ricardo Romo, David Matina, Eddie Canada and Dave Morton. Patterson presided over the integration of the UT track team, as walk-on sprinter James Means became the SWC's first black letterman in any sport during the spring of 1966.

As Littlefield had done, when Patterson retired from coaching after the 1970 season (to serve as AD at Baylor), he turned it over to his assistant, yet with much better results this time. Cleburne Price stayed on for 15 years, as Texas won seven conference titles before fading to relative mediocrity. The SWC had become such a track and field stronghold that the Longhorns could not win a conference title from 1982-1985, but they finished 12th or higher in the NCAA meet all four years. Price coached four national champions—Robert Primeaux in the 440-yard hurdles (1973), Jim McGoldrick in the discus (1975), Dana LeDuc in the shot put (1976) and Einar Vilhjalmsson in the javelin (1983 and 1984).

For a long time, UT charged admission for every track meet at Memorial Stadium. For example, if you wanted to see an early-season triangular meet between Texas, TCU and Baylor, you had to pay. Eventually, rising administrative costs and declining attendance led Price and the Athletics

Council to just open the gates and let people in for free to all but the biggest meets.

Partly due to health problems, Price resigned in 1985, and athletic director DeLoss Dodds brought in Stan Huntsman, three-time national coach of the year at Tennessee. During his 15-year tenure in Knoxville, the Volunteers won the Southeastern Conference crown 13 times and were NCAA champions in 1974. While Huntsman was surely a big-time coach, he was moving to a tougher league. UT immediately broke the Arkansas stranglehold on SWC championships, finishing third at the 1986 NCAA meet and second in both 1987 and 1988.

Huntsman has built strong teams, and some of his brightest stars—so far—include javelin thrower Dag Wennlund, long jumper Eric Metcalf, high jumper James Lott, hurdler Winthrop Graham, distance runner Harry Green and javelin thrower Patrik Boden. UT track and field got plenty of attention in 1988 when Huntsman and women's coach Terry Crawford headed the American Olympic effort in Seoul, South Korea.

It would be incorrect to claim that Memorial Stadium is the perfect track and field venue. Stadiums built for both football and track are less common today than in the 1920s, and some schools with older dual-purpose facilities have moved their tracks out, a notion that was contemplated at UT in 1968.

As mentioned earlier, the location of Memorial Stadium's east and west stands and the presence of a football field inside the track dictate somewhat long straightaways and tight turns. The stadium's track, converted from 440 yards to 400 meters in the summer of 1977, has 110-meter straightaways and 90-meter turns, whereas a "pure" track of modern design has both straightaways and turns that are 100 meters long.

Ever since the installation of synthetic surfaces at the stadium in 1969, some field events such as the discus and javelin throw must take place across Waller Creek at Clark Field (the former Freshman Field). But whatever drawbacks Memorial Stadium has as a track and field facility, it compensates with abundant seating and a tradition of great performances.

In 1963, as Clyde Littlefield was retiring, Sam Blair of the *Dallas Morning News* wrote " . . . the huge horseshoe on San Jacinto Blvd. has become a shrine of speed, spring and strength. Some lusty records and performances have been achieved there, and there'll undoubtedly be more in the future." As with football, it is impossible to document them all, so the following are highlights from some of the bigger track meets held at the stadium through the years.

TEXAS RELAYS (MARCH 27, 1925)

The origin of the Texas Relays is fairly well known. In 1923, the Longhorn medley relay team took part in the Kansas Relays, setting a world record in the process. Littlefield came back to campus with the idea of putting on a similar track and field meet, one in which schools from all over the country could compete in Austin's pleasant springtime weather.

Littlefield had no trouble selling Bellmont on such an annual event, although the UT administration was initially cool to it. The timing of all this is quite interesting, as it preceded by several months the initial thrust of funding and building Memorial Stadium. The Texas Relays would have had little chance of success at decrepit old Clark Field, so perhaps Littlefield's proposal spurred Bellmont and Stark to action.

What the *Austin American-Statesman* called "the first grand track and field carnival ever held in the South" drew around 400 athletes from 42 universities, colleges, junior colleges and high schools. Out-of-state institutions included Illinois, Drake, Oklahoma, Ohio State, Missouri, Butler and Kansas. Also invited were three Olympians: high jumper Harold Osborne, distance runner Joie Ray and sprinter Jackson Scholz.

Littlefield had put on a couple of minor track meets at the stadium before the first Texas Relays, and Austin was ready when the athletes arrived. Congress Avenue was decorated, and the hardware—$2,000 worth of loving cups, gold watches and gold, silver and bronze medals—were on display in a window of the Scarbrough Building.

Bellmont had hoped for attendance of 4,000, and he got 6,000, ensuring that the Texas Relays would be more than a one-year affair. It consisted of 30 events, beginning at 2 P.M. and concluding after 3 1/2 hours.

More than 60 officials, primarily UT faculty members, made sure the events ran on time and with minimal confusion. The starter of the inaugural Texas Relays was former Baylor hurdler Earl "Mule" Frazier, who did that job for 40 years. There was no honorary referee in 1925, but over the next four years, these notable men served in that position: Big 10 commissioner Major John Griffith, University of Chicago football coach Amos Alonzo Stagg, Michigan football coach Fielding "Hurry-Up" Yost and Notre Dame football coach Knute Rockne.

The Texas Relays did not choose an outstanding performer until 1946, or an outstanding team until 1956. Undoubtedly the best individual show the first year was put on by Osborne, who broke his own world record in the high jump with a leap of 6' 8 15/16". That record would last for another 10 years. Butler was probably the top team, since it won the 440-yard relay, the half-mile relay and the mile relay. The Longhorns were not entirely shut out, as the medley relay team, anchored by Jim Reese, took first place.

Friday night, in a banquet at the University Commons, President Walter Splawn served as toastmaster and handed out awards. Four months after the dedication football game against Texas A&M, UT had exposed Memorial Stadium to visitors from beyond Texas, and most were impressed.

Olympian Jackson Scholz, who liked the track so much that he stayed an extra week to train, said that the Texas Relays would soon rival the big meets at Kansas, Drake and Penn, and he proved to be right. Missouri coach Bob Simpson said "Believe me, we envy you. Down here, you can run outdoors almost all year round, while it will be two weeks before we'll leave our indoor track in Columbia. I predict that some day the University of Texas will be a Mecca for all outdoor athletic events."

SWC MEET (MAY 12-13, 1933)

The 1933 Southwest Conference track and field meet promised to be a heated, hard-fought battle for many reasons. The Texas Relays were in the midst of a three-year break due mostly to the Depression, and Littlefield was eager to have the conference meet back in Austin. Rice had hosted it in 1932, when disputes arose over the true winner of the 100-yard dash, possible cheating in shot-put measurement and the Owls' use of an ineligible athlete. Sprinters Ed Holloway of Rice and Edgar "Cotton" Meyer of Texas developed a grudge, as did 880-yard specialists Ray Harbour of Rice and George Adams of UT.

Texas, Rice and Texas A&M were the big three of the SWC at the time; in fact, between 1920 and 1959, no other school won a title. The Horns, Owls and Aggies conducted a close triangular meet in Houston the week before the 1933 conference showdown, so they were ready for some old-fashioned brotherly hate at Memorial Stadium.

After the Friday preliminaries, Rice was in a strong position, but it did not last. Meyer bested his old nemesis, Holloway, in the 100 (9.7 seconds) and 220 (21.3), and ran on two winning relay teams to earn high-point honors. Meyer, a senior who lost many informal races to UT freshman sprint sensation Chink Wallender, came through when it counted. Wallender, by the way, lost a special 100-yard dash event to future teammate H. V. Reeves of Schreiner Institute.

Longhorn Alex Cox won the 440 for the second straight year, as did O'Neal Archer in the mile and captain Lane Blakeney in the two-mile. Football star Harrison Stafford made a big contribution as well, finishing third in the broad jump, fourth in the javelin, fourth in the 220-yard low hurdles and running on the victorious sprint relay team.

Only two SWC records were set in the 1933 meet, as Honk Irwin of Texas A&M threw the shot 49' 8 3/4", and "Jumbo" Jim Petty of Rice threw the discus 154' 2 3/8". Weldon Hart of the *Austin American-Statesman* traced the Owls' collapse that day to Meyer's surprise win over Holloway in the 100.

"I am mighty proud over the outcome of the conference meet," said Littlefield, who again showed an ability to motivate his team members and have them peak for the big meets. "We hadn't expected victory. My boys won by the dint of hard work."

He could not have been too happy with the puny attendance at the meet, which was free on Friday, and cost 75 cents for adults and 40 cents for students and children on Saturday. But money was very tight in 1933, which was also a nadir in football attendance at the stadium.

TEXAS RELAYS (APRIL 5, 1941)

The genial Clyde Littlefield had a habit of forgetting people's names, of giving predictable pep talks before a meet, and of saying each year "This was the greatest Texas Relays ever." In 1941 at least, it was true, especially from a Longhorn perspective. The weather was ideal, there were many strong entries, and the meet ran with precision. One of the student volunteers was Rooster Andrews, beginning an association of more than 50 years with the Texas Relays.

From her throne in the middle of the field, UT Sweetheart Gloria Obar awarded medals and demure kisses to the various winners, many of them wearing orange and white. The top performance came from the Texas sprint-medley relay team, which consisted of Morris "Red" Barefield, Billy Seay, Fred Ramsdell and the long-striding Mac Umstattd. Their 3:24 set a national record.

A world record seemed in sight during the 440-yard relay. Seay, Carlton Terry and Ramsdell had given Lonnie Hill a big lead, but Hill suffered a muscle cramp halfway through his leg of the race and struggled to the finish line with a time of 42 seconds. It was good enough to win, but Southern California's world mark of 40.5 held up.

Olympic pole-vault champion Earle Meadows won his event, as did Billy Brown of LSU in the broad jump, breaking Jud Atchison's Texas Relays record. Brown also finished third in the 100-yard dash, behind Terry and Seay.

The Longhorns' Jack Hughes threw the discus a career-best 165' 9 1/2" for his third straight title. High jumper Don Boydston of Oklahoma A&M also sought to repeat, but had to settle for a tie with Dub Walters of Baylor, as both went 6' 7 7/8". Drake's runners broke the meet record in the two-mile relay by four seconds, and in the college division, North Texas set a new sprint relay record of 3:15.4. The high school sprint-medley relay record was broken, too, by Dallas Woodrow Wilson. That is important mostly because the anchor man was Jerry Thompson, soon to become one of UT's greatest distance runners.

Disappointment over the no-show of hurdle rivals Fred Wolcott and Boyce Gatewood was forgotten in the afterglow of the 14th Texas Relays, then billing itself as the "Olympics of the Southwest." *Austin American-Statesman* sports editor Wilbur Evans analyzed the performances in Memorial Stadium that day and proved that it had been a great meet. The results of common events in the 1941 Texas Relays and the 1940 Kansas, Drake and Penn relay meets showed that fully two-thirds of the best performances had taken place in Austin.

This proved to be a high-water mark for the Texas Relays, which was mostly a schoolboy meet during the war years.

TEXAS RELAYS (APRIL 6-7, 1951)

Sprint supremacy was usually conceded to UT in the Texas Relays, but not in 1951. The departed Charley Parker and Perry Samuels had won a lot of races for Littlefield over the past four years, and Dean Smith and Charlie Thomas were still freshmen, so junior Ralph Person was the main sprinter on the squad. The Longhorns' graying coach could only hope to win some field events.

Now conducted over two days, the 24th Texas Relays was part of a grand social whirl in Austin, as a huge crowd gathered downtown for the Round-Up parade. Unlike most schools, which pegged homecoming weekend to a fall football game, for UT it happened in the spring with Round-Up and the track meet.

Confirming Littlefield's fears, the host Longhorns were not much more than also-rans. Only broad jumper Charles Meeks won an event, while Ray Marek, winner of the javelin the past two years, took second place.

The big winners were UT's primary football rivals, Oklahoma and Texas A&M. The Sooners took the 440, 880, sprint-medley and two-mile relays, while the Aggies' Walter Davis and Darrow Hooper etched their names in the Texas Relays record books. Davis, who split time between basketball and track, elevated to 6' 9" to break Harold Osborne's 26-year old high-jump record.

Hooper was on his way to becoming one of the best weight men ever in the Southwest Conference. He threw the shot 53' 1" for a new meet record and won the discus with a heave of 148' 9 3/4". Named the outstanding performer, Hooper was one of six future Olympians competing in the 1951 Texas Relays.

Javier Montez of Texas Western (now UT-El Paso) successfully defended his 3,000-meter title and took third in the mile, an event Littlefield had named after Jerry Thompson in 1950. Those promising young UT sprinters, Smith and Thomas, competing in the freshman/junior college division, finished one-two in the 100-yard dash.

Littlefield knew that help was coming, but he needed it immediately. Whereas in earlier years, up to 200 students sought places on the UT track or cross-country teams, now the number was just 40. So he issued a call via the *Daily Texan*, asking for volunteers, especially football players. "I don't work the boys very hard, and the ones with natural ability don't have to work hard," he pleaded. But the Longhorns were to finish second to Texas A&M at the SWC meet the next month.

UIL MEET (MAY 6-7, 1955)

Every year since 1911, the University Interscholastic League (UIL) has held its state track and field meet in Austin, first at the original Clark Field and then at Memorial Stadium. High school athletes making it through district and regional meets got a chance to be part of the extravaganza. Winning an event, placing or simply taking part would remain a high point in the lives of many people long after youth had passed.

The UIL meet had a homogeneous air in the mid-1950s; integration was nearly a decade away, as black athletes competed in the Prairie View Interscholastic League. Likewise, the inclusion of girls in the "perspiring arts," in competition before a paying audience, was an idea seldom broached then.

Eddie Southern of Dallas Sunset was the subject of much parlor talk as the 1955 meet began. By far the best high school track athlete in the state, it was a foregone conclusion that he would win whatever three events (the maximum) he entered. While Southern had yet to decide where he would attend college, Clyde Littlefield's eyes lit up whenever he saw him run. A rumor had recently been floating around that Littlefield might retire, but Southern in a UT track uniform would probably keep him around for at least four more years.

Boys running in the 100-yard dash and 120-yard low hurdles were overjoyed to learn that the magnificent Southern would not compete in their events. Sunset coach Herman Scruggs had him in the 120-yard high hurdles and the 220 and 440-yard dashes. There had been other great individual performances at the UIL meet in recent times, by Ken Hall of Sugarland (1952 and 1953) and James Segrest of Bangs (1954), but nothing like this.

In Friday's 440-yard qualifying heat, Southern whipped around the stadium track like a greyhound, crossing the line 30 yards ahead of his closest competitor, in a time of 47.4 seconds. He cut .2 seconds off a seven-year old national record. The next day, in the finals, he broke his own record with a 47.2, the fastest quarter mile by *anybody* in the U.S. in 1955. For comparison, the SWC record was then 46.9, and the NCAA record was 46.2. Southern clearly demonstrated prodigious talent.

In the 220, he tied Jesse Owens' national record of 20.7 seconds and won the 120-yard high hurdles in a disappointing—for him—14.2. Track observers could not remember another one like the crew-cut Southern. After his final race, as sweat and cinder dust mingled on his cheeks, he just said "Well, it was quite a day."

He accounted for most of Sunset's 32 1/6 points, tying for second place behind Baytown. Although Southern got most of the spotlight, other athletes did well. Baytown's mile-relay team, anchored by future Longhorn Wally Wilson, set a national record of 3:17.9, and Troy Harber of Lubbock scored 22 points.

Within a week, Southern ended the suspense and declared that he would accept an athletic scholarship to UT. From 1956-1959, he won many 100, 220 and 440-yard dashes as well as hurdles events and was a key member of Littlefield's greatest relay team. A silver medalist in the 1956 Melbourne Olympics, Southern co-captained the 1959 Longhorn track squad and remains an esteemed figure in Texas sports history.

NCAA MEET (JUNE 14-15, 1957)

For years, Littlefield had sought to hold the national collegiate meet at Memorial Stadium. Despite his widespread reputation and many contacts throughout the NCAA, he was consistently turned down because of UT's adherence to racial segregation. The number of black athletes at non-Southern schools had grown, and Texas would never serve as host until it dropped the old policy. In 1956, the Board of Regents opened athletic facilities to people of all ethnic backgrounds. (This was something of an after-the-fact move, since interracial competition had begun at the stadium in 1954 with Washington State football player Duke Washington.) NCAA officials soon announced that the 1957 meet would be held below the Mason-Dixon line in Austin, Texas.

Southern California, national champions every year from 1949-1955, and UCLA, which won it in 1956, were on probation and would not be competing. Whether they could have beaten a talented team like Villanova is debatable, because the Mainliners, as they were then known, featured three Olympians; two of them had won gold medals at Melbourne.

The 1957 Texas team was the best in years, but it would do poorly in the most important meet yet held on its home track. Littlefield's athletes were tired from a long and strenuous season, sophomore sprint star Eddie Southern was injured, and no relay races were run. The NCAA then believed that such events would water down the meet, and preferred to measure only individual performances. This not only hurt the Longhorns' chances—they had a dynamite 440-yard relay quartet—but it irked the relay-conscious fans, too. As Lou Maysel wrote in the *Austin American-Statesman*, "Ending a meet with the 220-yard low hurdles is like topping off a meal with a helping of spinach."

Nearly 300 athletes from 79 schools were at the meet, which was conducted at night under the stadium lights. It produced few upsets, but most of the big stars came through with big performances. One world record was set, two were tied, and eight meet records fell, as did three national records and nine Memorial Stadium records.

Abilene Christian's Bobby Morrow, twice named outstanding performer at the Texas Relays and possessor of three Olympic gold medals, took no prisoners in the sprints. He won the 100-yard dash in 9.4 seconds and the 220 in 21-flat, both of them going away. Bob Gutowski of Occidental won the pole vault with a world-record 15' 9 3/4" and finished fifth in the broad jump, behind Gregg Bell of Indiana. Bell's leap of 26' 7" approached Jesse Owens' 22-year old world record. Kansas discus man Al Oerter, a three-time winner at the Texas Relays, took his event with a throw of 185' 4". He would go on to win four Olympic gold medals.

But it was Jumbo Elliott's Villanova team that won the NCAA meet with strong showings from middle-distance runner Ron Delaney, 440-yard specialist Charlie Jenkins, pole vaulter Don Bragg and high jumpers Phil Reavis and Charley Stead. With 47 points, Villanova led California (32), Fresno State (23) and all the rest. Texas scored 13 points for 11th place, as Joe Villareal took fourth in the mile, Pat McGuire was fourth in the broad jump, Bruce Parker was fifth in the javelin, Alvie Ashley tied for fifth in the high jump, and Hollis Gainey came in sixth in the 100-yard dash.

There was abundant praise for Memorial Stadium's track and field setup, and no record exists of any problems with accommodating black athletes in Austin. Attendance was fairly disappointing, however, as only 5,000 fans showed up for the Friday night preliminaries and 9,500 for the Saturday night finals. Seventeen years would pass before the NCAA again held its meet at UT.

TEXAS RELAYS (APRIL 5-6, 1963)

If the 1962 Texas Relays were not called "the sociological relays," they should have been. Stanley Wright's Texas Southern squad was a *tour de force* that year, winning five baton events in the college division, all in meet-record time. Never before had a black school been invited to UT's prestigious track and field carnival, and TSU was unanimously chosen as the outstanding team. To prove it was no fluke, the Tigers proceeded to win 15 of 17 such races in the Kansas and Drake relays.

Homer Jones had gone on to play pro football with the New York Giants, but speedburners like T. J. Bell, Ray Saddler, Overton Williams, Major Adams and Les Milburn were back in 1963, as good as ever. This time, though, the flying Tigers won *six* relay events and again copped outstanding team honors.

The 1963 Texas Relays were notable for other reasons. Clyde Littlefield was finally stepping down from his coach-emeritus position, and it did not pass unnoticed. The night before the meet, 450 friends and admirers gathered at the Driskill Hotel to honor him in an elaborate program. Governor John B. Connally declared April 4 "Clyde Littlefield Day" in Texas, and he was, naturally, the honorary referee of the meet.

Over the years, several things have sparked the Texas Relays. In 1927, Bellmont brought some Tarahumara Indians in to run from San Antonio to the stadium in Austin; famous non-collegians like Paavo Nurmi (1929) and Glenn Cunningham (1935) took part; there was the rather dubious 1941 "suitcase relay" in which porters from downtown hotels ran with suitcases in their hands; in the late 1940s, the "football relay" was instituted, in which football players wearing cleats and jerseys ran up and down Memorial Stadium's field carrying a pigskin rather than a baton; fraternity races and a masters' mile were attempted in the late 1960s; and a marathon was run around Town Lake in the 1970s.

What was in 1963 considered just another "special event" was the introduction of women's competition at the Texas Relays. Only two races were run, the 100-yard dash (won by Janice Rinehart in 11.8 seconds) and the 440-yard relay (won by the Texas Track Club of Abilene in 50.7).

Women's competition lapsed in 1964, but it resumed in 1965 with these same two events. Other sprints, relays, field events and distance races were gradually added to the program. But only in the mid-1970s, when Dr. Donna Lopiano arrived as women's athletic director, was women's competition treated with full respect.

The 1963 Texas Relays drew 12,000 people, who saw a record 1,474 entries competing on the black cinders and green grass of Memorial Stadium. Besides Texas Southern's high-stepping strutters, other fine performances included a 16' 1" pole vault by Fred Hansen of Rice, Emporia State's John Camien upsetting Dyrol Burleson and Bill Dotson in the mile and Texas A&M's Danny Roberts winning both the shotput and discus. Froggy Lovvorn's Longhorns did not win a single event, but Ohio University, under the tutelage of future Texas coach Stan Huntsman, took a pair of relay races.

SWC MEET (MAY 19, 1973)

Acrimony was the dominant theme of the 58th annual conference meet in 1973 at the stadium. Ever since UT spread-eagled the other SWC teams at the previous year's meet, there had been plenty of discussion, public and private, about the Longhorns' advantages. With 30 full scholarships, Cleburne Price had put together a big team, although not a great one, since Texas scored only one point in the 1972 national meet at the University of Oregon.

The NCAA had voted to limit track scholarships to 23 by 1976, but Baylor coach Clyde Hart complained that "Texas will still have too much of a dynasty going by 1976. They'll still have the finest track facilities, more money, three times as many coaches as anybody else and the state meet in Memorial Stadium."

Before the 1973 SWC meet, Price's team had won every outdoor meet it entered, set eight school records and had the conference's top marks or times in nine events. The only suspense was: How big of a landslide would it be? Under a new scoring system, UT won with 164 points, while Texas A&M was second with 77 1/2, and Rice came in third with 75.

Winners among the weight men were predictable, as SMU's Sammy Walker won his fourth SWC shotput title, Jim Pearce of Rice did the same in the javelin, and the Owls' Ken Stadel won for the third time in the discus, breaking Randy Matson's eight-year old record. The University of Houston, competing for the first time as a conference member, brought a skeletal team to Austin, but one that included former football player Wayne Johnson. He won the 100-yard dash and finished a close second in the 220.

SMU's 440-yard relay team (twins Gene and Joe Pouncy, Rufus Shaw and Mike Rideau) won in an impressive 39.8 seconds, while Texas (Ed Wright, Billy Jackson, John Lee and Don Sturgal) took the mile relay in 3:06.7. Longhorn sophomore Robert Primeaux was the winner of the 440-yard hurdles; a month later, he won that event in the NCAA meet in Baton Rouge.

Animosity was evident before, during and after the meet. Apart from Price and Hart sniping at each other, a disqualification in the three-mile race had Baylor's Pete Morales and UT's Tim Patton going nose-to-nose. There were accusations of bumping in both the preliminaries and finals of the 880-yard run, and SMU coach Jim Parr briefly disputed the results of the 100-yard dash.

"Every year there is controversy," said Hart. "If it doesn't stop, Southwest Conference track will be ruined." A bit of an overstatement, but Hart was right about the Texas track dynasty, since the Horns were in the early stages of a six-year rule over the SWC.

TEXAS RELAYS (APRIL 1-2, 1977)

Johnny Jones. The name still causes fluttering hearts among University of Texas track and field fans. An enormously talented athlete, Jones ran only one full season for Cleburne Price before concentrating on football, in which he had a fine career as a collegian and later as a pro with the New York Jets.

Nicknamed "Lam" for his hometown of Lampasas, Jones had quite a reputation before ever donning orange and white. In the 1976 UIL meet, he won the Class 3A 100 and 220-yard dashes, followed by a tremendous anchor leg to win the mile relay. Overcoming big odds, the 18-year old Jones made the U.S. Olympic team. At Montreal, he finished sixth in the 100-meter finals and helped the 400-meter relay team win the gold.

With little rest, he joined Earl Campbell and friends on the 1976 UT football team, and soon it was again time for track season, when he became the swiftest Longhorn ever. That growing belief was fueled by his performance in the 1977 Texas Relays, the golden anniversary of the meet. Jones would face some tough competition in the 100 meters, like Clifford Wiley of Kansas, Dwayne Evans of Arizona, 1976 event winner Ed Preston of Arkansas State and TCU-ex Bill Simpson. Price said "The quality of this meet is absolutely unbelievable. Realistically, we could run a school record in the 440-yard relay and still not win."

Between 15,000 and 20,000 fans, the biggest college track crowd at Memorial Stadium in a long time, gathered to witness a fine meet featuring over two dozen Olympians of various nationalities. Clyde Littlefield, then 85 and living in a retirement home, was in attendance.

Littlefield always loved the sprints, and this one was special. Jones and the others settled in their blocks, prepared for an all-out drag race down the stadium's west straightaway. As the gun went off, Jones jumped to a quick start, had a clear lead at 40 meters and with a slight tailwind, powered to the finish line. The electronic timer picked the worst possible moment to malfunction, because Jones had apparently broken the world record. Three hand-held watches had him at 9.80, 9.85 and 9.94 seconds, so the middle figure was given as Jones' time, although this precluded recognition as a world record.

"Every man has his day," said Jones. "It was a thrill to win here. The timer is just one of those things that happen." He would be named the meet's outstanding performer, although many other athletes did well, too. Niall O'Shaughnessy of Arkansas made up a deficit of 20 yards on Wilson Waigwa of UT-El Paso on the anchor leg of the distance-medley relay. Earl Bell of Arkansas State won his second consecutive Texas Relays pole vault title. UT's Paul Craig won the Jerry Thompson Mile in 4:01.17, while Henry Marsh of Brigham Young won the steeplechase in a meet-record 8:27.7. The Prairie View A&M Pantherettes dominated the women's competition with four first places and two seconds.

A few weeks later at the Southwest Conference meet in Austin, Johnny Jones put on another super performance: (1) fourth in the long jump, (2) anchor on the Longhorns' winning 440-yard relay team, (3) first in the 100-yard dash, (4) first in the 220 and (5) anchor on the winning mile relay team. He accounted for 29 points, as UT won its sixth straight conference title.

NCAA MEET (JUNE 5-7, 1980)

The American boycott of the Moscow Olympics (in response to the 1979 Soviet invasion of Afghanistan) had already been announced when 600 college athletes converged on Memorial Stadium for the 1980 NCAA meet. Although debate over the wisdom of the boycott was still going on, at least Cleburne Price was sure the athletes had no reason to hold back.

Price had declared this his best team yet, but he did not expect the Longhorns to contend for the national title. Even so, the SWC had several strong entries, including Texas A&M sprinter Curtis Dickey, SMU's Michael Carter in the shot put, Aggie pole vaulter Randy Hall, Baylor's Todd Harbour in the 1500 meters, UT's Oskar Jakobsson in the discus and shot put and a Houston freshman phenom named Carl Lewis in the long jump.

Lewis had qualified to compete in the 100 and 200-meter races, but he chose to focus on the long jump, calling himself "a long jumper who sprints." A future winner of six—and counting—Olympic gold medals, Lewis did run the anchor leg on the Cougars' 400-meter relay team.

Defending champion UT-El Paso and 1978 winner Southern California were the two favorites in the meet, much of which took place under 90° heat and high humidity. The Trojans' James Sanford, who came in with the best times in the 100 and 200 meters, won neither race. His reputation did not faze Auburn freshman Stanley Floyd, who won the 100 meters in 10.10 seconds and stated "I was the guy to beat. . . . This is a fast track, one of the better ones I've run on, and that's good because, man, it's hot."

Lewis captured the long jump with a wind-aided leap of 27' 4 3/4", Carter won the shot put, Hall won the pole vault, and Jakobsson took second in the shot put and third in the discus. UT's Desmond Morris tied for fourth in the high jump, and the Longhorn 1600-meter relay team of Ben Omodiale, Greg Watson, Ian Stapleton and Ricky Faggett was fifth.

UT-El Paso's Suleiman Nyambui (co-outstanding performer at the 1979 Texas Relays) won the 10,000 meters on Friday night and the 5,000 meters on Saturday night. Quite an achievement, considering the heat. The Miners roared to their second of four straight NCAA championships and an unprecedented sweep of the 1980 collegiate cross-country, indoor and outdoor titles.

Price did not conceal his unhappiness over the way UT-El Paso's "foreign legion" was dominating college track in the United States. Foreign athletes, some in their mid-20s, were a big part of the Miners' program (and many others, including UT, to lesser degrees), but coach Ted Banks made no apologies for it.

The 1980 NCAA meet was marked by a near-tragic incident. Tim Scott of Texas A&M, while practicing shot-put throws, hit official James Smith in the head with a 16-pound iron ball. Several athletes were visibly shaken as Smith received emergency treatment and was rushed to Brackenridge Hospital with a depressed skull fracture. Although doctors initially feared for his life, Smith survived and recovered. He also sued the university for $75,000.

Another footnote to this meet: Kansas State athletic director DeLoss Dodds served as running referee. One year later, he would become the AD at Texas.

AIAW MEET (MAY 28-30, 1981)

The Association of Intercollegiate Athletics for Women (AIAW) was an organization approaching demise in 1981, since its function would soon be taken over by the older, male-dominated NCAA. Women's track and field was undergoing rapid improvement at the time, as a slew of Memorial Stadium records were broken at the AIAW nationals.

UT coach Phil Delavan looked for a top-ten finish and possible victories by his 1600-meter relay team, Tammy Etienne in the 400-meter hurdles and Robbin Coleman in the 400 meters. But there were some high-powered teams coming to Austin that threatened to leave the Lady Longhorns far behind.

Tennessee, led by future Texas coach Terry Crawford, had won outstanding team honors in the Texas Relays earlier that season. The Lady Volunteers had such runners as Benita Fitzgerald, Cathy Rattray and AIAW 800-meter champion Delisa Walton. Their main rival was UCLA, with Jeannette Bolden, Sherri Howard, Oralee Fowler and two future stars of the first magnitude—Florence Griffith and Jackie Joyner.

The Lady Bruins were a solid favorite to win the team title, although other schools had their hopefuls. Could Louise Ritter of Texas Woman's University win her fourth straight high jump crown? Would Merlene Ottey of Nebraska break the women's 100-meter world record? Might North Carolina State distance star Julie Shea repeat her 3K/5K/10K triple whammy from last year's meet in Oregon?

Not many people showed up to learn the answers to those questions, and the weather did not help. Still wet and bruised from the Memorial Day floods that killed 13 people, Austin got more rain during this three-day meet. They ran, anyway.

The team championship came down to the 1600-meter relay, an intense duel between Tennessee and UCLA. On the anchor lap, the Lady Vols' Delisa Walton ran stride-for-stride with Oralee Fowler of UCLA and passed her in the final stretch for a 3:31.7 victory.

The 10-member Tennessee team took a victory lap at the end of the meet, just as the sky was clearing. Crawford pointed at the rainbow looming over the stadium and said triumphantly "That's for us. We found the pot of gold!"

Despite UT's 14th-place finish, Delavan could be optimistic. The next year in College Station, with some veterans and freshmen like Susan Shurr and Tara Arnold, the Lady Longhorns won the final AIAW national championship.

UIL MEET (MAY 10-11, 1985)

"With the caliber of athletes we have, I wouldn't be surprised to see some national marks set," said UIL director Dr. Bailey Marshall on the eve of the 1985 state meet in Austin. And he was right. Texas high school track and field had by then evolved into the strongest in the country. Crowds of more than 20,000 had become common at the meet, and 1985 (the first to fully include girls) proved one of the best.

Dallas Roosevelt, Class 5A champion the previous two years, was back with its main man, Roy Martin. The outstanding male performer in the Texas Relays in 1984 and 1985, he was the first high school athlete to be so honored. Roosevelt made it three titles in a row with a winning 400-meter relay time of 40.2 (tying the 1970 national record of Dallas Lincoln) and another victory in the 1600-meter relay. Martin anchored both of those races and won the 200 meters, as well.

On the 4A level, Joe DeLoach of Bay City was out to duplicate his 100 and 200-meter wins from 1984. He won the longer race in 20.44 seconds but lost the 100 in a photo finish to Corsicana's Byron Grant.

Reuben Reina of San Antonio Jay won the 5A 1600-meter run and the 3200 meters in a state-record 9:00.1. Another top performance came from Wanda Gardner of DeSoto, whose 47' 10" shot put broke the girls' state record by two feet.

Houston Sterling won the girls' 5A championship, as Tanya Davis busted the national record in the 100-meter hurdles with a time of 13.2, while teammate Carlette Guidry was the most amazing athlete, of either gender, in the stadium that day. The 15-year old sophomore won the long jump, the triple jump (barely missing the national high-school mark) and the 100 meters. She came in second in the 200 and ran on Sterling's winning 1600-meter relay team. Guidry's coach, Edward Robinson, said "She can improve in all the events. In the next two years, she could be phenomenal."

Among the other stars of the 1985 UIL meet, Reina became the third member of his family to run—and win—distance events at Arkansas, and DeLoach had a fine sprint career at Houston. Martin got off to a promising start at SMU, winning the Southwest Conference 100 and 200-meter titles as a freshman before slowing down and eventually dropping out of school.

SWC MEET (MAY 14-15, 1988)

The 73rd Southwest Conference track and field meet fell in an Olympic year, 1988. The head coaches of the two American teams, Stan Huntsman and Terry Crawford, split time between their regular gigs at UT and their once-in-a-lifetime Olympic opportunities.

A few athletes were sitting out the season (and thus the meet), preparing for the Olympic trials in July and, they hoped, the games in Seoul: three-time 400-meter champ Roddie Haley of Arkansas, shot put and discus man Randy Barnes of Texas A&M and Aggie sprinter Floyd Heard. Others in Austin were pacing themselves somewhat, although several turned in fine performances.

Among the men, it was a two-team race, between Texas, the conference winner in 1986 and 1987, and Arkansas, which was loaded with talent, especially distance runners like Joe Falcon, Matt Taylor, Chris Zinn, Reuben Reina and Richard Cooper. UT's Harry Green held the SWC 10,000-meter record of 28:19.5, but he had never beaten Falcon, and it happened again as the Hog star won both the 5K and 10K.

Greg West of Texas A&M vaulted 18' 3 1/4", and UT's Stefan Petersson won the javelin with a heave of 238' 2". Winthrop Graham, who would win an Olympic silver medal for Jamaica, set a meet-record 48.87 in the 400-meter hurdles and ran a blazing leg in the 1600-meter relay for Texas.

Baylor sophomore Michael Johnson brought the world's fastest 200-meter time of the year into the meet, but could only manage second place to Joe DeLoach of Houston (19.98). Future 100-meter world record holder Leroy Burrell of UH also finished second, to Raymond Stewart of TCU (10.01).

Surprise Arkansas victories in the long jump and triple jump made the difference, as the Razorbacks earned 155 points, just six more than Texas. The women's competition was not so close, as Crawford's track and field juggernaut won 12 of 19 events and ran away with the team title. Freshman Carlette Guidry, who had just led UT to the NCAA indoor championship, had another stupendous meet, winning the 100 meters (a meet-record 11.18), 200 (23-flat), long jump (20' 11 1/4"), and running on the Lady Horns' victorious 400-meter relay team.

For the third straight year, UT's Karol Davidson won both the 800 and 1500-meter races. Aisling Ryan, of Arkansas by way of Ireland, won both the 5K and 10K, and teammate Sally Ramsdale took the 3K.

After getting dunked by her athletes in the steeplechase water pit, Terry Crawford was asked about Carlette "Turbo" Guidry. She said "I think before she is finished, she'll be the dominant woman in the history of the conference."

TEXAS RELAYS (APRIL 4-6, 1991)

Francie Larrieu-Smith's reputation in women's distance running was firmly established long before the 1991 Texas Relays. First as a 13-year old California *wunderkind*, then as a collegian, a four-time Olympian and a road racer, few women had run so fast and for so long. She had not done badly at the Texas Relays, winning the 1500 meters in 1974, 1975 and 1979, the

10K in 1987 and the 5K in 1990. At an age (38) when most runners have lost speed, Larrieu-Smith was not only maintaining, but getting faster.

Under a light rain on the meet's first night, she toed the line with a dozen other women in the 10,000 meters. Although defending champion Lisa Stone of Baylor was there, she had little chance to win, as Larrieu-Smith broke to a big early lead. She hit the tape 31 minutes, 28.92 seconds later, the new holder of the American women's record, cutting more than six seconds off Mary Decker-Slaney's nine-year old mark.

Larrieu-Smith revealed that the race was basically a tuneup for the London Marathon three weeks hence. "I knew I was in good shape. I came in at a peak," she said. "I felt so good, I got in a rhythm and kept going."

Some observers were perplexed when she did not receive female outstanding performer honors, which went instead to high schooler Stacy Swank of Texas Military Institute for winning the 1500 and 3200-meter races. Another likely candidate was Carlette Guidry, whose 11.2-second 100-meter win was then the second fastest of her brilliant career. A few weeks later at the NCAA meet, she won both the 100 and 200 meters.

The outstanding performer among men was Gordon McKee, formerly of Southwest Texas, who flew 27' 3/4" for a new Texas Relays long-jump record. That is farther than well-known people like Ernie Shelby, Ralph Boston, Bob Beamon, Carl Lewis, Mike Conley and Eric Metcalf ever jumped at the stadium.

For the fifth time in six years, the 400-meter relay went to TCU (39.23), and Baylor won the 1600-meter relay for the third straight year. Perhaps the biggest surprise was the showing made by junior colleges. Barton County JC of Kansas and Blinn JC both had a crew of fleet athletes that compared with any in the university division. Scholarship and coaching-staff reductions brought on by NCAA rulings showed their effect at the 1991 Texas Relays, putting the future of college track and field in some doubt.

The meet referee was Charlie Thomas, the Longhorn sprint star of the early 1950s, recently retired from a 32-year coaching stint at Texas A&M. During that time, Thomas' Aggie teams won five conference titles and had six top-six finishes in the NCAA meet. He coached 124 SWC champions, 101 all-Americans, 22 individual national champions, eight world record holders and several Olympians. The long and successful record Thomas put together would have made his old coach, Clyde Littlefield, quite proud.

Memories of Memorial Stadium

Who knows just how many people have attended and participated in athletic events at UT's Memorial Stadium over a span of almost seven decades? Counting every football game and every track meet, 25 million may be a conservative estimate. And each one has a story to tell.

The following recollections about the stadium come from letters and interviews held in 1990 and 1991. Some of the interviews took place in the stadium's stands or press box, as will be evident.

There has been no attempt to emphasize one particular viewpoint (in fact, some stories flatly contradict each other) or to embellish the history of the stadium. With only light editing and in alphabetical order, here are the memories of 89 athletes, coaches, alumni, administrators, faculty members, sportswriters and others regarding Memorial Stadium and the events it has hosted.

Fred Akers, Arkansas football player (1957-1959), UT assistant coach (1966-1974) and head coach (1977-1986): "While I was at Arkansas, we played in Austin once, in 1958. I just remember that Memorial Stadium was large, and it was a good football atmosphere. The tradition that engulfs the place has to rub off on you, whether you are a player, a coach or a fan. And there have been some great athletes, great teams and great games at that stadium. . . . By the time I came back as head coach in 1977, the old locker room was a dinosaur, so in my first meeting with the Athletics Council, I told them that we ought to take a bulldozer, flatten it and start over. They didn't realize that other schools had much nicer player facilities than the University of Texas. It was hurting us in recruiting, so we just had to have Neuhaus-Royal."

Marty Akins, UT football player (1972-1975): "As both a fan and participant in athletic events at Memorial Stadium, I've always felt its overpowering spirit and tradition. That exemplifies my feelings about the stadium."

Rooster Andrews, UT student manager, football and baseball player (1941-1944) and Texas Relays official: "I started coming down here for football games and track meets while I was in high school in 1939. I was here when Jack [Crain] made his run against Arkansas. . . . The University of Texas has been my life, no two ways about it, and a lot of it has taken place in the stadium. Really and truly, it doesn't seem that much different to me today. It's still the same joint."

Ed Barlow, 1927 UT graduate and former physical education professor: "Mr. Bellmont just worked with Lutcher Stark, and the rest of the Board of Regents went along. There were two or three times when the thing got bogged down, and Mr. Bellmont asked Lutcher to get the payroll done. . . . I watched the stadium going up. They were still using mules at the time, but everybody in Texas athletics knew that with the building of the stadium, we were moving out of the 19th century."

Skip Bayless, former *Dallas Times Herald* sportswriter: "Access to Memorial Stadium on the day of a game is awful, but it always is for on-campus stadiums. The press box is nice, but it's pretty high and a little bit cramped. To me, the stadium reflects the school itself: It's huge, stately and rather imposing."

Hub Bechtol, UT football player (1944-1946): "Those plaques in the stadium portals mean a great deal to me. I lost two brothers in World War II, and I just felt like I was playing for them. You don't hear many people talk about it any more. . . . I have the same old feeling every time I walk in. It's home. It's my stadium, but I never had such affection for it that I would have objected to them moving, because I've always felt that we ought to have first-class athletic facilities at the university."

Fred Bednarski, UT football player (1956-1958): "When I was in high school, attending University of Texas football games, it was my dream just to be on the team. I used to ask the players for their chinstraps . . . guys like Herb Gray and Tom Stolhandske. I didn't want to go anywhere else. . . . The locker rooms in the 1950s weren't anything fancy. The freshmen were separated from the varsity, and when you got your name put on a locker, there was a real feeling of pride. Playing for UT was the memory of a lifetime, and the stadium is the key to the whole thing."

Ted Bellmont, 1947 UT graduate: "My father [L. Theo Bellmont] knew that building Memorial Stadium would bring enormous business into the community and stimulate much interest among alumni. He was proud of the stadium, but it was a modest kind of pride. . . . He, like anyone who does monumental things, was the subject of controversy. He held no bitterness in his heart toward those who brought him down as athletic director. But I know this. He contributed more to student life at the University of Texas as the director of physical training than he had in prior years."

Dr. Margaret C. Berry, 1937 UT graduate: "When I came to the university as a freshman in the fall of 1933, I saw my first home football game, against the School of Mines (now UT-El Paso). What a thrill to walk into Memorial Stadium that first time! We didn't have a Bevo that year—or a Big Bertha, or a Smokey, or the big Texas flag. We didn't even know the 'Hook 'em, Horns' sign! But Memorial Stadium, which held only 40,500 fans then, was breathtaking on that warm September afternoon."

Jim Bertelsen, UT football player (1969-1971): "The stadium wasn't as impressive in 1968 as it is today because the upper deck wasn't there. When they were putting it in, I thought the jackhammering would go on forever. . . . Once you're here a while, you kind of get familiar with it, and you lose perspective of the stadium's size. If I had a choice, I'd prefer that the track not be there. I'd rather have the fans right down on you. . . . I'm kind of surprised they've let the stadium get as dirty as it is, with the water leaks and things like that. It's just going to speed up the deterioration, especially on the old part."

Joe Bleymaier, UT football player (1935-1937): "I was eight years old when we moved into that house on the stadium grounds. I've got some great memories from those days. My buddies would come around on the morning of a football game and stay until they closed the gates. We had a cow, some chickens, dogs, and a mackaw bird on a chain who would mimic the umpire calling balls and strikes in Clark Field across the street. . . . My father [Jake Bleymaier] was so dedicated to that place, he knew every blade of grass. He worked from sunup to sundown, and he also took care of the tennis courts, Clark Field and Freshman Field."

Fannie M. Boyls, 1925 UT graduate: "I recall one occasion—I believe it was just before our first football game in the new stadium—when the Women's Athletic Association director [Anna Hiss] called a meeting of the members and advised us as to how we should conduct ourselves at the football games. We could applaud by clapping our hands, but it would be unladylike for us to yell. I was so incensed at this admonition that I stood and made what must have been a very moving speech, favoring the right of women to yell at the games, just as the men were doing. I received a standing ovation and, as a result, we did attend the games and yell as loud as we could."

Glenn Brown, 1951 UT graduate and former public address announcer for track and radio broadcaster for basketball and football: "College track is probably not as popular today as it was 20 years ago, but it's still close to my heart. . . . We've got a group of track officials who have been here 10, 15, 25 years, some of them longer. They've run so many big meets, they just know how to do it, and that helped get the NCAA meet here in 1992. And the facilities had a lot to do with it. I think Memorial Stadium is a very good place to see a football game or track meet."

Quinton Bunton, former grounds crew worker: "I worked there from 1946 until about 1965, helping Bleymaier and the others. We'd mark off the field, cut the grass, clean the stadium up and line the track and tennis courts. We'd take the flags down after a game, but there was a different crew that put the tarp on the field or took it off. That was a big-ass chore [laughter]. We took care of the baseball field, too. . . . It was just a damn job, nothing special, and I haven't been to a game since, even though I like football and baseball."

Mike Campbell, UT assistant football coach (1957-1976) and coordinator of the Texas Longhorn Education Foundation: "I was right by Frank Erwin on the day of the Waller Creek incident. Frank brought in a guy with a chainsaw, who must have been 6' 5" and 230 pounds, who looked like Little Abner [laughter]. Frank said 'OK, let her go!' and that boy started up his chainsaw. The people in the trees jumped down so fast, they looked like monkeys."

David C. "Bobby" Cannon, UT baseball and football player (1916-1917, 1919): "People were really enthusiastic about Memorial Stadium. It was a godsend to the university to have that stadium there. . . . The momentum of the stadium created a building program for the university. It was a focal point. Having that big stadium right there made people appreciate new buildings, and they were willing to pay for it. Now, we've got one of the finest campuses in the country."

Liz Sutherland Carpenter, 1942 UT graduate: "Oh, I went to all the football games. It was a part of the social scene. You wore a big chrysanthemum with orange and white ribbons, and you yelled for your team. I saw Jack Crain make his big run . . . he just lit out, and we went wild, absolutely wild. . . . The snap of autumn brought this excitement. It was a glorious time of youth, when UT wasn't oversized, and you did chants until you were hoarse. Football would absorb us on the weekends, but it didn't devour us. It's always been a big part of Texas life."

Harley Clark, 1957 UT graduate and former cheerleader: "When they put in lights at the stadium, there was the usual grumbling that it wouldn't be the same and speculation that you wouldn't be able to see. I suppose people thought of country high school stadiums with dim lights. But everybody was surprised how clear it was, and it was accepted quickly. There's a certain mystique about playing at night, with everything focused on a lighted stadium."

Sam Coates, Baylor football player (1924-1926): "Yes sir, I played tackle, end and fullback for Baylor from 1924 to 1926, and I was all-Southwest Conference every year. I was in the first game ever played in that stadium. It was about half finished when we played. There was no question about us winning."

Jerrie Hejl Collins, 1952 UT graduate: "I went to UT during the late 1940s and early 1950s, and never even stopped to imagine what a behemoth the stadium was or wonder what it took to keep it up. I remember sitting on the wooden bleachers in the broiling afternoon sun and in a snowstorm. Neither instance was pleasant. . . . The whole campus has changed so much since I was there, but the stadium stands—like the Coliseum in Rome—a reminder of glorious times, past and present. I'm so glad it wasn't moved!"

Dan Cook, *San Antonio Express-News* sports editor: "I don't put great trust in any stadium that's a year older than I am. However, Memorial Stadium is well built, with far better facilities than 95 percent of all the other stadiums I've visited. The press box must be among the best in the country. If they could just figure a way to get the bats—and the odor they create—out of the bowels of that plant, they'd have a near-perfect setup."

Margaret Cousins, 1926 UT graduate: "News about the new stadium appeared in the *Daily Texan* consistently, and the whole student body was excited about it. Everybody was thrilled that we were going to have such a facility on the campus. No demands were made on us to give to the stadium drive. . . . Well, the stadium was finally finished, and we were all so proud. It was so new, modern and big. I believe the first football game ever played in it was with Baylor University. We got ourselves all dressed up and swarmed over there. And what do you think happened? They beat us! Baylor! It was too ignominious to be borne!"

Jack Crain, UT football player (1939-1941): "In 1938, when we were freshmen, the varsity won one ball game. In 1939, we won five, which was a tremendous improvement. In my first game, there were only a few thousand people in the stands and most were on the west side. Over the next three years, I saw the stadium full. . . . I think there was just a growing interest among fans and the student body because of a winning ball club. Texas became a powerhouse and the No. 1 team in the nation for a while."

Terry Crawford, UT women's track coach: "The track itself is very good, and the stadium gives us the ability to hold major meets like the Texas Relays, the UIL meet and the NCAA meet. The major drawback is that with the football field's artificial turf, it restricts us from holding some throwing events there. So Memorial Stadium isn't an ideal track and field facility. . . . The Texas Relays has had its ups and downs, but the legacy remains strong. It's still one of the top three relay meets in the country."

Moton Crockett, 1947 UT graduate and former Longhorn Band director: "I think the Longhorn Band definitely increases spirit on game day, with the crowd and so forth. A lot of people don't care that much about football, but they like the band, and they stay to see the halftime performances."

Pat Culpepper, UT football player (1960-1962): "I remember Memorial Stadium and the way you went from our dressing room to the playing field before the big games, where Longhorn fans were tightly packed, making a one-man passage to the steps, and how they would yell your name."

Joe Dixon, UT football player (1962-1964): "The stadium is basically the same as when I played, but it's different. . . . One change is that we dressed under the stands. The band would be outside the locker room, playing in a canyon-like atmosphere, making a tremendous roar. People were generally in a good mood, because we usually won, and we could hear them while we were showering."

Noble Doss, UT football player (1939-1941): "The week before the 1940 Texas A&M game, my thought was 'Man, I don't want to be a member of the football team at the University of Texas that doesn't uphold the tradition of never losing to them.' That meant a lot. . . . There's no question they did the right thing in leaving the stadium where it was. The main thing is for the student body. They can walk to the games, and that's who you play football for, the students. And it keeps the alumni involved."

Margaret Ellison, Texas Track Club coach: "It was at the end of the 1963 Texas Relays when Froggy Lovvorn let us run a couple of women's events for the first time. The announcer said 'And here is the Powder-Puff Derby' or something like that. Clyde [Littlefield] liked to die when he saw us about to run. But I saw him at a meet in Houston later, and he said some nice things. He had changed his attitude."

Gover "Ox" Emerson, UT football player (1929-1930) and assistant coach (1951-1956): "When I came to the university in 1927, Memorial

Stadium was larger and more impressive than any of the others we played in. It held 40,000 people. Gosh, that was a big place! It certainly set a pace for other buildings on campus, but there were no dressing facilities in the first few years. We'd dress in an old wooden building on Speedway and walk down 21st Street, which was just a gravel road. . . . Clyde Littlefield was a fine track coach, but he wasn't so good for football. We respected him and liked him, but he didn't make somebody jump up, grab their helmet and run on the field."

Doug English, UT football player (1972-1974): "I came down for the Aggie game my senior year in high school on a recruiting trip, and I remember it being very powerful . . . all the people, the Longhorn Band taking the field, the power of the team as it rolled over other teams. I was enthralled. As a player, you had to keep the blinders on, despite 78,000 screaming fans. You remember it with fondness."

Happy Feller, UT football player (1968-1970): "Coming to the University of Texas from Fredericksburg was a large step by itself, and entering Memorial Stadium prior to our first game was an experience that I will never forget. The excitement, the crowd reaction, the color and the lines of people that you had to wade through to get to the playing field were all unforgettable. I feel very privileged to have had the opportunity to play in Memorial Stadium on a national championship team coached by Darrell Royal."

Dr. Joe B. Frantz, 1938 UT graduate, former Athletics Council member and history professor: "Memorial Stadium is part of the mystique that's here. When people wanted to move it off campus, Darrell [Royal] shot that down. They'd never know there was a university to go with it. If it was off campus, you'd drive in to the stadium, park, maybe see the Tower and go back home. Here, it's a central part of the campus. I love this place. . . . The bats just give it character. If it rains on Wednesday before a game, it's going to smell like all get out, but you know you're home [laughter]."

Hollis Gainey, UT track athlete (1957-1959): "Clyde Littlefield was an easy-going guy who coached on an even keel. We had some rigorous workouts there, but you enjoyed it because he had an innate ability to put people at ease. . . . Memorial Stadium was as congenial an environment as you'd find anywhere. Once, coach Royal stopped football practice, and they all watched us run a 440-yard time trial. Things like that really made you feel good about competing for UT."

Chris Gilbert, UT football player (1966-1968): "Any UT football player who was involved in a 'Medina session' can tell you that there was nothing more difficult than completing one of Frank Medina's workouts. They were conducted in Memorial Stadium, and the hardest part consisted of running the entire bleachers from bottom to top, several times, with a fellow player on your back!"

Dr. Norman Hackerman, former UT president: "Frank Erwin was the driving force behind the expansion of the stadium. We had come to the same conclusion, and he pushed it pretty hard. . . . If I were in his position, I wouldn't have been down by the creek that day. The students were truculent in those years, and this gave them a focal point for their feelings. There was restlessness about the Vietnam war, and their attitudes about authority. . . . There was a lot of noise on this campus at the time. The basic reason for the incident was not a football stadium, but much deeper social problems."

Don Hood, former Abilene Christian University track coach: "The Texas Relays is like a reunion for track exes and fans. I've been going there since 1952, and even today, the sight of the stadium makes your heart leap. There have been some fantastic races and meets there. . . . Coach Littlefield was an imposing figure. He was accommodating and friendly to all the coaches, big or small, and he carried himself with dignity. He *was* University of Texas track."

Ralph Huber, 1936 UT graduate and former superintendent of construction and maintenance: "I inspected the addition to the stadium in 1948 and part of the last go-around. I did a lot of maintenance there and at several other campus buildings. We fixed water leaks, sanded the wooden bleachers, rebuilt the field once [in 1959] and all sorts of things. . . . Thinking back, it was run down a little, and it just wasn't well taken care of. The problems kind of grew, from the things that don't turn a buck. They'd hire a couple of guys to mow the grass on the field and ignore the rest of it."

Stan Huntsman, UT men's track coach: "I competed here in 1953 with Wabash College, and I remember throwing the javelin in the middle of Memorial Stadium. My Ohio University team had real good success in the Texas Relays, and we won nationals here in 1974 for Tennessee. . . . The tradition, the crowds and the marks that have been set here are exceedingly impressive. The atmosphere here is great, where you can seat 40,000 for a track meet, while some modern facilities seat only 2,000, and it's usually set out in a field somewhere. I think the Texas Relays is an indicator in the Southwest of what the University of Texas has done in the past and continues to do."

Craig James, SMU football player (1979-1982): "Our game in 1980 against Texas was one of the highlights of my sports career. Playing in front of 80,000 people, knowing the history and the tradition of all the great teams and players to come through there was unbelievable! . . . Memorial Stadium is there on campus, in the city of Austin, which is just the epitome of a college town. Some stadiums don't have that collegiate atmosphere, but it does."

Margaret Kennedy, 1926 UT graduate: "I entered the university as a junior in the summer of 1923, boarding with friends across the street from what became the north end of the stadium. Several of the construction men took their meals with us, and one or two had rooms there. We received a report each day on the progress or lack of it. By the end of the summer of 1924, I felt as if I had had a hand in the erection of Memorial Stadium."

John Knaggs, 1961 UT graduate: "I was sports editor of the *Daily Texan* in the fall of 1955 and felt honored to cover the first Longhorn game under the lights at Memorial Stadium. There had been some grumbling about it, not only from the standpoint of tradition, but the more practical concern of fans accustomed to driving to and from afternoon games in Austin without sustaining the expense of staying over. However, most fans and players were weary of the sweltering September heat and welcomed the lights. . . . Dame Fortune wasn't so kind that night with the Longhorns losing to Texas Tech, 20-14, but the lights worked well, and a new era was launched at the stadium."

Willie Kocurek, 1933 UT graduate: "Everybody viewed the stadium with great delight when I was a student. It was one of the largest, and we were proud of it. People looked upon it as a Mecca of sports. . . . Bellmont didn't lose prestige at the university after he was deposed, because he was loved by the people. And Lutcher Stark, he was the commander in chief of all forces, so to speak. Whatever he said, went. And if it didn't go, Lutcher would turn the water off somewhere. He was a powerful person."

Ernie Koy, Sr., UT football and baseball player (1930-1933): "In 1930, we were the first ball club that had a dressing room at the stadium. The visitors dressed at their hotel and came out in cabs. . . . There was quite a contrast between it and other schools' stadiums."

Ted Koy, UT football player (1967-1969): "I can't remember *not* coming to this stadium to see football games. My roots are here, because my father and brother played here. . . . The most distinct thing to me, as a player and as a fan, is when the Longhorn Band plays 'Texas Fight.' There's something electric about it. Even a non-football fan could come here and appreciate the color, the excitement and everything that goes on. It's that burnt orange factor."

Tom Landry, UT football player (1947-1948): "The year I remember most is 1947. The Longhorn team was one of the best teams in the history of the university, and Bobby Layne was our quarterback. . . . My first game was against North Carolina and Charlie Justice. It was an early game in the season, and the temperature was in the 90s with high humidity. The North Carolina team 'melted' in the heat, and we ran away with the game. . . . The most disappointing game was in 1948 when Texas A&M tied us. This, as I remember, was the first time we were ever tied or beaten by them in Memorial Stadium."

Al Lundstedt, 1951 UT graduate and former athletic business manager: "Considering the construction abilities of the time, I think they did a marvelous job in 1924. I'm almost positive that the stadium is here for good. And if it's ever not structurally sound, the solution I see is to rebuild it right here."

John Mackovic, UT head football coach: "Stadiums are known more for the spirit within them than for the bricks and mortar they're made of. It means a little more at Texas than at other places. Before I came here, people told me about the enthusiastic spirit of Memorial Stadium. . . . I'm glad to be part of the history and tradition of the University of Texas. I look forward to the excitement of the Longhorn football centennial. There have been so many championships here, and great players and coaches."

Jack Maguire, 1944 UT graduate and former executive director of the Ex-Students' Association: "Alums are always accused of being football-mad, but not a large percentage give a damn about football. They're interested in other things. In 1968, we didn't object to the expansion of the stadium, because it indicated the moving issue had been settled once and for all. . . . Today, there's not an alumni center that compares with ours. There's always a mob on game day. It's marvelous. With Waller Creek on the back and the stadium in front, it's like having a townhouse in New York City amid all the skyscrapers."

Ray Marek, UT track athlete (1949-1951) and Texas Relays official: "The Texas Relays were more of a carnival then than now. There was more recognition of people, you had the support of the Greeks, and Round-Up was going on. They always had a parade down the Drag on Friday morning, and it sort of swept across campus and into the stadium."

Randy Matson, Texas A&M track athlete (1965-1967): "My most vivid memory of Memorial Stadium was at the state high school track and field meet in 1963. Sticky orange paint on the discus prevented me from setting a national high school record. That was the beginning of my dislike for the color orange, and becoming an Aggie only intensified that dislike. . . . But my experiences at Memorial Stadium weren't all negative. I enjoyed competing there during the Texas Relays, SWC meets and other meets. Probably my greatest thrill there was at a 1965 triangular meet. I threw the shot 69', when the world record was 67' 10". It was never ratified as a world record because shortly after that, I threw 70' 7" at Kyle Field in the SWC meet."

Stan Mauldin, Jr., UT football player (1969-1971): "Prior to the 1970 Texas-Arkansas game, one of our lettermen from the 1969 team, George Cobb, climbed up on one of the light poles on the east side of the stadium and tied an orange jersey with a number 28 on it. . . . George showed me the jersey that was flapping like a flag on the light pole, close to the top. I couldn't imagine someone climbing up that pole without some safety backups. George told me that he had done it the previous night in honor of Freddie Steinmark."

B. J. "Red" McCombs, 1950 UT graduate: "It's not just a stadium, but a happening, because of what has taken place there. For three hours, it's a mix of people who have one thing in common. I get goose bumps at the stadium. It was awesome when I was a student, and it still is."

David McWilliams, UT football player (1961-1963), assistant coach (1970-1985) and head coach (1987-1991): "I didn't know the history of the stadium, but it always seemed bigger and shinier than other stadiums we played in. We hardly ever practiced here, so when it was game day, we were really ready. We knew we were wearing the orange and white, representing the University of Texas."

Willie Morris, 1956 UT graduate: "When I was a freshman at UT in 1952, and in subsequent years until the lights were installed, the stadium had an air of shabby gentility to it in those afternoon games. It needed a paint job, and I recall more than a few splinters in the seats. There was a relaxed quality to it, and I loved it. . . . I was at the Washington State game in 1954 when Duke Washington broke the stadium color barrier. He scored their only TD late in the game on a long run, and the UT student section stood and applauded."

Tommy Nobis, UT football player (1963-1965): "Probably my biggest thrill was every Saturday, coming out onto the field when the band was playing 'The Eyes of Texas,' and there were 60,000 people standing, most of them singing it and doing the 'Hook 'em, Horns' sign. . . . I remember when they discussed moving the stadium. Most of the guys who sweated and bled to build that tradition, we would have been upset if they had torn it down and moved somewhere else. And to lose that . . . well, we'd have wanted our voices to be heard."

Charley Parker, UT track athlete (1947-1950): "I ran in the state track meet there in 1942, 1943 and 1944, winning the 100 and 220-yard dashes all three years. At first, I was almost awe-stricken at the size of the stadium, but by the time I got through, it became home to me. . . . It was the fastest track in Texas, excellent for sprinters. The only ones better, that I ran on, were in Fresno and Modesto [California], which had banked curves."

Jubal R. Parten, 1917 UT graduate and former member of the Board of Regents: "Memorial Stadium gave the university a first-class athletic field. It was a big venture, and a lot of people were opposed to it. They thought the university was emphasizing the wrong thing, but I thought football was fine."

Eddie Phillips, UT football player (1969-1971): "My lasting impressions from the 1970 UCLA game: The pandemonium of our fans! The picture in the next day's newspaper indicating total disbelief by UCLA. The confidence [offensive lineman] Bobby Wuensch felt that UT would win that game. The immense pride that a team with average overall ability and size could win through a will to succeed and execution. And that was the day I grew up as a successor to James Street."

Wally Pryor, 1951 UT graduate and public address announcer for football at Memorial Stadium and basketball at the Erwin Center: "I'm not sure what year this was, but here's a funny story. Kern Tips, the best radio announcer in the world, had a booth next to me. One time, the Longhorn Band came into the stadium, and he said 'When Vince DiNino and his troops take the field, it's like Hannibal and his army crossing the Alps. The only thing missing is the elephants.' What he didn't know was that the Shrine Circus, with three elephants, was following the band [laughter]. They were raised up on their back legs, too. That's the only time I saw Kern Tips at a loss for words."

Nelson Puett, Jr., UT football player and track athlete (1938-1940): "My daddy was on the team that beat the Aggies in 1911, and he would take me to Texas football games as early as I can remember. To me, Memorial Stadium was just tremendous. I had never seen anything like this. It was just overwhelmingly big. . . . It was right there in the south end zone where I scored against Texas A&M in 1938, and in that corner, I let a guy from SMU get behind me, and the coaches took me out of the game. I won the Southwest Conference broad jump 50 years ago down there. To me, this place has a lot of nostalgic meaning."

James Raup, 1968 UT graduate: "I'm about as orange as anybody. When I was a kid, I sat in the knothole section in the north end zone, then as a student, I sat on the east side, and played baseball over at Clark Field. And now, as an alumnus, I sit on the west side, where it's not as rambunctious, but you have more armchair quarterbacks."

Travis Raven, UT football player (1941-1942, 1946): "When I first put on a University of Texas uniform, and we were under the stadium before coming out for a ball game, I had this feeling of exhilaration. My heart was pumping, and the blood was really flowing through my veins."

Bob Rochs, 1942 UT graduate and executive director of the T Association and Longhorn Hall of Honor: "I was attending some football games here in the 1930s when my brother was a student. Then, the stadium held 40,500 people. It was much better than any of the others, and we were real proud of it. When I came back from the service in 1946, I just stayed on and never left. I haven't missed a home game since, or any game since 1955."

Dr. Ricardo Romo, UT track athlete (1964-1966), history professor and Athletics Council member: "My first visit to Memorial Stadium was the 1961 Texas-TCU football game, and I recall walking in and being awed by this vast structure. . . . I was most impressed with the energy that came out of the stadium. It was an experience, and it helped in my coming to the University of Texas. The true center of campus is the west mall, except for five Saturday afternoons every fall. While there will always be a variety of opinions, a consensus feeling is that the stadium has served the university very well, and that many great moments in sports history have taken place here."

Lawrence Sampleton, UT football player (1978-1981): "It was kind of breathtaking and amazing the first time I saw the stadium. Playing here gave the members of the team a little bit more hype and mystique. All of the guys who played here were aware of the tradition UT had in the Southwest Conference, all the history behind it. We felt like we couldn't be beat here."

Bill Sansing, 1941 UT graduate and former sports information director: "The Cotton Bowl was the only stadium in this part of the country that even compared to Memorial Stadium. We had an excellent press box, and the best turf you've ever seen. It was like a golf course . . . you could sleep on it. Jake Bleymaier really took care of that place. I believe Memorial Stadium has been the centerpiece around which UT ex-students come back. One of the greatest assets of college football is that it keeps alumni involved with the institution, but that's in direct proportion to how much you win."

James Saxton, UT football player (1959-1961): "The stadium looks a lot different today. It's kind of like the transitions we've all gone through with automobiles, clothes and everything else. I think that today, Memorial Stadium is a more noticeable symbol of the university because of the upper deck, and it's so visible from the highway. I'm not sure it stood out that much when I was in school. . . . Moving the stadium would have been a huge mistake. To me, it needs to be a part of the university community, and I don't care if it creates parking problems or what."

Billy Schott, UT football player (1972-1974): "I was born the Tuesday before the 1952 Arkansas game. The first place I stopped on the way home from the hospital was right here. My father bundled me up and brought me in for a while and was showing me off. . . . I know every nook and cranny of this place. These seats we're sitting on, I was on the crew that put them in during the summer of 1970. You've got different degrees of caring, from guys who've gone out and spilled blood on the field, to kids in school who are coming for a social event. The stadium ought to be preserved and maintained. You look around today, and you see things chipped and corroded. If I was in charge, I'd do a lot of things different."

Wally Scott, UT football player (1940-1942) and former Athletics Council member: "It was getting kind of crowded around there by the 1960s when the talk about moving came up, but it never really got serious. I can recall vividly the reasons we didn't do it. We didn't think it would be a good recruiting tool to bring our athletes here, load them up on buses and go way out to Balcones. We felt it would disassociate football from the campus. The alumni liked it here, and this is where everybody wanted it."

Jerry Sisemore, UT football player (1969-1971): With coach Royal, when you walked out there, your ears were ringing, and you were pretty pumped up. It was a special place, with all the tradition, the pressure, the national championship and never losing. . . . I really didn't know that it was a memorial to World War I veterans. To me, it was just Memorial Stadium, where Texas plays football."

Dean Smith, UT track athlete and football player (1952-1955): "Some of the other tracks in the Southwest Conference were poor, but Memorial Stadium was like the Olympic stadium in Rome. It was a wonderful track, and they kept it immaculate. That old stadium has a feeling of depth, and it's 10 times bigger and better now. I love that place, and I'll always have a good feeling from those days."

Weldon Smith, 1934 UT graduate and Athletics Council member: "Oh, I was strongly in favor of not moving the stadium. It was very important to have the stadium right there on campus. The cost of tearing it down and building a new one just didn't make sense to me. We were horrified at first and certainly relieved when it was decided to keep it there."

Harrison Stafford, UT football player and track athlete (1930-1933): "I remember the stadium real well, and I was enthused about playing there. But I'm not sure if we ever filled it, to tell you the truth. . . . In the 1932 SMU game, they were right near our goal line. I intercepted a pass and started running down the field. They never put a hand on me."

Homer Stark, Texas A&M graduate: "My dad [H. J. Lutcher Stark] really loved that stadium. He was still talking about it years later. He never said 'I built it,' just 'us' and 'we.' When Dana Bible told him to get off the bench, I thought he would blow up, but he didn't. He just said 'That's the way it is.' He had a violent temper, and sure, he was upset, but there was no cussing Bible or the university. The university was his life, but after that, he stopped going to all the games, and he shifted his attention to other things."

Tom Stolhandske, UT football player (1950-1952): "Memorial Stadium was like the Roman Coliseum as far as I was concerned. It's a great facility. There's something about it, walking in there on game day, when the band is playing and the stands are full. Even in 1950, you didn't find anything else like it. There's history at the stadium, a legend, something galloping through there. It's more than just a football field. . . . That's where we used to do our courting, in the stadium. We'd drive cars up the ramps, overlooking San Jacinto. It was just you, the girls and the bats [laughter]. . . . The expansion of the stadium is a semblance of the success the university has had. I think it looks great. They've done it in a very pleasant manner and kept the design of the original bowl. In fact, one of these days, they may dome the damn thing. I'd just like to see them put grass back in there."

Carlton Stowers, UT track athlete (1961-1962): "I still say there are few athletic competitions in the country that can match the drama and intensity of the state high school track and field championships. When I was running for Abilene High School, the walk into Memorial Stadium for the state meet was the sign of a reached goal which all high school runners set for themselves. . . . Then, as a student-athlete at Texas, the stadium became something of a comfortable home away from home. Daily workouts weren't a drudgery; rather they were a welcome escape from the pressures of class and the confines of dorm life. After practice, we would hang around, lounging on the (then) grass infield, enjoying the spring sun."

Jerry Thompson, UT track athlete (1943, 1947-1948): "I never ran on a better track than the one at the University of Texas. Coach Littlefield would have it plowed up in early spring to keep it from packing. It was fine on top, so your spikes would catch, but not too much. . . . I always felt that competing at Memorial Stadium meant more than at other places. It was our home stadium and the most impressive stadium in the Southwest Conference, no doubt about it. It had a special aura because of the history of athletics there."

Dr. John Treadwell, UT football player (1960-1962): "I started coming to games here around 1950, and I still have John David Crow's chinstrap. The grass field took a hell of a beating out there. Toward the end of the season, there were places with no grass, especially in the middle. . . . This stadium doesn't look tired to me. I think it's got a lot of character, and it looks pretty solid. It needs a facelift every once in a while, but I don't see why you'd want a plastic toy of a stadium. The north scoreboard looks a little bit gaudy and out of place, but hey, things change."

Roy Vaughan, executive director of the Ex-Students' Association: "I never did think that moving the stadium was a viable option, just an idea that got a lot of emotional heat. . . . Everybody said 'Are they seriously thinking about moving the stadium? Surely not.' And they didn't. . . . We had good reason to think this area was going to become the attendance focus of the campus, even before the Art Building, Drama Building and Performing Arts Center were built. And being across the street from where 60,000 to 80,000 people come five days a year was no drawback."

Harvey "Chink" Wallender, UT track athlete (1934-1936): "Memorial Stadium was at the top. The track was as good as any in the east or in California. Coach Littlefield was a fine gentleman who would beat you at every meet. He knew how to place his runners and peak for the big ones. He started the Texas Relays back up in 1935 because he wanted to show off his facilities and his track team. It was good for prestige and recruiting."

Etta Bain Ward, 1924 UT graduate: "I saw my first Texas game when I was very young, sitting with my parents in our horse-drawn buggy in Hyde Park. Now I'm 87 and still get goose bumps when they play 'The Eyes of Texas.' . . . I went to the first football game at Memorial Stadium, but before the game, a bunch of us got together and cried because we weren't going to Clark Field. Of course, it was progress, but there was an empty feeling when we went into this huge new stadium."

Jeff Ward, UT football player (1983-1986): "The whole University of Texas thing didn't hit me until the 100-year celebration in 1983, and I saw what a big deal it is, this uniform, this school, this town. It's pretty impressive. It was an honor to play here, and I think most of the guys who have played here treat it that way."

Dr. Mike Wetzel, UT football player (1957-1958) and referee: "To me, the stadium was more than just a stadium. It was an awesome shrine, a symbol of Texas football prowess and a gathering place for all kinds of people. On game days, there were lots of Longhorn people at Moore-Hill Hall, trying to get tickets. . . . For referees, it's a big old stadium, and most guys like to work there because they know it's going to be a full house. You always look forward to being in front of a big crowd."

Bobby Whilden, UT track athlete (1955-1957): "It's been 34 years since I ran track on the cinders of Memorial Stadium, but I obviously have fond memories of it. . . . Although I had the good fortune of winning many races in Memorial Stadium, it was the Friday night of the 1957 Texas Relays when Wally Wilson, Hollis Gainey, Eddie Southern and I set a new world record in the 880-yard relay that I will never forget. The crowd was screaming and as I broke the tape, I thought the stadium would collapse."

Bill Whitmore, 1942 UT graduate and former Rice sports information director: "The single most electrifying play I saw there was the Jack Crain 67-yard touchdown in the final seconds, plus extra point, against Arkansas in 1939. The best game? The 1940 upset by UT over a great Aggie team. The 'Immortal 13,' the Noble Doss catch, Pete Layden, Malcolm Kutner, Chal Daniel, et al. Drama at its finest and SWC football at its best. So much history there!"

Hugh Wolfe, UT football player and track athlete (1935-1938): "The hardest I was ever tackled in Memorial Stadium was by Nelson Puett, Jr. when we had a scrimmage with the freshman team. I was a senior at about 200 pounds and Nelson weighed every bit of 140 pounds. My caustic reprimand drew an appropriate response from the little freshman, quote: 'If the Big Bad Wolfe can't take it, turn in your uniform!'"

Steve Worster, UT football player (1968-1970): "My first time at Memorial Stadium was in 1967 on a recruiting visit, and I was in total awe and amazement when they took us down on the field. I'd never been in such a big stadium. . . . I'm not a great Texas ex or fan, but I took my kids back for the 20th anniversary of the 1969 national championship team, and the first thing we did was go to the stadium. We were drawn to it; it's a fascinating place. The feeling of standing in the middle of the field was great. It brought back the electricity of those years."

Martha Robertson Zivley, 1926 UT graduate: "Clark Field was just a grass field with bleachers, and you could reach down and touch the players if you had the nerve. It was like a little high school field, and now we had this great stadium. You could get more attention for the university by having a nice big football stadium than you could with a new biology building. At least if people came to the games, they could see the condition of the campus, and that would facilitate changes. . . . I remember when they added the lights. It was spectacular!"

The Stadium, Today and Tomorrow

Memorial Stadium will be here long past my time. I think it's good for at least another 40 years if it's properly maintained," said J. Neils Thompson, who played football in the stadium during the 1930s and nurtured its growth as chairman of the Athletics Council in the 1960s and 1970s. "This is a beautiful facility, and there's a lot of history tied to it."

A gray heirloom from some angles and a sparkling jewel from others, the stadium rests on a bed of limestone and rock, ready to serve the University of Texas well into the 21st century. For reasons of economics, campus space and tradition, Memorial Stadium will remain the epicenter of Longhorn athletics for the foreseeable future. You will hear no "build a new stadium" talk emanating from the first- and second-floor offices of Bellmont Hall. As Thompson suggested, the stadium seems likely to reach its 100th birthday in 2024 because the UT athletic department, in concurrence with the university's administration, is committed to maintaining and possibly expanding it.

If we may call the stadium "old," we should not be surprised to learn that it has a few aches and pains, and requires more attention than when it was young. The same could be said about virtually any other old college athletic facility, such as Washington's Husky Stadium (built in 1920), Tennessee's Neyland Stadium (1921), Stanford Stadium (1921), Ohio State's Ohio Stadium (1922), LSU's Tiger Stadium (1924), Colorado's Folsom Field

(1924), Michigan Stadium (1927), Georgia's Sanford Stadium (1929) or Notre Dame Stadium (1930).

Such facilities need perpetual upkeep and must be adapted to changing times. Once a building falls too far behind, bringing it up to date is difficult and tedious—not to mention expensive. Few schools have built new stadiums in the last two decades. Four of the newest NCAA Division I on-campus stadiums are Kentucky's Commonwealth Stadium (built in 1973 for $12 million), West Virginia's Mountaineer Field (1980, $22 million), Syracuse's Carrier Dome (1980, $28 million) and Vanderbilt Stadium (1981, $10.6 million). All four are rather low-budget facilities, since some recently erected pro stadiums have cost well over $100 million. It surely behooves any university with an old but solid facility to provide the necessary maintenance and modifications.

When 75,000 people converge on Memorial Stadium for a Longhorn football game, not many of them even think about its appearance or condition. But in recent years, the Texas athletic department has heard more frequent expression of concern, particularly when several small chunks of concrete fell on cars parked under the west stands.

Lest we criticize the work performed by architects, engineers and day laborers on Memorial Stadium in the 1920s, we should realize that they actually did a fine job, given the technology of the time. Aided by Austin's mild climate, the stadium has already lasted longer than many others erected in that era.

From the beginning, most of the maintenance done on Memorial Stadium has been day-to-day work or stopgap measures not addressing its long-term needs. When Dana X. Bible (1937), Darrell Royal (1957) and Fred Akers (1977) became Longhorn head football coaches, all three expressed a need to better maintain the stadium. And today, some fairly serious problems have developed in a building expected to remain in service for many more years. But the stadium is assuredly not, as some alarmists have claimed, "falling apart."

JASTER-QUINTANILLA REPORT

In late 1990 and early 1991, the Austin structural engineering firm of Jaster-Quintanilla & Associates (J-Q) did a thorough study of the stadium, putting its methods and conclusions into a 200-page report. While affirming the health of the stadium's infrastructure, the engineers enumerated its various defects, and they recommended solutions.

They saw few problems with the 20-year old upper deck, but they estimated that 15 percent of the seating area in the lower stadium was in need of replacement. Recommending that work begin quickly on urgent matters such as repairs on steel support beams under the west stands, J-Q came up with an eight-point rehabilitation program for Memorial Stadium: a waterproofing system for the top surface of the entire stadium; treatment of expansion joints; epoxy injection of cracks; restoration of beams, girders and decks, including new reinforcing bars where necessary; repair of ramps and stairs; miscellaneous cosmetics; replacement of deteriorated decks with new precast concrete risers; and installation of a sloping concrete topping to facilitate drainage of water. The last item would, of course, go in prior to the waterproofing treatment.

The cost of this work, J-Q estimated, would be $1.445 million on the north end, $1.325 million on the east side, $1.190 million on the west side, and $565,000 in the upper deck, for a total of $4.525 million. If begun immediately and everything went according to plan, the entire project would be complete in time for the 1994 Longhorn football season.

"The stadium is well maintained, as far as I know," said Dr. James Vick, UT vice president for student affairs, and chairman of the Athletics Council since 1988. "There are knowledgeable people looking at it who will tell us what needs to be done, and I don't think there will be any reluctance to follow it."

The J-Q report does not specify, but presumably included in the "miscellaneous cosmetics" category is the exterior of Memorial Stadium's north-end horseshoe. Built in 1926, just two years after the east and west stands, this is the only part of the stadium with a stucco covering, lending itself to further water infiltration. The north end's 13 graceful arches and main entrance patterned after the Alamo pose no immediate structural danger, but their appearance leaves much to be desired. Fungus, stains and peeling paint have contributed to an aesthetic downer just across 23rd Street from the beautiful, modern Performing Arts Center.

"Part of our long-range plan is to look at the exterior and interior of the facility," said Doug Messer, associate AD for business affairs. "There's a good bit of sandblasting, repainting, sealing and other work that needs to be done. No final date has been set. We'll have to build a needs list and quantify it in such a way that we can go out into the marketplace and find companies to provide those services."

Since Jaster-Quintanilla limited its study to the stadium's structure, it did not address several other things in need of attention. Restroom facilities come first. In the summer of 1991, some of the older restrooms got a makeover (a coat of paint, sinks, toilets and stalls), but these remain barely adequate.

And there simply are not enough, as attested by the long lines outside women's restrooms at most games. The plumbing is old, and water lines sometimes break during the winter. To significantly upgrade existing restrooms and build several new ones would cost between $2-$2 1/2 million, Messer estimated.

Of less importance than the restrooms are the concessions facilities, where fans purchase the standard fare of soft drinks, peanuts, popcorn, hot dogs, coffee, hot chocolate and candy, recently augmented by such items as yogurt and nachos. The concessions facilities tucked under the west, east and north stands are in the same places as 60 years earlier. Those in the upper deck are newer and somewhat roomier. Gene Seaton ran stadium concessions from 1964 until his retirement in 1991, when Jim Baker succeeded him. Baker and his many workers need more space, more modern facilities and perhaps a wider menu.

When construction workers finally completed Bellmont Hall in February 1973, it was more than big enough for the athletic department, the UT police, the Kinesiology and Health Education Department and a portion of students' recreational needs. In just a few years though, the extra space was devoured as the women's athletic department started up, staffs grew, and the Dana X. Bible Academic Center opened.

The departure of the UT police from Bellmont Hall in 1989 eased the crunch briefly, but soon the building was again "maxed out," in DeLoss Dodds' words. That is not unusual on the crowded Texas campus.

"Space is at a premium," said Messer, "but it's not so bad that we can't do our jobs."

The one-level Memorial Stadium press box, first used in 1971, was never as big as sports information directors Jones Ramsey and Bill Little wanted. But today, it is noticeably small and outdated. For some football games, reporters spill onto the photo deck, resulting in a less-than-ideal working environment. You can contrast it with the plush, spacious press boxes to be found, for example, at Oregon's Autzen Stadium, Colorado's Folsom Field, Arizona State's Sun Devil Stadium, Notre Dame Stadium, Wisconsin's Camp Randall Stadium, Tennessee's Neyland Stadium or Maryland's Byrd Stadium.

One more drawback to Memorial Stadium as it is today: The public address system, with speakers located in the Freddie Steinmark scoreboard, is due for replacement. "It was a booming, impressive one in 1972, but in today's market, it's weak," said Dodds. "The scoreboard itself is permanent, as far as I'm concerned. We might modernize it at some time, but it will stay."

These items and a few others give us reason for concern, but a responsible, proactive stance by the UT athletic department assures the facility's short-term and long-term needs. Let's now look to the future and to some changes that might take place at Memorial Stadium.

THE STADIUM'S FUTURE

First, however, a few things that have been proposed, discussed and rejected with some finality.

• A return to natural grass at Memorial Stadium is very unlikely. In recent years, Michigan, Ohio State, Iowa, Mississippi, Florida, South Carolina and some other schools have ripped up the artificial turf at their respective stadiums and planted specially designed grass fields. But Texas probably will not follow suit, in part because the football team uses Memorial Stadium regularly for practice. If grass were installed, UT would have to keep the stadium—a beehive of runners and other athletes—closed most of the time. The Longhorn Band and ROTC would have to find other places to practice, as well. Advocates of a return to grass may have forgotten the trouble and maintenance costs involved.

• Despite the presence of the Dallas Cowboys' training camp in Austin and that of the Houston Oilers in San Antonio, Memorial Stadium will not be hosting any pro football exhibition games. Regents' rules allow pro basketball in the Erwin Center, which is available for rent. But the stadium is another matter, and since a three-year experiment in the late 1950s, the Texas athletic department has seen no benefit in having the NFL on campus.

• While it would surely raise some serious revenue, do not look for the sale of beer to the public at Memorial Stadium. Restroom facilities are already overloaded without the extra flushing beer sales would bring. Keeping beer out of the hands of minors (including many students), boisterous behavior and the specter of drunken fans hopping into their cars after a game will keep the stadium technically "dry," although clandestine drinking has been going on there since 1924.

• There is no apparent solution to the bat problem at the stadium. Large amounts of time, money and effort were expended on getting rid of the flying mammals in the 1950s, 1960s and 1970s, but with little success. Environmental laws now prohibit some of the more aggressive means of bat eradication, so UT seems to have accepted their massive presence, doing a periodic clean-up of bat guano.

• The UT-Texas A&M football game will continue to be played in Austin on even-numbered years. San Antonio's Alamodome is due to open in 1993, and its backers have expressed interest in hosting the game, at least occasionally. Although Dodds is amenable to an "away" game there, he has clearly stated that he does not want yet another out-of-town "home" game. Playing Oklahoma in Dallas every October is fine, but that is enough. While Arkansas can play half of its home games in Little Rock, much like Alabama (Birmingham) and Mississippi (Jackson), Austin is home for the Horns.

Other than the rather substantial maintenance work mentioned earlier and replacement of synthetic surfaces every six years or so, what changes are likely at Memorial Stadium in the near and intermediate future? Among the various options open to Texas athletics, the big question is expansion. Any alteration to the stadium would be costly, and university funds will not help pay for it. Yet the Board of Regents and UT System would have to give their approval before any work is done on a project of more than $300,000.

Texas currently has the 13th largest on-campus stadium in the country, with a permanent seating capacity of 75,504. It trails Michigan (101,701), Penn State (93,000), Tennessee (91,110), Ohio State (86,071), Stanford (86,019), Georgia (85,434), Auburn (85,214), Florida (83,000), LSU (80,140) Clemson (79,854), Wisconsin (77,745) and Michigan State (76,000).

Frequency of football sellouts at UT depends on the fortunes of the team and the quality of home schedule played. Longhorn fans do not flock to the stadium with the faithful regularity of fans at places like Nebraska, Oklahoma, Tennessee, Notre Dame, Michigan, Ohio State and Penn State, where sellout streaks go back for decades.

Perhaps it is folly to consider expansion of Memorial Stadium until fans pack it for every game, and for several consecutive seasons. But Dodds, his staff and the Athletics Council are responsible for looking to the future, making sure the facility does not become obsolete.

DeLoss Dodds: "It comes down to this—the public always dictates. You've got to do market studies and surveys to find out what people think. . . . Would they pay $250 or $500 for a seat option? Over a period of time, the stadium is going to get fuller and fuller, and if Austin continues to grow, you've got to think that the University of Texas can handle a bigger stadium."

Doug Messer: "It's in the think-tank mode right now, so some of these things may not happen until the year 2000. You take it one step at a time and figure out what you gain economically by making major changes to the stadium. You see how people feel about it, and they no doubt feel strongly about tradition at Texas and about Memorial Stadium. . . . You sure don't want a large number of empty seats."

James Vick: "I'm not a demographer, a marketer or a seer, but I think our program is developing well. I think we'll continue to have good attendance at home games. . . . We've discussed expansion, mostly on an individual basis, and doing something creative. And we've looked at what other schools have done with their stadiums."

EAST-SIDE OPTIONS

If attendance warranted, *if* market studies and surveys looked favorable, and *if* the UT athletic department, administration and Board of Regents all agreed, how might Memorial Stadium be enlarged? The most obvious plan and the one most often discussed calls for a matching upper deck on the east side, boosting seating capacity to around 90,000.

This would offer a big chunk of good—though not prime—seats for watching football games and would present options to keep the stadium viable well into the 21st century. One potential stumbling block to an east-side upper deck goes back to 1968, when the LBJ Library was under construction. Regent Frank Erwin, AD and head football coach Darrell Royal and Athletics Council chairman J. Neils Thompson envisioned a second level on the stadium's east side. But Lady Bird Johnson pointed out that such an addition would obstruct the view from the presidential library southwest to the state Capitol. For that reason and others, Bellmont Hall and the upper deck went west, leaving the "Capitol view corridor" intact; a state law codified it in 1985. So if Memorial Stadium were expanded on the east side, UT would have to get a variance declared.

(It is somewhat ironic that the 12-story Lyndon Baines Johnson State Office Building, constructed in 1973 at 17th and Brazos streets, partially blocks the view corridor between the stadium and the Capitol.)

Not only would an east-side upper deck give Memorial Stadium symmetry, more important, it would offer tantalizing possibilities. A modern, multi-level press box could be erected, allowing the conversion of the west-side press box into revenue-producing luxury skyboxes. Several other schools have built such skyboxes at their stadiums, and with good success. Like it or not, this is one way a university's athletic department can balance the budget.

If construction of an entire upper deck proved too costly or if the Capitol view corridor issue precluded it, a row or two of skyboxes on the east side might work, suggested former regent and Athletics Council member Howard Richards. "I'd like to see us do something on the east side," he said.

So would a lot of people, but whether it is an upper deck, a press box, skyboxes or some combination, another problem remains. Since UT plays three and sometimes four of its five home games each season in the afternoon, people in these new east-side locations would be facing west, into the sun. Of course, Memorial Stadium already has about 24,000 seats there, and most of them are filled on game days, so it should not be a critical matter.

An upper deck on the stadium's east side might have a Bellmont Hall-style building underneath, making university (that is, non-athletic) financial participation feasible. It would also address an old problem, since the stadium's east side has long been regarded as an ugly stepchild to the west. A cursory look at the stadium from the intersection of Manor Road and East Campus Drive shows dull, featureless architecture. Double-decking the east side would cover that and might require an eastward shift of East Campus Drive, similar to the westward shift of San Jacinto Boulevard in 1969.

NORTH-END OPTIONS

Probably the worst seats in Memorial Stadium are located in the north-end horseshoe, where fans must do without yard-line viewing of football games. While the track and high jump area put them a long way from the north end zone, they practically need high-powered binoculars to see a goal-line stand in the south. So it is no wonder that general-admission seats (the knothole section) have always been in the north end.

Just as with large-scale alteration of Memorial Stadium's east side, nothing is imminent in the north end. But because it holds 13,500 relatively poor seats, Dodds and others in the Texas athletic department wonder if that is not an area for change in the future. Hold on to your hat and consider Dodds' scenario: "The north-end seats aren't very good and there's not much you can do about it. So our goal would be to deck the east side, take the north end off completely, take the track out and lower the field, then put a building on the north end that would house all of athletics. That's our dream.

"What we have in mind somewhere down the road is to have a museum with the T Room, open to the public at times, similar to the NFL Hall of Fame. You could look at Earl Campbell's Heisman Trophy, old jerseys or film clips. It would be a whole thing of Texas athletics, maybe in a stand-alone building at the northwest corner of the stadium.

"It's just conversation at this point, looking ahead and saying 'What would we do if. . . .' There may be five other athletic directors here before it happens, and me saying something doesn't make it true. These kinds of things raise political questions, emotional questions. You know, tearing down the north end would be emotional because it's a landmark, and it's got memorials all over it. And taking the track out—that's an emotional question. These are not decisions to be made lightly."

Certainly not, and yet similar things have happened at other college stadiums, particularly Georgia Tech's Grant Field. Ten years older than

Memorial Stadium, Grant Field got a radical makeover in 1986. The track was taken out, and the 12,000-seat south end-zone stands were demolished and replaced by a six-level multi-use facility that includes 42 skyboxes for well-heeled Yellow Jacket fans.

An end-zone facility of this sort at Memorial Stadium could be built with modest seating and with steel-and-glass skyboxes overlooking the field. These might be in conjunction with, or in place of, skyboxes on the east or west sides. Moving the T Room to a new spot might invigorate it, also allowing for expansion of the Dana X. Bible Academic Center.

Dodds alluded to the various war memorials at the stadium's north end: plaques on the exterior and in the portals, those on the walls of the main entrance, the 47' × 7' chunk of bronze atop the horseshoe and the nearby granite marker. What would be done with these memorials to long-dead Texas soldiers? Would they be moved elsewhere in the stadium or consigned to the junkyard like the Louis Jordan flagpole that meant so much in 1924? If the north end experiences a big conversion as described here, we can only hope these markers will be part of the new Memorial Stadium.

Incorporation of the original outer wall, with its multiple arches and ceremonial gateway, into such a scheme is not beyond the range of possibility. Architects call this "adaptive re-use."

AND THE TRACK . . .

At the stadium's conception, H. J. Lutcher Stark and L. Theo Bellmont wanted a dual-purpose facility, one for football as well as track and field. That crucial decision, for better or for worse, dictated the architecture of Memorial Stadium, and for nearly 70 years now, football and track have been compromised by the need to share space. Not really ideal for conducting track meets (especially after the installation of artificial turf in 1969), Memorial Stadium also suffers in terms of football fans being so far removed from the field.

It is not unique in that regard. A sampling of other schools with football/track stadiums includes Texas A&M, Stanford, Washington, Missouri, Ohio State and Duke. Of course, some schools can boast that fans on the front rows of their (trackless) stadiums are virtually within arms' length of the sidelines: Rice, Oklahoma, Oklahoma State, Colorado, Iowa, Notre Dame, Michigan and Purdue, among others.

Following the 1968 decision not to build an off-campus facility, Thompson explored the possibility of removing the Memorial Stadium track, lowering the field significantly and adding perhaps a dozen new rows there. But hard rock, combined with stadium plumbing under the track and concern about fans' sightlines, ended that pretty quickly. Furthermore, the track coaches, athletes and fans liked being in the stadium, not in a remote location.

Again, no major changes are pending, but you occasionally hear discussions of removing the track, the oval where Clyde Littlefield coached, where runners like Harvey "Chink" Wallender, Jerry Thompson, Eddie Southern, Johnny "Lam" Jones, Carlette Guidry and so many others have competed. Although Memorial Stadium is primarily a football facility, a great deal of athletic history is bound up in the track, and taking it out would be a sensitive matter.

Without resorting to an elaborate geometrical explanation, it should suffice to say that simple removal of the track might have no effect on fans watching football at Memorial Stadium. This has to do with the gentle grade of the stadium's risers, an essentially permanent aspect of its architecture. Lowering the field—if that were feasible—could result in many fans losing sight of a portion of the field, or having their views blocked by those in front. Such an unacceptable situation would ensure that the familiar space remain between the sidelines and the first rows on the east and west stands. Osborn and LAN discovered this in their 1968 study of the stadium.

Still, a north-end complex of the type discussed earlier would sit very close to the football field, rendering the track useless. What, then, happens to Longhorn track and field? A new facility, designed expressly for that sport, would most likely be built on university-owned land east of Interstate 35. Disch-Falk Field, the offices of UT Press and the UT Physical Plant headquarters reside there already.

This facility (possibly to be named after Clyde Littlefield) would have a 400-meter track with international parameters, room for all field events and a grandstand for 10,000-15,000 spectators. Although the track program would lose its central location, it might benefit, since moving off campus has actually helped the Longhorn baseball, basketball and tennis programs. But if a new track facility were reserved for scholarship athletes, the university would not pay a dime for its construction. Such a move might also be a public relations problem, since so many people are accustomed to using the track at Memorial Stadium.

And what effect would a smaller track facility have on the Texas Relays or the UIL high school meet? The schoolboys and schoolgirls have drawn more than 30,000 fans in recent years, and if a new facility held only half that, the meet might well be staged elsewhere.

Afficionados of the sport would hope not, but taking the track out of Memorial Stadium might lead to the demise of the Texas Relays and de-emphasis of track and field at UT. Attendance at college track meets in Austin during the last three decades, ranging from low-key triangular meets to the NCAA championships, has been uniformly disappointing. And despite quality teams under coaches Stan Huntsman and Terry Crawford, track is a financial loser for UT. These facts, in conjunction, could cause future athletic administrators to view it with a hard eye if the track were to be taken out of the stadium.

OTHER POSSIBILITIES

The condition of the locker rooms at Memorial Stadium has never been better. The Longhorn football team has its state-of-the-art facility in the south end, visiting teams share the old home locker room directly under the west stands with men's track, and women's track makes good use of the former visitors' locker room in the southwest corner of the stadium.

Some people have suggested building a new locker room for visiting football teams, perhaps on the east side of the stadium, but Dodds sees no need: "We treat people here better than we are treated on the road. We're not going to put money into a new visitors' locker room, to be used five times a year."

What are now the visitors' and UT men's track locker room (built in 1930) and the women's track locker room (1953) both have a lot of years on them, and sometimes the roofs leak. But they have been maintained and brought up to date enough to provide sufficient accommodation.

The Neuhaus-Royal Athletic Center, a huge step forward for the Longhorn football program and its image, is an excellent facility that will serve Texas well for years to come. More debatable, however, is the rooftop 70-yard practice field, which gets some use by the football team during the season and spring training, but not much. The Longhorn Band and ROTC march there occasionally, and the Texas Longhorn Education Foundation hosts some catered pre-game parties.

Since space is at such a premium around the stadium, this might be a site for future expansion. The roof would probably require extra support, but all kinds of things could be erected there. Athletic offices, the new T Room, skyboxes or a "bubble" athletic field—any (or maybe none) of these may end up on top of Neuhaus-Royal.

"We've spent a lot of time trying to figure out how to better use the stadium," said UT sports information director Bill Little. "I doubt that you could come up with anything we haven't already discussed. But the one suggestion I've made is to go back to having a fence around the stadium. That way, you could do things with the grounds out there—concessions, restrooms and even tailgate parties. People would enter at the street, like they used to. . . . I don't know of any other stadium that's open like this one, practically 24 hours a day."

While Little's idea has merit, it is unlikely to become reality since a seven-foot fence running along the west, north and east sides of the stadium stood until 1967, and it was roundly disliked. And the stadium's accessibility to all should be seen as a plus rather than a minus. Step inside the place at 6:30 A.M. on almost any day of the year, and weather permitting, you will find a dozen walkers or runners working out. On a spring evening, the number is closer to fifty. Memorial Stadium is a major resource in Austin, reaching far beyond Longhorn football.

Parking near the stadium on game days is still "the great adventure" according to the *Daily Texan*, but the situation is improving. A park-and-ride bus system begun in the early 1970s helped, as did construction of a parking garage two blocks north of the stadium in 1986. Another parking garage just south of Jester Center is due within five years. This will further alleviate vehicle congestion, although most Texas fans are accustomed to parking and then walking a good distance. All game-day parking from San Jacinto Boulevard to Red River Street, and from Martin Luther King Boulevard to 26th Street is reserved for VIPs such as donors and UT administrators.

WHOSE NICKEL?

We have looked at a number of things in this chapter, some of which are almost certainly a part of Memorial Stadium's future, while others have varying degrees of likelihood. All of them come with price tags, and (with the exception of a parking garage) the University of Texas athletic department is responsible for the entire bill.

In 1928, after the stadium had been built and mostly paid for, the Texas Memorial Stadium Association deeded it over to the university. The stadium became UT property, but because intercollegiate athletics was deemed auxiliary to education, the university has not maintained it like other campus buildings.

"Besides the university helping pay for a new track, we have to underwrite everything 100 percent," said Messer. "That's probably not going to change. I think it's pretty well understood that if we need money for the stadium, the men's athletic department has to come up with it."

Dodds, Messer and associate AD Larry Franks now administer a $16 million budget and have accrued a $4 million surplus. In the 1950s, Dodds ran track at Kansas State; in the 1960s, Messer played football at Florida State, and Franks played basketball and baseball at UT. While these three former athletes still love sports, it is their business and financial acumen that has UT in good shape. They know that football continues to have a dominant role in the economic health of the entire athletic program. Therefore, the home base of Longhorn football, Memorial Stadium, must be properly maintained and kept current. Dodds, Messer, Franks and their successors in the future will decide on the pace of that work and how to finance it.

If the proposed work on existing and new restrooms went ahead and all of Jaster-Quintanilla's recommendations were followed, a conservative cost estimate would be $7 million. Those are the stadium's most immediate needs, but what of the other options examined here?

An east-side upper deck, skyboxes, a new press box, a north-end office/museum complex, you name it, what would these items cost? Depending on inflation and how much of the "wish list" were enacted, it would run between $20-$50 million, maybe higher, according to some estimates. A capital improvements project of this magnitude will cause the UT athletic department to proceed methodically.

Whether for renovation, expansion or both, the following schools have invested heavily in their stadiums over the past decade: Baylor, Texas A&M, Arkansas, LSU, Tennessee, Auburn, Georgia, Georgia Tech, Clemson, South Carolina, Florida, Florida State, North Carolina, Maryland, Penn State, Michigan State, Illinois, Purdue, Washington, Oregon and Arizona State. Construction of the $7 million Neuhaus-Royal Athletic Center in 1986 puts UT on that list, but plenty more work remains to be done with Memorial Stadium.

"Some of these things we're talking about are 15 or 20 years down the road, or they may never happen," said Dodds. "Nothing's on the agenda right now, but if we got clearance to build another upper deck, we'd have to sell bonds and then retire them over a number of years. We've already made the decision that the money we raise will be for scholarships only. Even with a seat option plan, it would be hard to pay off the bonds.

"Memorial Stadium is such a landmark on this campus. . . . It's famous. Kids come here from all over Texas to run in the UIL state meet, and they probably look up at that stadium and their breath is taken away. It's majestic.

"The stadium is safe today, but we're going to have to put a lot of money into it. To do some of these things, you need to make wise business decisions, you need to be able to forecast the economy, and you need a consistently winning football program."

CONCLUSION

According to a 1926 UT football game program, "Memorial Stadium is built of everlasting concrete, defying age, fire and the elements. It will still be sound and strong when this generation's great, great grandchildren are out there winning for Texas."

Even before the first game held there, Texas football coach E. J. "Doc" Stewart spoke affectionately of "these great, gray walls." The students, alumni and others who worked and gave money for its construction in 1924 knew the significance of what they had done.

If they had simply provided a large facility for UT football and track, their pride would have been justified. But it has been so much more. The building of Memorial Stadium and its use in those early years gave the university a new, grander vision of itself. Within a decade, the UT campus was transformed, and the stadium was a prime catalyst.

As is the tendency with human beings, they eventually grew accustomed to the huge facility and even took it for granted. By the 1950s, Memorial Stadium seemed in decay, and barely avoided the wrecking ball in the 1960s. But it caught a second wind and charged on into the latter part of the century. Today, while the stadium's needs have been identified and partially addressed, it stands tall on the UT campus, as if aware of its own place in the history of the institution.

Memorial Stadium has been the scene of so many stirring athletic events, we are tempted to call it hallowed ground. Go take a seat in the stadium on a nice day, and with a little imagination, you can see Jack Crain beating Arkansas in the last 30 seconds in 1939; Bobby Layne flinging touchdown passes right and left; Darrell Royal's teams rampaging to a pair of undisputed national titles; Earl Campbell showing Heisman Trophy form. You can see Clyde Littlefield's runners tearing up the cinder track; Wes Santee of Kansas almost breaking the four-minute mile in the 1955 Texas Relays; Johnny "Lam" Jones sprinting to victory as a high schooler and a Longhorn; Carlette Guidry doing the same.

But Memorial Stadium is more than just a place for staging football games and track meets. Practically the entire gamut of human activity has transpired there at one time or another. People have died at the stadium and pregnant women have gone into labor, although we have no record of anyone giving birth there. Business deals have been made, as well as marriage proposals, and a few informal weddings have occurred on the 50-yard line. Within its walls, students have laughed, cried, listened to musical concerts, engaged in fistfights, sunbathed, imbibed bootleg whiskey and studied for final exams.

Bold expression of an ambitious future in 1924, the stadium today reflects the image and character of Texas' premier educational institution. Even the oldest UT alumni still recognize it, despite repeated expansion and alteration. Because of its unifying influence through the years, Memorial Stadium remains, arguably, the most significant building on the University of Texas campus.

Appendix

Attendance at UT Football Games in Memorial Stadium

[Author's note: Every effort has been made to provide a complete and reliable list of attendance figures, although for a handful of games, no information is available. Especially in the early years, the 1920s and 1930s, we should beware too many round numbers, which were often little more than a sportswriter's offhand guess. Even later, attendance figures could be inflated by Band Day, children in the knothole section or other variables. And sometimes tickets sold have far exceeded the number of people actually in attendance.]

1924
Baylor (November 8)—13,500
Texas A&M (November 27)—33,000

1925
Southwestern (September 26)—8,000
Mississippi (October 3)—10,000
Rice (October 24)—6,000
Baylor (November 7)—12,000
Arizona (November 14)—7,000

1926
SW Oklahoma Teachers (September 25)—6,500
Phillips (October 9)—6,000
SMU (October 30)—15,000
Southwestern (November 11)—3,000
Texas A&M (November 25)—35,000

1927
SW Oklahoma Teachers (September 24)—not available
TCU (October 1)—6,000
Trinity (October 8)—not available
Rice (October 22)—10,000
Baylor (November 5)—10,000
Kansas A&M (November 11)—12,000

1928
St. Edward's (September 29)—4,000
Texas Tech (October 6)—5,000
Arkansas (October 20)—12,000
SMU (November 3)—20,000
Texas A&M (November 29)—42,571

1929
St. Edward's (September 28)—20,000
Centenary (October 5)—10,000
Rice (October 26)—not available
Baylor (November 9)—25,000
TCU (November 16)—20,000

1930
San Marcos Teachers (September 21)—2,000
Texas Mines (September 28)—not available
Centenary (October 4)—7,000
Howard Payne (October 11)—not available
SMU (November 1)—30,000
Texas A&M (November 27)—40,000

1931
Simmons (September 26)—8,000
Missouri (October 13)—10,000
Rice (October 10)—15,000

212

Baylor (November 7)—10,000
TCU (November 14)—18,000

1932
Daniel Baker (September 24)—4,000
Centenary (October 1)—8,000
SMU (October 29)—20,000
Texas A&M (November 24)—25,000

1933
Texas Mines (September 30)—4,500
Rice (October 28)—10,000
Baylor (November 11)—7,000
TCU (November 18)—7,000
Arkansas (November 24)—5,600

1934
Centenary (October 20)—10,000
SMU (November 3)—15,000
Baylor (November 10)—10,000
Texas A&M (November 29)—33,000

1935
Texas A&I (September 28)—6,000
Centenary (October 19)—6,000
Rice (October 26)—27,000
TCU (November 16)—10,000
Arkansas (November 22)—7,000

1936
LSU (October 3)—15,000
Baylor (October 17)—9,000
SMU (October 31)—16,000
Texas A&M (November 26)—33,000

1937
Texas Tech (September 25)—11,000
Arkansas (October 16)—16,000
Rice (October 23)—21,500
TCU (November 13)—17,500

1938
LSU (October 1)—18,000
SMU (October 29)—not available
Baylor (November 5)—10,000
Texas A&M (November 24)—35,000

1939
Florida (September 30)—12,000
Arkansas (October 21)—17,000
Rice (October 28)—27,000
TCU (November 18)—17,000

1940
Colorado (September 28)—17,000
SMU (November 2)—25,000
Baylor (November 9)—17,000
Texas A&M (November 28)—45,000

1941
LSU (October 4)—18,000
Arkansas (October 18)—21,000
Rice (October 25)—42,000
TCU (November 15)—23,000
Oregon (December 6)—30,000

1942
Corpus Christi Naval Air Station
    (September 19)—7,500
Kansas State (September 26)—13,000
SMU (October 31)—19,000
Baylor (November 7)—24,000
Texas A&M (November 26)—43,000

1943
Blackland Army Air Field (September
    25)—9,000
Southwestern (October 2)—15,000
Arkansas (October 16)—10,000
Rice (October 23)—12,000
TCU (November 13)—12,000

1944
Southwestern (September 30)—14,500
Randolph Field (October 7)—18,000
SMU (November 4)—13,000
Oklahoma A&M (November 11)—16,000
Texas A&M (November 30)—43,000

1945
Bergstrom Field (September 22)—16,000
Southwestern (September 29)—10,000
Texas Tech (October 6)—15,000
Rice (October 27)—21,000

Baylor (November 10)—30,000
TCU (November 17)—27,000

1946
Missouri (September 21)—38,000
Colorado (September 28)—28,000
Oklahoma A&M (October 5)—44,000
Arkansas (October 19)—37,000
SMU (November 2)—33,000
Texas A&M (November 28)—48,000

1947
Texas Tech (September 20)—33,000
North Carolina (October 4)—47,000
Rice (October 25)—48,000
Baylor (November 8)—39,000
TCU (November 15)—43,000

1948
LSU (September 18)—47,500
New Mexico (October 2)—31,000
Arkansas (October 16)—46,000
SMU (October 30)—66,000
Texas A&M (November 25)—68,000

1949
Texas Tech (September 17)—28,000
Idaho (October 1)—23,000
Rice (October 22)—60,000
Baylor (November 5)—57,000
TCU (November 12)—40,000

1950
Purdue (September 30)—40,000
Arkansas (October 21)—40,000
SMU (November 4)—66,000
Texas A&M (November 30)—66,000
LSU (December 9)—38,000

1951
Kentucky (September 22)—47,000
North Carolina (October 6)—32,000
Rice (October 27)—50,000
Baylor (November 10)—58,000
TCU (November 17)—55,000

1952
Notre Dame (October 4)—66,390
Arkansas (October 18)—44,000
SMU (November 1)—55,000

Texas A&M (November 27)—64,000

1953
Villanova (September 26)—27,000
Houston (October 3)—30,000
Rice (October 24)—48,000
Baylor (November 7)—57,000
TCU (November 14)—42,000

1954
LSU (September 18)—36,000
Washington State (October 2)—28,000
Arkansas (October 16)—42,000
SMU (October 30)—52,000
Texas A&M (November 25)—60,000

1955
Texas Tech (September 17)—47,000
Tulane (September 24)—30,000
Rice (October 22)—45,000
Baylor (November 5)—42,000
TCU (November 12)—55,000

1956
Southern California (September 22)—47,000
West Virginia (October 6)—30,000
Arkansas (October 20)—40,000
SMU (November 3)—35,000
Texas A&M (November 29)—62,000

1957
Tulane (September 28)—35,000
South Carolina (October 5)—38,500
Rice (October 26)—50,000
Baylor (November 9)—42,000
TCU (November 16)—30,000

1958
Georgia (September 20)—32,000
Texas Tech (October 4)—33,000
Arkansas (October 18)—46,000
SMU (November 1)—55,000
Texas A&M (November 27)—52,000

1959
Maryland (September 26)—47,000
California (October 3)—20,000
Rice (October 24)—57,000
Baylor (November 7)—40,000

TCU (November 14)—43,000

1960
Nebraska (September 17)—40,000
Texas Tech (October 1)—52,000
Arkansas (October 15)—35,000
SMU (October 29)—34,000
Texas A&M (November 24)—50,000

1961
Texas Tech (September 30)—43,000
Washington State (October 7)—40,000
Rice (October 28)—62,310
Baylor (November 11)—62,000
TCU (November 18)—50,000

1962
Oregon (September 22)—52,000
Tulane (October 6)—50,000
Arkansas (October 20)—64,350
SMU (November 3)—51,000
Texas A&M (November 22)—57,000

1963
Texas Tech (September 28)—50,015
Oklahoma State (October 5)—50,280
Rice (October 26)—59,000
Baylor (November 9)—64,307
TCU (November 16)—56,658

1964
Tulane (September 19)—60,000
Army (October 3)—65,700
Arkansas (October 17)—65,700
SMU (October 31)—59,000
Texas A&M (November 26)—65,000

1965
Tulane (September 18)—40,000
Texas Tech (September 25)—65,310
Indiana (October 2)—57,000
Rice (October 23)—63,000
Baylor (November 6)—57,500
TCU (November 18)—51,000

1966
Southern California (September 17)—42,000
Indiana (October 1)—56,000
Arkansas (October 15)—65,000

SMU (October 29)—58,000
Texas A&M (November 24)—65,500

1967
Texas Tech (September 30)—65,200
Oklahoma State (October 7)—51,000
Rice (October 28)—65,000
Baylor (November 11)—55,000
TCU (November 18)—51,000

1968
Houston (September 21)—66,397
Oklahoma State (October 5)—51,000
Arkansas (October 19)—66,397
SMU (November 2)—66,397
Texas A&M (November 28)—66,397

1969
Texas Tech (September 27)—65,200
Navy (October 4)—63,200
Rice (October 25)—61,500
Baylor (November 8)—51,000
TCU (November 15)—51,000

1970
California (September 19)—61,000
UCLA (October 3)—65,500
SMU (October 31)—66,500
Texas A&M (November 26)—66,400
Arkansas (December 5)—68,447

1971
Texas Tech (September 25)—76,639
Oregon (October 2)—61,969
Rice (October 23)—62,000
Baylor (November 6)—54,673
TCU (November 13)—64,109

1972
Miami (September 23)—62,000
Utah State (October 7)—58,127
Arkansas (October 21)—80,844
SMU (November 4)—72,500
Texas A&M (November 23)—68,000

1973
Texas Tech (September 29)—77,809
Wake Forest (October 6)—51,700
Rice (October 27)—62,300
Baylor (November 10)—64,500

TCU (November 17)—50,000

1974
Wyoming (September 21)—53,800
Washington (October 5)—50,250
Arkansas (October 19)—67,700
SMU (November 2)—58,500
Texas A&M (November 29)—77,584

1975
Colorado State (September 13)—46,000
Texas Tech (September 27)—77,809
Utah State (October 4)—40,130
Rice (October 25)—55,000
Baylor (November 8)—75,500
TCU (November 15)—34,500

1976
North Texas (September 18)—60,130
SMU (October 23)—50,000
Houston (November 6)—77,807
Texas A&M (November 25)—70,000
Arkansas (December 4)—49,341

1977
Boston College (September 10)—50,000
Virginia (September 17)—41,000
Rice (October 1)—47,500
Texas Tech (October 29)—78,809
TCU (November 12)—50,150
Baylor (November 19)—60,000

1978
Wyoming (September 23)—60,000
North Texas (October 14)—63,000
Arkansas (October 21)—78,000
SMU (October 28)—65,289
Houston (November 11)—83,053
Texas A&M (December 1)—78,413

1979
Iowa State (September 22)—73,652
Rice (October 6)—65,227
Texas Tech (November 3)—77,809
TCU (November 17)—61,597
Baylor (November 24)—63,288

1980
Arkansas (September 1)—70,660
Utah State (September 20)—60,923

Oregon State (September 27)—60,381
SMU (October 25)—73,535
Houston (November 8)—79,154
Texas A&M (November 29)—72,537

1981
Rice (September 12)—68,497
North Texas (September 19)—58,638
Miami (September 26)—74,653
Texas Tech (October 31)—67,439
TCU (November 14)—60,038
Baylor (November 21)—72,806

1982
Utah (September 18)—70,158
Missouri (September 25)—76,438
SMU (October 23)—80,157
Houston (November 6)—76,657
Texas A&M (November 25)—72,368
Arkansas (December 4)—67,903

1983
North Texas (September 24)—71,202
Rice (October 1)—70,005
Texas Tech (October 29)—75,401
TCU (November 12)—61,156
Baylor (November 19)—76,208

1984
Auburn (September 15)—78,348
Arkansas (October 20)—77,809
SMU (October 27)—80,759
Houston (November 10)—80,348
Texas A&M (December 1)—81,309

1985
Missouri (September 21)—76,437
Rice (October 5)—69,471
Texas Tech (November 2)—65,137
TCU (November 16)—66,397
Baylor (November 23)—78,912

1986
Stanford (September 13)—74,372
Arkansas (October 18)—67,344
SMU (October 25)—65,481
Houston (November 8)—60,650
Texas A&M (November 27)—75,623

1987
Brigham Young (September 12)—65,102
Oregon State (September 26)—53,389
Texas Tech (October 31)—74,984
Rice (October 3)—54,740
TCU (November 14)—63,642
Baylor (November 21)—61,331

1988
New Mexico (September 17)—55,630
North Texas (September 24)—60,152
Arkansas (October 15)—73,451
Houston (November 5)—69,600
Texas A&M (November 24)—77,809

1989
Penn State (September 30)—75,232
Rice (October 7)—57,038
Texas Tech (November 4)—81,826
TCU (November 18)—50,882
Baylor (November 25)—49,081

1990
Colorado (September 22)—75,882
Arkansas (October 21)—72,657
SMU (October 27)—65,128
Houston (November 10)—82,457
Texas A&M (December 1)—82,518

1991
Auburn (September 21)—77,809
Rice (October 5)—67,328
Texas Tech (November 2)—74,873
TCU (November 16)—57,656
Baylor (November 23)—61,310

Bibliography

Interviews

Lou Maysel, April 16, 1990; August 8, 1990; June 9, 1991
Ed Bluestein, April 20, 1990
Betty King Barker, May 23, 1990
Dr. Margaret C. Berry, May 28, 1990; June 18, 1990; December 5, 1991
Malcolm Gregory, June 9, 1990
T. H. Johnson, June 11, 1990
Dr. Cecil Hale, June 26, 1990
Margaret Bellmont Gray, July 1, 1990; September 17, 1990
Roy Vaughan, July 4, 1990; May 15, 1991
Fred Bednarski, July 6, 1990
David C. Bland, July 11, 1990
Ted Koy, July 11, 1990
Willie Kocurek, July 17, 1990
Robert Levy, July 18, 1990
Tom Stolhandske, July 19, 1990
Jerry Thompson, July 19, 1990
Etta Gilbert Marley, July 25, 1990
Dr. Byron Short, July 25, 1990
Dr. J. Neils Thompson, July 30, 1990; August 27, 1990; September 21, 1990; April 23, 1991;
    September 24, 1991
Martha Robertson Zivley, August 1, 1990
Dr. John Treadwell, August 2, 1990
Al Lundstedt, August 6, 1990; September 6, 1990; February 28, 1991; March 20, 1991; June 10,
    1991; December 5, 1991
Travis Raven, August 7, 1990
Liz Carpenter, August 7, 1990
David McWilliams, August 8, 1990
Dr. Joe B. Frantz, August 9, 1990
Wally Pryor, August 9, 1990
Ted Bellmont, August 10, 1990
Weldon Smith, August 10, 1990
Mallie Coker, August 13, 1990
Jeff Ward, August 14, 1990
Bob Rochs, August 15, 1990; February 28, 1991; April 16, 1991
Nelson Puett, Jr., August 17, 1990
Hugh Wolfe, August 19, 1990
Malcolm Kutner, August 19, 1990

Dr. Joseph Jones, August 20, 1990; March 26, 1991
Robert Brewer, August 20, 1990
David C. "Bobby" Cannon, August 22, 1990; January 13, 1990
Clyde Littlefield, Jr., August 23, 1990; June 17, 1991
Jerry Sisemore, August 23, 1990
Ed Barlow, August 27, 1990
Gover "Ox" Emerson, August 27, 1990
Tommy Ingram, August 28, 1990
Quinton Bunton, August 29, 1990
Clint Small, August 30, 1990
Lawrence Sampleton, September 4, 1990
Bill Sansing, September 4, 1990; January 31, 1991
Moton Crockett, September 5, 1990; December 11, 1991
Harley Clark, September 11, 1990; March 2, 1991
Jim Bertelsen, September 11, 1990
D. Harold Byrd, Jr., September 12, 1990
Tommy Nobis, September 12, 1990
Noble Doss, September 14, 1990; July 27, 1991
Rooster Andrews, September 15, 1990; July 26, 1991
Billy Schott, September 18, 1990
Stan Huntsman, September 20, 1990
Homer B. Stark, September 24, 1990
J. R. Parten, September 25, 1990
Mike Campbell, Sr., September 27, 1990
Hub Bechtol, September 30, 1990
Bill Little, October 2, 1990
Dr. Ricardo Romo, October 3, 1990
Jack Sparks, October 4, 1990
Etta Bain Ward, October 8, 1990
Harry Badger, October 24, 1990
Darrell Royal, October 31, 1990; June 26, 1991
Craig James, November 7, 1990
Bob Miller, November 11, 1990
Sam Coates, November 24, 1990
Steve Worster, November 27, 1990
Jones Ramsey, December 4, 1990
Doug English, December 6, 1990
Wally Scott, December 11, 1990
Dr. Mike Wetzel, December 11, 1990
Kermit E. "Dutch" Voelkel, January 2, 1991
Jon Bible, January 11, 1991
Constance Douglas Reeves, January 13, 1991
Bradley Davis, January 13, 1991
James R. Cole, January 18, 1991
Morris Breazeale, January 18, 1991
Pat Kelly, January 23, 1991
Lex Acker, February 9, 1991; February 16, 1991; February 23, 1991; March 2, 1991; September
     10, 1991; September 23, 1991
Dr. Norman Hackerman, February 20, 1991
Joe Bleymaier, February 23, 1991

Perry Giles, March 2, 1991
Jack Maguire, March 3, 1991
Dr. Demetri Vacalis, March 5, 1991
Fred Steinmark, March 9, 1991
Roland G. Roessner, May 1, 1991; August 16, 1991
Roy Vaughan, March 11, 1991
Harrison Stafford, March 12, 1991
Ethel Lee Tracy, March 12, 1991
Bobby Lackey, March 13, 1991
Karl Kamrath, Jr., March 14, 1991; January 6, 1992
Joe Ternus, March 20, 1991
Charles M. Harris, March 21, 1991
Gerald Lyda, March 21, 1991
Mel Stekoll, March 28, 1991
Dr. William Cunningham, April 8, 1991
B. J. "Red" McCombs, April 16, 1991
Dr. David Deming, April 18, 1991
Dr. David Fowler, April 23, 1991
Mike Korth, May 14, 1991
Dr. Roland Rust, June 2, 1991
Dr. Rhea Williams, June 3, 1991
Dr. Bailey Marshall, June 3, 1991
Ray Marek, June 4, 1991
Dean Smith, June 8, 1991
Harvey "Chink" Wallender, June 9, 1991
Phil Delavan, June 9, 1991
Don Hood, June 10, 1991
DeLoss Dodds, June 10, 1991; August 28, 1991; September 5, 1991; October 3, 1991
Steve Brougher, June 10, 1991
Dr. Mike Quinn, June 12, 1991
Joe Dixon, June 19, 1991
Margaret Ellison, June 23, 1991
Olan Brewer, June 25, 1991
Glenn Brown, July 1, 1991
Hollis Gainey, July 8, 1991
Jack Crain, July 22, 1991
Ralph Huber, July 23, 1991
James Saxton, August 1, 1991
James Raup, August 1, 1991
Charley Parker, August 2, 1991
Ken Dabbs, August 20, 1991
Leon Manley, August 22, 1991
Dale Swearingen, August 23, 1991
John Pastier, August 23, 1991
Skip Bayless, August 25, 1991
Dr. James Vick, August 27, 1991; September 4, 1991
H. C. Lott, August 30, 1991
Doug Messer, September 3, 1991
Howard Richards, September 4, 1991
Terry Crawford, September 5, 1991

Dr. Donna Lopiano, September 5, 1991
Fred Akers, September 13, 1991
Dave Snyder, November 21, 1991
Jeff Moore, November 21, 1991
Gordon Wilkerson, December 6, 1991
John Mackovic, December 22, 1991
Dr. John Breen, January 13, 1992

Letters Received

Crockett English, June 20, 1990
Ted Bellmont, June 25, 1990
David C. Bland, June 26, 1990
Carl J. Eckhardt, July 2, 1990
Tom Landry, July 9, 1990; July 31, 1991
Jane S. Boldrick, July 10, 1990
Sally Prince Martin, July 11, 1990
Elizabeth E. Vestal, July 12, 1990
Robert Levy, July 13, 1990; January 17, 1991
Ina Maye Carothers, July 13, 1990
Joe Goldstein, July 17, 1990
Margaret Cousins, July 23, 1990; August 25, 1990
Alice Lundy, July 25, 1990
Fannie M. Boyls, August 12, 1990
Hugh Wolfe, August 14, 1990
Stan Mauldin, Jr., August 20, 1990
Marvin Kristynik, August 22, 1990
H. Allen Alderson, August 24, 1990
Fred Sarchet, August 26, 1990
Vincent DiNino, August 30, 1990
Del Bradford White, September 5, 1990
Etta Bain Ward, September 24, 1990; October 13, 1990
Joe McGuire, January 28, 1991
Willie Morris, March 11, 1991
John B. Connally, March 20, 1991
Jack S. Blanton, May 29, 1991
Glen Halsell, June 5, 1991
Happy Feller, June 6, 1991
Bobby Whilden, June 6, 1991
Carlton Stowers, June 8, 1991; June 20, 1991
Pat Culpepper, June 9, 1991
George Breazeale, June 19, 1991
Bill Whitmore, June 21, 1991
Charles Brewer, June 25, 1991
Dr. Terry Todd, July 9, 1991
Jerry Thompson, July 14, 1991
Chris Gilbert, July 19, 1991
Dan Cook, August 14, 1991
David McNabb, August 19, 1991
Bernie Esunas, August 22, 1991

Eddie Phillips, August 24, 1991
Jack Vickrey, September 13, 1991
Marty Akins, October 16, 1991
Randy Matson, October 31, 1991

Books

Tips, Kern. *Football Texas Style*. Garden City, NY: Doubleday, 1964.
Maysel, Lou. *Here Come the Texas Longhorns*, volume I. Fort Worth: Stadium, 1970.
Morse, Frederic C. *The Ex-Students' History of the University of Texas in Pictures*. Austin, 1970.
Dugger, Ronnie. *Our Invaded Universities*. New York: Norton, 1974.
Freeman, Denne. *Hook 'em Horns!* Huntsville, Ala.: Strode, 1974.
Maysel, Lou. *Here Come the Texas Longhorns*, volume II. Austin: Burnt Orange, 1978.
Stowers, Carlton, and Wilbur Evans. *Champions: University of Texas Track and Field*. Huntsville, Ala.: Strode, 1978.
Berry, Dr. Margaret C. *The University of Texas: A Pictorial Account of Its First Century*. Austin: UT Press, 1980.
Forsyth, John D. *The Aggies and the Horns/86 Years of Bad Blood*. Austin: Texas Monthly, 1981.
Jones, Dr. Joseph. *Life on Waller Creek*. Austin: AAR/Tantalus, 1982.
Frantz, Dr. Joe. *The Forty Acre Follies*. Austin: Texas Monthly, 1983.
Campbell, Dave, ed. *The Best of Dave Campbell's Texas Football, 1960-89*. Dallas: Taylor, 1989.
Maher, John, and Kirk Bohls. *Bleeding Orange*. New York: St. Martin's, 1991.

Newspaper Articles

"Bellmont Prods Longhorn Budget Up with Success," *Dallas News*, October 23, 1921.
"Victory Thanksgiving Day May Mean New Stadium," *Daily Texan*, November 23, 1923.
"Drive Starts to Give University of Texas Huge Sport Stadium," *San Antonio Express*, December 4, 1923.
"Stewart Predicts 40,000 Will See 1924 Classic Here," by L. L. Engelking, *Austin American*, December 11, 1923.
"Stadium Construction to Start Much Talked Campus Improvements," *Daily Texan*, February 19, 1924.
"Athletic Facilities Out of Harmony with Record of Longhorns," *Daily Texan*, February 19, 1924.
"Work Begins on Stadium Site," *Daily Texan*, February 25, 1924.
"For Texas, We Will," *Daily Texan*, February 26, 1924.
"Bonfire Tonight to Close Stadium Drive," *Daily Texan*, March 4, 1924.
"Varsity Stadium Becomes Reality," *Austin American-Statesman*, April 5, 1924.
"San Antonio Firm Gets Stadium Contract," *San Antonio Express*, May 8, 1924.
"Fichtenbaum Says Students Are Paying Stadium Pledges," *Daily Texan*, May 18, 1924.
"Varsity Stadium Will Be a Monument to War Heroes who 'Went West'," *Daily Texan*, May 18, 1924.
"Lutcher Stark Resignation Demanded," *Daily Texan*, May 20, 1924.
"Stark Told to Pay for Stadium as Penance for Picking Neff," *San Antonio Express*, May 20, 1924.
"Ex-Students Here Refuse to Aid in Stadium Drive," *El Paso Times*, May 26, 1924.
"Stadium Concrete to Be Poured Monday," *Austin American-Statesman*, May 30, 1924.
"McGill to Succeed Stark in University Stadium Drive as Factions Call Truce," *San Antonio Express*, June 2, 1924.

"Shacks and Stadium," *Hillsboro Mirror*, June 11, 1924.

"Visitors Flock to Site of Stadium," *Austin American-Statesman*, June 27, 1924.

"Work Proceeds Swiftly on South's Greatest Athletic Field," *Daily Texan*, June 29, 1924.

"Stadium Great Move to Build Big University," *Marshall Morning News*, September 19, 1924.

"World Record Broken in Construction of Memorial Stadium," *Daily Texan*, November 2, 1924.

"B. U. Strategy Beats Texas Longhorns as Bears Take 28-10 Tilt," *Dallas News*, November 9, 1924.

"Stadium Presents Breath-Taking Scene" by Pop Boone, *Fort Worth Record*, November 28, 1924.

"Allen Races Over for Winning Score/37,000 Fans in New Stadium," *Dallas News*, November 28, 1924.

"The Stadium Fulfills its Promise," *Austin American-Statesman*, November 28, 1924.

"President Splawn Gives Official Approval to Varsity Relay Carnival," *Daily Texan*, February 19, 1925.

"Designs Accepted for Stadium 'Horse Shoe'," *Daily Texan*, May 5, 1926.

"Steers Lose Bitter Fight to Mustangs," by Dick Vaughn, *Daily Texan*, October 31, 1926.

"Greater Stadium Crowns Vast Campus Improvements," by Duby Dubose, *Austin American-Statesman*, (date uncertain), 1926.

"Authorities Silent on Ousting of Bellmont," *Austin American-Statesman*, October 2, 1928.

"Texas Longhorns Cop Conference Title," by Lloyd Gregory, *Houston Post*, November 30, 1928.

"Rice Crumbles and Longhorns Carry Off Track Title," by Weldon Hart, *Austin American-Statesman*, May 14, 1933.

"Crushing Attack of Purple Horde Buries UT, 28-0," by Weldon Hart, *Austin American-Statesman*, November 17, 1935.

"Students Gave Flesh and Blood to Build Memorial Stadium," *Daily Texan*, September 19, 1937.

"Steers Come Back to Whip Farmers," by Weldon Hart, *Austin American-Statesman*, November 25, 1938.

"Happy Crowd Mobs Crain as Texas Wins, 14-13," *Daily Texan*, October 22, 1939.

"13 Longhorns End Aggies' Rose Bowl Dream," *Houston Post*, November 29, 1940.

"New Relays Records Climax 2nd Day of Round-Up," by Bill Sansing, *Daily Texan*, April 6, 1941.

"Randolph Bombs Longhorns, 42-6," by Jack Gallagher, *Daily Texan*, October 8, 1944.

"Stadium Won't Get Lights for 1946 Football," *Daily Texan*, June 7, 1946.

"Odessa's Gridsters Rip Jeff's Mustangs by 21 to 14 for Title," by Jimmy Banks, *Austin American-Statesman*, December 29, 1946.

"Amazing Longhorns Stun Carolina, 34-0," *Daily Texan*, October 5, 1947.

"SMU Rolls Past Texas, 21-6," *Daily Texan*, October 31, 1948.

"Fired-Up Texas Carves Prime Bear Steak, 21-20," by Mark Batteson, *Austin American-Statesman*, November 8, 1953.

"New Stadium Lights Hit Research Phase," by J. C. Goulden, *Daily Texan*, November 19, 1954.

"Eddie Southern Record Tops 1955 State Meet," by Orland Sims, *Austin American-Statesman*, May 7, 1955.

"Swink Stampedes for 4 Scores! Frogs Win, 47-20," by Flem Hall, *Fort Worth Star-Telegram*, November 13, 1955.

"Relays History Dates Back 30 Colorful Meets to 1925," by Jim McIntyre, *Daily Texan*, April 5, 1957.

"Ramirez and Longhorns Upset Owls, 19-14," *Daily Texan*, October 27, 1957.

"Olle Announces Plan for Lounge Under Stadium," *Daily Texan*, February 7, 1960.

"Memorial Stadium to Have New Turf," *Daily Texan*, May 17, 1960.

"Longhorns Race Clock on 90-Yard Push, Capture 7 to 3 Triumph Over Arkansas," by Lou Maysel, *Austin American-Statesman*, October 21, 1962.

"For Texas, They Did," by Carolie Baity, *Daily Texan*, April 5, 1963.

"Texas Southern's Cloud Covers Relays; Rice's Hansen Soars to Texas' Record," by Carlton Stowers, *Daily Texan*, April 7, 1963.

"UT Chokes Last Bear Gasp, 7-0," *Daily Texan*, November 10, 1963.

"Texas Gamble Fails; Arkansas 14-13 Victor," by Lou Maysel, *Austin American-Statesman*, October 18, 1964.

"Stadium Relocation Eyed," by Sam Keach, Jr., *Daily Texan*, July 20, 1965.

"Time to Move," *Daily Texan*, October 6, 1965.

"Regents Ask Study of Stadium Location," by Nancy Kowert, *Daily Texan*, October 10, 1965.

"Proposal to Move Stadium Arouses Student Opinion," by Christopher Dann, *Daily Texan*, October 12, 1965.

"Chancellor to Request Delay on Stadium Location Decision," *Daily Texan*, November 23, 1965.

"Regents Veto Plans to Raze UT Stadium," *Houston Chronicle*, November 25, 1965.

"Relays, Littlefield Span Track History," *Daily Texan*, April 1, 1966.

"Memorial Stadium May Be Enlarged," *Dallas Morning News*, October 24, 1967.

"Bellmont Architect of UT Athletics/His Deeds Stagger Imagination," by Lou Maysel, *Austin American-Statesman*, December 28, 1967.

"Top O' Morn," by Lou Maysel, *Austin American-Statesman*, August 8, 1968.

"UT Longhorns, Cougars Settle for 20-20 Deadlock," by Lou Maysel, *Austin American-Statesman*, September 22, 1968.

"Whew! 'Horns Slip by Bruins, 20-17," by Andy Yemma, *Daily Texan*, October 4, 1970.

"Memorial Stadium Addition Speeding Toward Completion for Home Opener," *Austin American-Statesman*, May 16, 1971.

"Plano Captures AAA Crown," by Fred Sanner, *Austin American-Statesman*, December 19, 1971.

"Stadium Completion Delayed by Striking Iron Workers," *Austin American-Statesman*, August 31, 1972.

"Regent 'Shocked' at Stadium Cost," by Robert Schwab, *Austin American-Statesman*, March 24, 1973.

"UT, Other Kings Repeat in SWC," by Lou Maysel, *Austin American-Statesman*, May 20, 1973.

"Horn Defense Broils Razorbacks, 38-7," by Kelley Anderson, *Daily Texan*, October 20, 1974.

"Balky Clock Foils Jones' Record Try," by George Breazeale, *Austin American-Statesman*, April 3, 1977.

"Records Fall as UTEP Runs Away with NCAA Title," by Scott Sudduth, *Daily Texan*, June 9, 1980.

"Ex-UT Coach Gets Ovation at Last Rites," by Dick Moore, *Fort Worth Star-Telegram*, May 24, 1981.

"Lady Vols Nab AIAW Title," by Suzanne Michel, *Daily Texan*, June 1, 1981.

"TLEF Finances VIP Booth in Stadium," by Frank Januzzi, *Daily Texan*, June 15, 1982.

"Ponies Ride Infractions to Big Time," by David McNabb, *Daily Texan*, October 23, 1982.

"SMU Soars Past Texas, 30-17," by Temple Pouncey, *Dallas Morning News*, October 24, 1982.

"Texas' Athletic Facilities Have Come a Long, Long Way," by George Breazeale, *Austin American-Statesman*, September 14, 1983.

"Texas Holds Off Auburn, 35-27," by Stan Roberts, *Daily Texan*, September 17, 1984.

"Stadium History Rich after 60 Glorious Years," by Audray Bateman, *Austin American-Statesman*, November 23, 1984.

"Martin, Davis Set National Marks," by George Breazeale, *Austin American-Statesman*, May 12, 1985.

"Longhorns Limp Over Frogs to Stay in SWC Race," by Schuyler Dixon, *Daily Texan*, November 15, 1987.

"Lady Horns Use Guidry's 4 Golds to Win SWC Meet," by Mark Wangrin, *Austin American-Statesman*, May 16, 1988.

"Bush Commencement a Waste of Money," by Kerry O'Brian, *Daily Texan*, July 2, 1990.

"Horns Wake Up Coogs, 45-24," by Gene Duffey, *Houston Post*, November 11, 1990.

"Larrieu-Smith Sets American Record," by Mark Rosner, *Austin American-Statesman*, April 5, 1991.

"'Turbo' Time: Guidry Runs to 100 Crown," by Randy Riggs, *Austin American-Statesman*, April 6, 1991.

"Mackovic: The Man, The Mission," by Rick Cantu, *Austin American-Statesman*, December 13, 1991.

Magazine Articles

"Editorial/A Stadium," *Alcalde*, December 1920.

"Stadium Movement," by Moulton "Ty" Cobb, *Alcalde*, February 1924.

"The $500,000 Memorial Stadium Campaign, How and Why It Is to Be Put Over," by H. J. Lutcher Stark, Harry E. Moore and L. Theo Bellmont, *Alcalde*, April 1924.

"History of the Stadium," by Nowlin Randolph, *Alcalde*, November 1924.

"Construction Notes on Texas University Stadium," by A. T. Granger, *Engineering News Record*, October 1, 1925.

"Vale, Football!" *Alcalde*, April 1926 (reprinted from *Columbia Alumni News*).

"Shall We Have Athletics for Pay or Athletics for Play?" by Roy Bedichek, *Alcalde*, January 1927.

"Is Intercollegiate Athletics Wrong?" by Dr. Daniel Penick, *Alcalde*, January 1927.

"Men's Gym Destroyed by Fire," *Alcalde*, April 1928.

"A Farewell to Football," by James L. McCamy, *Alcalde*, June 1931.

"Open Season Declared on Football Drunks," *Alcalde*, December 1935.

"The Bible Program," *Alcalde*, October 1937.

"Archangel and His Bible," by Kenneth Foree, Jr., *Saturday Evening Post*, October 9, 1937.

"Regents Plan Enlargement of Stadium," *Alcalde*, June 1947.

"Bellmont Will Retire," *Alcalde*, November 1951.

"Light the Stadium?" *Alcalde*, March 1955.

"Then Came D. X. Bible," by Oscar Griffin, *Alcalde*, October 1957.

"Hall of Honor," *Alcalde*, January 1959.

"Reminiscences 1912-1963," by Clyde Littlefield, *Alcalde*, June 1963.

"Where are We Going Next?" by Anita Brewer, *Alcalde*, October 1965.

"Stadium Should be on Campus," *Alcalde*, November 1965.

"Misplaced Stadium," by Jack Maguire, *Alcalde*, November 1965.

"Memorial Stadium to Stay Put," *Alcalde*, February 1966.

"Since '24—Eyes of Texas on the Stadium," by Kathy McLaughlin, *Austin*, September 1966.

"Stadium Enlargement Studied," *Alcalde*, December 1967.

"14,000 Seats to Be Added to Stadium," *Alcalde*, November 1968.

"The Trees Have Fallen," *Alcalde*, December 1969.

"Stadium Forecast," *Alcalde*, May 1971.

"Over the Years at Memorial Stadium: The Magic Moments," by Lou Maysel, *Dave Campbell's Texas Football Newsmagazine*, September 23, 1972.

"Finally, A Flashy New Home for the 'Horns," by Vaughn Aldredge, *Dave Campbell's Texas Football Newsmagazine*, September 23, 1972.

"A Tradition Began with Memorial Stadium," *Alcalde*, March/April 1975.
"What One Football Weekend Does to Austin Cash Registers," *Alcalde*, January/February 1984.
"The Eyes of Texas," by Alexander Wolff, *Sports Illustrated*, December 6, 1986.
"Empty Seats," by Gregory Curtis, *Texas Monthly*, November 1990.
"The Center of Attention," by Valerie Davis, *Alcalde*, May/June 1991.

Miscellaneous

Minutes, University of Texas Athletics Council, 1913-1990.
Minutes, Texas Memorial Stadium Association, January 1924-May 1927.
Accounting report by Rankin & McAlpine to Texas Memorial Stadium Association Board of Directors, March 5, 1926.
Minutes, University of Texas Board of Regents, March 12, 1965; July 16, 1965; November 23, 1965.
"Site Comparison Study/Off-Campus Athletic Complex/The University of Texas," by Osborn Engineering Co. and Lockwood, Andrews & Newnam, July 1968.
"Feasibility Study/Memorial Stadium Expansion/The University of Texas," by Osborn Engineering Co. and Lockwood, Andrews & Newnam, September 1968.
"Football/Baylor vs. Texas, November 8, 1924," (self-published paper) by T. H. Johnson, 1984.
"History of Intercollegiate Athletics for Women/The University of Texas," July 25, 1990.
Memorial Stadium structural report by Jaster-Quintanilla & Associates, September 1991.
Strategic Plan, 1994-1999/The University of Texas at Austin.

Index